Series in Recreation and Leisure

The purpose of the Prentice-Hall Series in Recreation and Leisure is to provide an innovative conceptual framework for the study of leisure and to communicate expert programmatic and management knowledge on the delivery of leisure services in contemporary society. The Series authors are distinguished leisure scholars, researchers, and practitioners.

Each volume presents original ideas and synthesizes and communicates recent knowledge in an understandable and operational form for the reader. Books published in the Series are designed to be of interest and use for students, educators, and practitioners.

Joseph J. Bannon and
James F. Murphy

Series Editors

Christine Z. Howe
University of Georgia

Gaylene M. Carpenter
University of Oregon

Programming Leisure Experiences

PRENTICE-HALL, INC.   Englewood Cliffs, New Jersey 07632

Library of Congress Cataloging in Publication Data

Howe, Christine Z.
   Programming leisure experiences.

   (Series in recreation and leisure)
   Includes index.
   1. Leisure—Study and teaching.   2. Leisure—
Management.   I. Carpenter, Gay.   II. Title.   III. Series.
GV14.5.H65   1985   790′.01′35068   84-24924
ISBN 0-13-729286-4

Editorial/production supervision:
  Cyndy Lyle Rymer
Manufacturing buyer: Harry P. Baisley
Cover designer: Diane Saxe

Printed in the United States of America

10   9   8   7   6   5   4   3   2   1

ISBN 0-13-729286-4

PRENTICE-HALL INTERNATIONAL, INC., *London*
PRENTICE-HALL OF AUSTRALIA PTY. LIMITED, *Sydney*
EDITORA PRENTICE-HALL DO BRASIL, LTDA., *Rio de Janeiro*
PRENTICE-HALL CANADA INC., *Toronto*
PRENTICE-HALL OF INDIA PRIVATE LIMITED, *New Delhi*
PRENTICE-HALL OF JAPAN, INC., *Tokyo*
PRENTICE-HALL OF SOUTHEAST ASIA PTE. LTD., *Singapore*
WHITEHALL BOOKS LIMITED, *Wellington, New Zealand*
PRENTICE-HALL HISPANOAMERICANA, S.A., *Mexico*

Contents

Preface

Programming, the process of planning and delivering leisure experiences to an individual or a group of individuals, is one of the areas that is truly unique to the body of knowledge in park, recreation, and leisure services. Good programming is a way of managing play without putting constraints on its joy and spontaneity. Skill in programming is a basic necessity for all contemporary park, recreation, and leisure professionals and, as such, is an essential part of professional preparation curricula in the field. Programming is an art and a science, and a good book on the subject can help make the reader a better program artist or scientist.

A cyclical approach to programming leisure experiences implies that there is indeed a systematic way of identifying and meeting people's leisure needs and interests. The leisure programming cycle begins with the assessment of constituent needs and interests and moves to the planning of the program. This is followed by the provision or implementation of the program, evaluation, and revision. Then the cycle begins again. It is this cyclical approach that constitutes the theme of this book. The chapters that follow thoroughly address each of the phases of the leisure programming cycle in a new and exciting way. The chapters also address the different contexts in which programs occur and, as appropriate, the special characteristics of diverse populations that are served.

In his book *Future Shock*, Alvin Toffler stated that the recreation industry will continue to grow as the nature of leisure is defined in experiential terms. Park, recreation, and leisure professionals, he said, may be called the "experience makers" as the primary responsibility of their jobs becomes just that—providing leisure experiences and environments that enhance the well-being and quality of life of the participants. Toffler goes on to say that the experience makers will form a basic sector of the postservice economy of the future. Leisure, as an experience industry, will provide psychological "extras" to its "consumers." Experiences will be sold just as if they were goods or services.[1] Whether one believes that scenario or not, the point is that the past, present, and future of the park, recreation, and leisure profession are connected to the act of programming. This book is an attempt to examine that connection thoroughly, for now and for the future.

ACKNOWLEDGMENTS

Each of us has many persons to whom we are indebted for their help in the completion of this book. In the beginning there was Raymond T. O'Connell at Prentice-Hall, Inc. Throughout the process there was series editor Joseph J. Bannon, who was unfailing in his encouragement. Doris S. Michaels of Prentice-Hall gave us our head and let us run. In the end, there was Linda Edwards, who cheerfully typed word after word, and my colleagues in the Department of Recreation and Leisure Studies and in the Division of Health, Physical Education, Recreation and Dance at the University of Georgia and my friends in Athens, who offered me their fullest support and resources. Cyndy Lyle Rymer of Prentice-Hall was a most supportive production editor, and Janet Podell, through her copy editing, helped us to say what we meant. This book could not have been written without them and I thank them very much.

C.Z.H.

I would especially like to thank my colleagues in the Department of Leisure Studies and Services in the College of Human Development and Performance at the University of Oregon for their interest, encouragement, and support. I am also indebted to my former colleagues at Temple University and to dozens of professional recreators in the Philadelphia area and throughout California who graciously shared their programming experiences.

G.M.C.

[1] Alvin Toffler, *Future Shock* (New York: Bantam Books, Inc., 1970), pp. 219-237.

chapter 1

Introduction to Leisure and Recreation

INTRODUCTION

During times such as these, when financial and other resources are constrained, it makes sense to cut back on items previously considered to be essential to daily life. But what we're finding is that nationally reported figures on leisure expenditures are reflecting an upward trend. Increases in leisure spending in the United States over the past several years have taken place at the same time that expenditures in other facets of life have leveled off and, in some cases, proportionally dropped or declined. An estimated $300 billion was spent on entertainment in 1984. These American dollars paid for vacations, electronic games and equipment, sporting goods, theater, movies, spectator sports, and other forms of recreation.[1]

The number of participants involved in leisure experiences has also increased. More and more people are involved in lifetime sports and lifelong education during their free time. Not only do more children go to camp each summer, they also choose from a wider variety of camping experiences. Travel in this country and abroad has steadily increased. Employees in many large corporations participate in leisure experiences provided by their employers. Citizens by the millions visit theme parks and complexes across North America. More and more housing developments are being constructed with fully equipped recreation spaces and environments. The high technology of the 1980s has added to the consumer mania for acquiring such leisure amenities as electronic devices, including video games, television watches, and personal stereos.

An emerging leisure-centeredness within segments of North American society is clearly observable. There are increasing numbers of individuals seeking employment near sites that offer leisure opportunities consistent

1

with their needs and interests. Families are relocating to communities or sections within communities in order to take advantage of recreation options geared toward each family member.

Thousands of leisure professionals work in a variety of agency settings. All are engaged in the delivery of programs and services designed to provide individuals with optimal leisure experiences. The park, recreation, and leisure profession consists of public, quasi-public, private, and commercial agencies. While the number of employees in this field has decreased somewhat in the public sector, there has been an increase in the total number, owing in particular to the provision of additional leisure experiences by private organizations, businesses, and corporations. It is not our intent to elaborate on the various park, recreation, and leisure agencies or the diversity of their program offerings. Rather, the intent of this book is to focus on that which is generic to each of these unique settings—the programming of leisure experiences for and with potential and returning participants.

SOME THOUGHTS ON LEISURE AND RECREATION

Because the focus of this text is on programming leisure experiences, it is necessary for us to share with you the concepts of leisure and recreation in which we believe. Rather than reiterate the volumes of published material related to the terms "leisure" and "recreation," we have selected those definitions and descriptions of recreation and leisure that form the basis of our philosophy and thus provide a foundation for this book.

There is no one definition of leisure that satisfies all who label leisure as their profession or who experience leisure in their lives. The definitions of leisure are as variable as people are variable. To most North Americans, leisure means free time. To be at leisure means to have time at your disposal that is free from other obligations of living. To other people, leisure is holistic. It is that element of freedom, growth, and interrelatedness that is found within all of life's spheres. The authors believe that the descriptions of leisure offered by David E. Gray,[2] John Neulinger,[3] and Seppo E. Iso-Ahola,[4] offer the richest means for exploring the programming dimensions of leisure.

Neulinger's concept of leisure places it within the context of the quality of life. For Neulinger, leisure is not a thing that you have or accumulate, such as free time, but rather an "experience, a process, an ongoing state of mind."[5] Neulinger describes his psychological model of leisure in these words: "Leisure [is] a state of mind [and] is brought about by activities engaged in under conditions of perceived freedom. The quality of this leisure is further affected by the motivation for the activity, intrinsic as opposed to extrinsic."[6]

Gray's work in identifying common elements within leisure further supports the "perceived freedom" and "intrinsic motivation" aspects of Neulinger's work. He finds that leisure is inner-directed, that is, intrinsically motivated. Leisure facilitates the cultivation of the free mind; leisure is an expression of values; leisure is nonutilitarian, that is, having no motivation but its own; leisure provides potential for personal growth; and leisure is existential, in that it is an exercise of free will.[7]

Stressing that perceived freedom and freedom of choice are key attributes of leisure, Iso-Ahola focuses on the importance of perceived competence being "at the heart of intrinsic motivation."[8] "For the pursuit of and involvement in leisure activities to become intrinsically motivated, a person has to be able to participate in them freely and to feel competent because of engagement.[9]

Iso-Ahola believes that the feeling of competence is the major intrinsic reward linked with leisure behavior. Other intrinsic rewards, such as relaxation, novelty, escape from daily routine or stress, and social interaction, are obtained by people in leisure activities in which they feel a sense of success. The desire to obtain optimal arousal or a state of self-satisfaction in leisure stimulates people to seek novelty and variety within ongoing leisure activity. Obtaining optimal arousal, according to Iso-Ahola, is intrinsically motivating to leisure participants. Social interaction is also an intrinsic motivator in leisure expression. Leisure behavior occurs in social settings, and a desire for social interaction is often a prime motivator for leisure behavior.

Recreation, as traditionally defined, is the activity (either passive or active) that people engage in while in a state of leisure. A leisure programmer produces or facilitates recreational activity in a manner that allows participants to arrive at a leisure state. People typically engage in recreational activity during periods of free time. Much recreational activity is self-directed rather than truly organized, and is not necessarily the sole responsibility of the leisure programmer to initiate or direct. In either a self-directed or a programmed setting, recreation can be diversionary, passive, active, social, remedial, educational, and so on.

The term "recreation" is also used to designate the organized profession of park, recreation, and leisure services. The recreation profession is made up of persons who are either direct program providers or who assume support roles in leisure programming.

It is imperative that leisure programmers be knowledgeable regarding the concepts of leisure and recreation. They must understand the nature of their "product" in order to deliver their service—leisure experiences. It is also important for them to understand the role that leisure plays throughout the lives of people.

THE PROGRAMMER AND HUMAN DEVELOPMENT

Several of the major theories of human development, including life-cycle and life-course theories, have emerged from developmental psychology. Understanding concepts related to developmental psychology and the human life course can enable you to apply these concepts in the delivery of programs designed to address the leisure needs, interests, and demands of your clientele.

Developmental Psychology. Developmental psychology is concerned with understanding human growth and development. Although human individuality is clearly a reality, there is much evidence to support the concept of developmental phases or cycles that operate universally and consistently. That is, there are some aspects of living, growth, and development that are common to all people. It is also generally accepted that human behavior undergoes cyclical periods of change and stability throughout the life-course. Developmental psychologists use an interdisciplinary approach, encompassing both the social and the biological sciences, to address the multifaceted nature of human development. Leisure programmers can use the theories and findings of developmental psychology to aid themselves in understanding people whom they serve. The characteristics found in common for age graded groups or cohorts can help programmers to understand the life experience that participants bring with them to their leisure engagements. Leisure programmers, both as individuals and according to the identifiable characteristics that are common to them as a group, can use the theories and findings of developmental psychologists to aid themselves in understanding the people whom they serve.

In order to provide you with a look at some of the factors that influence human development, we will examine a paradigm developed by George Kaluger and Meriem Fair Kaluger.[10]

Kaluger and Kaluger speak of *determinants* of development—that is, factors having an influence on human growth, development, and behavior. Their work divides these determinants into four categories: physiological, environmental, psychological, and metaphysical (see Figure 1-1).

Physiological determinants are biological and include factors related to heredity, the nervous system, the glandular system, and the physical maturation process, including prenatal and postnatal development.

Environmental determinants include the cultural forces or norms that the socialized individual experiences. Families, peer groups, and other social groups encourage the individual to behave in ways that are acceptable to them. Social attitudes and role expectations are examples of environmental determinants. It is within this determinant area that leisure programmers can have a major influence on human development, because many leisure experiences take place within the context of family, peer, and group relationships. Other environmental determinants are physical, geographic, and climatic. Whether one lives in a rural or urban community can influence one's growth and development, for example.

Psychological determinants refer to the intrinsic and extrinsic (or internal and external) elements that influence people. Factors such as self-concept, values and attitudes, and behavioral responses are critical components of the psychological development of individuals.

The Kalugers indicate that *metaphysical determinants* are interesting to ponder but they are difficult to analyze because of their abstract nature and because of the impossibility of empirical verification.[11] Evolving theories of adult development suggest that metaphysical influences do have importance and can emerge as forces as late as adulthood. The metaphysical determinants include factors related to life forces, life choices, and the individual's understanding of the basis of life (as the result either of divine creation or of evolution). Life forces are the inner drives that influence the individual's

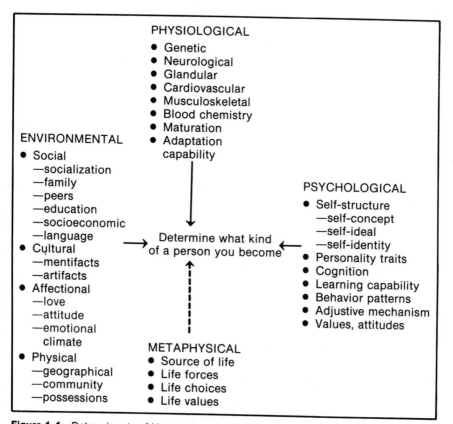

ENVIRONMENTAL
• Social
—socialization
—family
—peers
—education
—socioeconomic
—language
• Cultural
—mentifacts
—artifacts
• Affectional
—love
—attitude
—emotional
climate
• Physical
—geographical
—community
—possessions

PHYSIOLOGICAL
• Genetic
• Neurological
• Glandular
• Cardiovascular
• Musculoskeletal
• Blood chemistry
• Maturation
• Adaptation
capability

→ Determine what kind
of a person you become ←

PSYCHOLOGICAL
• Self-structure
—self-concept
—self-ideal
—self-identity
• Personality traits
• Cognition
• Learning capability
• Behavior patterns
• Adjustive mechanism
• Values, attitudes

METAPHYSICAL
• Source of life
• Life forces
• Life choices
• Life values

Figure 1–1   Determinants of Human Growth and Development
From George Kaluger and Meriem Fair Kaluger, *Human Development: The Span of Life*, 3rd ed. (St. Louis: Times Mirror/Mosby College Publishing, 1984), p. 47.

survival values, social values, and self-realization values. Life choices involve the nature and responsibility of individual decision making—that is, the degree of self-determination in the destiny and direction of an individual's life.

Programmers must consider these determinants of human development when engaged in the process of leisure program planning. They must, for example, consider physiological determinants when planning leisure experiences that are consistent with the capabilities of their clientele. Clearly, one would not plan activities requiring mature hand-eye co-ordination for tiny tots. Programs that involve the entire family are affected by environmental determinants, as are trips and excursions within and outside the participants' town or province. Programmers in organizations serving youth have a long history of creating leisure experiences designed to stimulate positive self-concepts, values exploration, personal development, and other psychological determinants. Finally, programs in leisure educa-tion encourage participants to examine life choices, engage in decision making, and become self-directed in their own leisure experiences—all of which are consistent with metaphysical development.

These examples illustrate the relationship between determinants of human development and the leisure programmer. While each example has been placed within one of the determinant categories, programmers should recognize that a carefully created program could easily contain elements from each category for any given group of participants. We can identify a number of ways in which a comprehensive set of leisure programs can contribute to human development.

Application Section.   Take a few moments, alone or with others, to identify some additional leisure programming examples that could evolve from applying the developmental determinants to program ideas. To begin, you might consider each area—physiological, environmental, psychological, and metaphysical—separately. Then try to identify some leisure programs that would address two areas. For example, a noncompetitive sports program for children addresses both the physiological (musculoskeletal and adaptation capability) and the environmental (socialization) determinant areas. A leisure education workshop for teens addresses both the environmental (peers and education) and the metaphysical (life choices and life values) determinant areas. If you are feeling particularly creative, try to combine three or all four determinant areas into one leisure program.

The Human Life Course.   According to Douglas C. Kimmel, developmental theories of the human life course are aimed at explaining the nature of growth and patterns of change experienced by individuals throughout their life-spans by focusing on the interaction of biological, psychological, and social factors.[12] As the individual ages biologically, he or she experiences a certain amount of physiological deterioration. Psychological aging refers to behavioral indicators of aging, such as self-awareness or the ability to adapt to changes. Social influences include the individual's relationship to socializing agents and institutions—for example, friends and family. The four developmental theories that are briefly examined in this chapter suggest that individuals move through developmental phases. Each of these theories has received a good deal of attention and is generally accepted as a plausible view regarding human development throughout the life course.

Charlotte Buhler's view of human growth and development emphasizes a parallel between the biological process of growth, stability, and decline and the psychosocial process of expansion, culmination, and contraction in activities and accomplishments.[13] During the 1930s, Buhler and her associates collected and studied four hundred biographies. These life stories were analyzed in terms of external events (profession, friends, family, hobbies), internal reactions (subjective experience of external events), and accomplishments over the course of life.[14] This psychosocial information was analyzed within the context of the following biological developmental phases: (1) progressive growth up to age 15; (2) continued growth combined with the ability to reproduce sexually during ages 15 to 25; (3) stability of growth during ages 25 to 45; (4) loss of sexual reproductive ability around ages 45 to 65; and (5) regressive growth and biological decline from age 65

Age	Phase
0–15	Child at home; prior to self-determination of goals.
15–25	Preparatory expansion and experimental self-determination of goals.
25–45	Culmination: definite and specific self-determination of goals.
45–65	Self-assessment of the results of striving for these goals.
65 up	Fulfillment of goals or experience of failure; previous activities continue, but in late life there may be a re-emergence of short-term goals focusing on satisfying immediate needs.

Figure 1–2 Buhler's Phases of Life

From Douglas C. Kimmel, *Adulthood and Aging*, 2nd ed. (New York: John Wiley and Sons, 1980), p. 9. Reprinted by permission of John Wiley and Sons, Inc.

on. From this analysis there emerged five phases of life that correspond with Buhler's biological time frame.[15] Figure 1-2 shows these psychosocial phases in approximate chronological age categories.

Carl Jung was another early researcher who contributed greatly to our present understanding of the human life course. Jung's view of the stages of human life was based primarily on his clinical work and his own theory of psychology.[16] Believing that growth is not finished and maturity is not reached by the end of adolescence, Jung emphasized that the individual continues to develop throughout the life course. His theory suggests that the life course is made up of two stages, with the first lasting until approximately age 40. A major developmental task for the individual is eliminating the last remnants of childishness by finding lasting solutions to earlier childhood experiences. In life's second stage, the individual is involved in a process of inner growth and development that Jung calls individuation. In Jung's view, the aim of this process of individuation is self-realization and self-discovery.[17] This self-analysis process occurs as one's values are reevaluated, physical energy is displaced by psychic energy, vigor is replaced by wisdom, and the individual is transformed into a more spiritual being.[18]

Erik Erikson, another developmental theorist, also concluded that personality development does not end with puberty but continues throughout adulthood.[19] Erikson postulated eight psychological stages of ego development from infancy to old age. Each of Erikson's stages is an area of resolution or problems for the self in relation to the external world. Each stage also requires the individual to acquire a favorable balance between opposing concepts in order to move to succeeding developmental stages. Figure 1-3 illustrates Erikson's eight stages of human development.

Finally, Robert Havighurst views human growth as a series of developmental tasks. The notion of developmental tasks acknowledges that certain skills, abilities, or tasks must be mastered by a person during a specific time period of life. Havighurst identifies three origins of inner and outer forces which structure these tasks: (1) physical maturation, such as learning to walk or adjusting to menopause; (2) societal demands and expectations, such as learning to read or learning to participate as a socially responsible citizen; and (3) the individual's personal values and aspirations, such as choosing and preparing for an occupation.[20] To illustrate, developmental tasks of middle age include:

Assisting teen-age children to become responsible and happy adults.

Achieving adult social and civic responsibility.

Reaching and maintaining satisfactory performance in one's occupational career.

Developing adult leisure-time activities.

Relating oneself to one's spouse as a person.

To accept and adjust to the physiological changes of middle age.

Adjusting to aging parents.[21]

SOME THOUGHTS ON PLAY

There is a behavior that is fundamental to the leisure experience. That behavior is called play. At least that is what it is called for children. Play for adults is usually referred to as recreation, possibly because some people believe that the latter term sounds more grown-up. The word "play" applies in this text to the leisure behavior of both children and adults.

There are several textbooks that are devoted exclusively to theories of play, including one by Michael Ellis[22] and one by Joseph Levy.[23] We encourage you to read them in order to get an in-depth understanding of the phenomenon of play. Our purpose here is to share with you some of the things that we find to be true about play as it relates to leisure.

Our vision of play is that it is enjoyable, optimally arousing, and intrinsically motivated behavior that may assume many forms and may occur at any time and in any place. Play is engaged in voluntarily in both structured and unstructured situations. However, some element of spontaneity must be present. That is, we do not look upon totally controlled leisure engagements as being play. Within play there is freedom. There is also pleasure, optimal challenge, opportunities for socialization, and growth and development. Play may range from the bubbling and gurgling behavior of infants to the highly competitive intramural/recreational sports behavior of college youths to the reading done by older adults. In today's world, play

Opposing Issues of Each Stage	Emerging Value	Period of Life
(1) Basic Trust versus Mistrust	Hope	Infancy
(2) Autonomy versus Shame and Doubt	Will	Early childhood
(3) Initiative versus Guilt	Purpose	Play age
(4) Industry versus Inferiority	Competence	School age
(5) Identity versus Identity (Role) Confusion	Fidelity	Adolescence
(6) Intimacy versus Isolation	Love	Young adulthood
(7) Generativity versus Stagnation (Self-Absorption)	Care	Maturity
(8) Integrity versus Despair (and Disgust)	Wisdom	Old age

Figure 1-3 Erikson's Eight Stages of Human Life

From Erik Erikson, "Reflections on Dr. Borg's Life Cycle." Reprinted by permission of *Daedalus*, Journal of the American Academy of Arts and Sciences, *Adulthood*, Spring 1976, Boston, MA.

may be the optimum means of reducing stress, whether through vigorous physical activity, engaging in fantasy, or merely taking the time out to breathe deeply, stretch, or smell some flowers. As such, play is an essential part of our lives.

SUMMARY

In this first chapter, we have begun by pointing out the importance of leisure to North American life; by introducing the role that leisure programmers play in facilitating or providing leisure experiences to clients or constituent groups; and by presenting the concepts of leisure and recreation that guide programming, underlie the leisure programming cycle, and recur within this book.

The four theories of human development described in this chapter have implications for leisure programming. In the next chapter, we will continue to examine leisure programming within the context of human development. After all, it is people who play! While programmers must be conscious of individual differences, we are suggesting that you also need to know about some commonly shared characteristics in order to find the balance in programming that will realistically allow you to be both effective and efficient. This is especially important in an era of limited resources. We also feel that this kind of information gives you better insight into constituents without leaning back on stereotypes.

Application Section. Take a few moments to think about the synopses of the developmental theories that you have just read. Choose the one or two that have the most relevance to you. Discuss any of the life-course experiences that you have had or observed in others. Then, unobtrusively, watch some people at play and try to infer the meaning underlying what they are doing.

FOOTNOTES

1. "Tomorrow," *U.S. News & World Report,* July 9, 1984, p. 20.
2. David E. Gray, "This Alien Thing Called Leisure," paper presented at the California State University at Long Beach, May 4, 1970.
3. John Neulinger, *To Leisure: An Introduction* (Boston: Allyn and Bacon, Inc., 1981).
4. Seppo E. Iso-Ahola, *The Social Psychology of Leisure and Recreation* (Dubuque, Iowa: William C. Brown Company, Publishers, 1980).
5. Neulinger, *To Leisure,* p. xiii.
6. Ibid., p. 34.
7. Gray, "This Alien Thing," pp. 3-4.
8. Seppo E. Iso-Ahola, "Intrinsic Motivation: An Overlooked Basis for Evaluation," *Parks & Recreation,* February 1982, p. 32. Reprinted by special permission of the National Recreation and Park Association.
9. Ibid., p. 32.
10. George Kaluger and Meriem Fair Kaluger, *Human Development: The Span of Life,* 3rd ed. (St. Louis: Times Mirror/Mosby College Publishing, 1984), p. 47.

11. Ibid., p. 73.
12. Douglas C. Kimmel, *Adulthood and Aging*, 2nd ed. (New York: John Wiley and Sons, 1980), pp. 7–8. Reprinted by permission of John Wiley & Sons, Inc.
13. Ibid., p. 10.
14. Else Frenkel-Brunswick, "Adjustments and Reorientation in the Course of the Life Span," in *Middle Age and Aging*, ed. Bernice L. Neugarten (Chicago: University of Chicago Press, 1968), p. 78.
15. Kimmel, *Adulthood and Aging*, p. 8.
16. Ibid., p. 12.
17. Wilbur Bradbury, *The Adult Years* (New York: Time-Life Books, 1975), p. 13.
18. Alan B. Knox, *Adult Development and Learning* (San Francisco: Jossey-Bass, Inc., Publishers, 1977), p. 329.
19. Erik Erikson, *Childhood and Society*, 2nd ed. (New York: W. W. Norton and Co., Inc., 1963).
20. Robert J. Havighurst, *Human Development and Education*, 3rd ed. (New York: Longmans Inc., 1972), p. 5. Copyright 1972 by Longman Inc. Reprinted by permission of Longman Inc., New York.
21. Ibid., pp. 96–106.
22. Michael Ellis, *Why People Play* (Englewood Cliffs, N.J.: Prentice-Hall, Inc., 1973).
23. Joseph Levy, *Play Behavior* (Melbourne, FL: Robert E. Kreiger Publishing Co., Inc., 1983).

chapter 2

The Life Course
and Leisure

INTRODUCTION

In designing programs to meet the leisure needs, interests, and demands of participants, leisure programmers must understand the role of leisure in relationship to the human life course. You can and should tap into the vast amount of information available on the populations you serve, no matter what their age, disability, or developmental stage of life.

In earlier times, the greatest amount of information available to programmers was specifically related to childhood and adolescent development. An abundance of research and knowledge about child's play has been recorded by a variety of people in many occupational fields. Because of this, it has been possible for park, recreation, and leisure agencies to offer leisure programs for children and teens that are many, varied, and based on the expressed needs and interests of those in the earlier years of their life-course.

More recently, the recreational offerings made available to older adults have grown in quantity and quality because older people have received more research and public attention since the 1960s. Current census data show that North Americans are an aging population. But the middle years, roughly between ages 30 and 60, are still experiencing a lack of public and research attention. Middle adults lack leisure choices more than any other age group within Western society, owing to a variety of factors.

Our overview of leisure throughout the life course is offered from a life-span developmental perspective, from childhood through late adulthood. We will take a close look at the middle years, particularly, because of the growth of that population and the lack of previous attention to it.

CHILDHOOD

There are vast amounts of free time available to youngsters during their childhood years. In the preschool years, children's lives are filled with opportunities for exploration and stimulation through play. In summarizing data on play in relationship to socialization through leisure, Douglas A. Kleiber and John R. Kelly say: "The conditions that support play in early childhood can be extended to leisure behavior in general."[1] Children, like persons of any age, seek optimal arousal in their leisure experiences.[2]

Programmers' interest in children continues as they grow older and approach school age. The ages of 3 to 6 are typically when youngsters begin participating in "tiny tot" programs offered by leisure and human services organizations, especially if both parents are employed. However, most children of this age still find their leisure experiences in the home or in locales near home, such as in the neighborhood or on the playground. Parents and other family members such as siblings exert a tremendous influence on children. Kleiber and Kelly write: "Family structures lead children into certain kinds of leisure experiences that prepare them for the acquisition of certain roles with a predisposition to subsequent leisure experiences."[3]

The family provides a context for recreational activities, games, and handicrafts, for the time-consuming pastime of watching television, for outings, and for holiday-related functions and celebrations. Shared leisure experiences can bring divorced parents together with their children. The leisure experience for both the child and the parent takes on great importance within the family as a means through which the child masters developmental tasks.

By the time children are 6 or 7 years old, their play is becoming increasingly organized.[4] Once in school, they are still fortunate in having free time. With this free time and through leisure experiences, the child's early social learnings take hold and become established. Kleiber and Kelly report: "Extensive involvement in games and sports often emerges during this period. However, there is also expansion into other forms of play, as well as into expressive, creative, and constructive activities. All of these activities are influenced by such factors as the family, peers, schools, the media cultural values, and social systems."[5]

Leisure programmers often design leisure experiences that influence and promote socialization during childhood. The leisure programmer serves as an agent in a social system that functions in concert with other social systems (especially the schools) that affect children's lives. You play an important role in providing programs that facilitate cognitive, social, personality, and physiological development throughout the childhood years. Iso-Ahola states: "The acquisition of favorable attitudes toward leisure during formative years lays the foundations for satisfactory socialization in later stages of the life span."[6]

Organized games and group sports activities are found in most leisure programs. Adventure Playgrounds, New Games, and other innovative programs offer children opportunities to explore, experiment with, and manipulate their leisure environment in novel ways. This offers them enjoyment and opportunities for success and variety, thereby enhancing optimal arousal or incongruity in their leisure experiences. According to Iso-Ahola, a child's early leisure experience is strongly related to his or her leisure patterns later in life. "Thus, if an individual's play and recreation is poor in stimulation throughout childhood, the person may become accustomed to a low level of arousal and may regard it as optimal. This in turn may impair the tendency to seek novel incongruous and complex experiences in adulthood."[7]

ADOLESCENCE

The teen years, generally ages 13 to 19, are often considered to be a very difficult time for the individual, whose personal identity search and role as a student consume tremendous energy. Often several life-styles are experimented with, varying from childish to adult. Kaluger and Kaluger remark: "In some ways adolescents are like squirming, wiggling caterpillars engaged in the agonizing fight to escape childhood's cocoon and enter into adulthood's full flight. The world will soon be full of beautiful butterflies. They cannot wait to break out and fly."[8]

This is an age group that provides diversity, refreshment, and woes to the leisure programmer. Peer-group affiliation plays a major role and is seen as contributing to the adolescent's identity. Further, the peer group is greatly responsible for the modification of behavior.[9] Adolescents have a strong tendency toward social conformity with their peer group.[10] Significant bodily changes at puberty and the psychological reaction to these changes create dissonance and the need to reevaluate one's self in relationship to one's body. These bodily changes are accompanied by psychosexual development. The Kalugers write: "Early adolescence begins with gangs or groups made up of members of the same sex and ends with a coming together of the two sexes in crowd activities and possibly with some dating."[11] Later adolescence usually does include dating. Leisure experiences provide a setting for the individual to establish social relationships, especially heterosexual ones.[12]

Parental influence continues throughout adolescence, but this relationship becomes clouded by the importance teenagers place upon members of their peer group. One developmental task during adolescence is the attempt to achieve emancipation from the home.[13] The adolescent tends to pull away from parental influence in order to accomplish this. The influences of school and leisure agencies can serve as substitutes for parental influence, particularly if the teenager's peers are involved with the same agencies.

Leisure is frequently when the adolescent can seek status and affirmation or establish social position and social differentiation with selected others[14] and organized leisure programs can provide that context. It is especially in their leisure, apparently, that teens want to interact under minimal adult supervision. "Symbols of identification" for "group-oriented youth" can be obtained in leisure activities such as listening to music or dancing, or in joining voluntary associations such as clubs, religious groups, and service and fraternal organizations. Kleiber and Kelly state:

"The importance of leisure in adolescence generally is that it is a primary context for self-expression and social integration. It is thus critical in obtaining feedback relative to role learning and individual identity. It provides an optimum setting for 'experimenting' with social relationships and individual potentials."[15]

Facilitating leisure experiences that give the participant feelings of independence and perceived competence are particularly important in enabling him or her to surmount the developmental difficulties associated with adolescence.

As we examine the individual's movement across what might be labeled the "preparatory" stage of life, we see the maturing of the child through preadolescence to adolescence. We find that the child is occupied with exploration and initial learning, whereas the preadolescent is intent on establishing a personal identity and the adolescent a place in his or her social group. In terms of leisure, the child seeks to discover things about the world and himself or herself. This exploration continues for the preadolescent with an even deeper questioning or seeking. For the adolescent there is an emerging independence and sexuality.

Early childhood socialization, including the formation of the child's fundamental attitudes toward leisure, occurs within the family. Later, peers, schools, and other organized community groups continue this process. Leisure plays an important role in socialization, from the earliest "let's make believe" play experiences (through which social roles may be learned) to more structured group activities (through which cultural values and skills needed for successful interpersonal functioning are practiced).

ADULTHOOD AND LEISURE

Adulthood makes up the majority of the life course, roughly from age 30 to 60. Because this portion of life is only now being given the same degree of attention that childhood, adolescence, and later adulthood have been given in the past, we are examining it here in more depth. We will begin by considering life changes and personality during adulthood. Then we will examine adulthood life stages, drawing upon the literature in leisure that describes adult leisure pursuits, leisure-related changes, and the importance of leisure experiences during this stage of life.

Adult Life Changes. Developmental psychologists have focused their research into adult development within the context of the family (leaving one, raising one), work (occupation or lack thereof), and self (value reorientation, attitude reassessment, personal relationships, development, and intimacy). Leisure has yet to be fully examined in a developmental context. However, as the developmental periods of life become more clearly understood and as the interest in leisure research on adulthood continues to grow, you can expect to be able to do your job in the future with more knowledge regarding the functions of leisure in adulthood. It is known that patterns of leisure engagement, as well as meanings and motivations for participation, are related to physiological, psychological, and social changes and the interaction of these phenomena as they occur at various points in the life course of the individuals.[16] It is also known that developmental changes occur throughout adulthood.

Adulthood is a dynamic time of life. Internal occurrences, as well as social influences and life events, bring about change and growth during adulthood. In the social context, adults are influenced by the norms of the communities in which they live, the value society places on people at various ages, the rate of social change, their social class, their living arrangements, and the opportunities available to them. Functioning within the traditional social roles related to family, work, and community, adults are repeatedly involved in a variety of transactions with other individuals. Life events create experiences and expectations that emerge from societal contexts. According to Alan B. Knox, major socially related changes occurring during adulthood include changes in job or career, divorce or remarriage, moving to a new dwelling, and what has been termed the "empty nest," the time when the youngest child leaves home.[17]

Successful adjustment to these social influences and life events requires adults to adapt. Knox points out that there are interweaving threads of stability and change that occur during adulthood.[18] These threads or trends, whose existence is supported by the research of others such as Havighurst, Daniel J. Levinson, and Gail Sheehy, revolve around the adult's performance in family, work, and community settings. Do these threads of stability and change also revolve around leisure during adulthood?

In our opinion, the answer is "yes." To illustrate this, it is helpful to think of leisure as a "career" or major life endeavor in which some elements remain stable and others change as the individual moves through the life course.[19] This happens in much the same way as job-related experiences. Let's say that a businesswoman takes on a challenging three-year work assignment, or finds parenting a full-time demand for an extended period of time, or moves across the country to take a promotion with new and greater responsibilities. Any of these job-related occurrences can effect other facets of her family or leisure life. Let's say that this same businesswoman begins to take an interest in a time-consuming, long-term, and highly involving leisure pursuit. The resultant "leisure career" may then, in various ways, intersect with and impact on the family and work spheres of her life.[20]

One of the most useful concepts in understanding growth and development during adulthood is suggested by Levinson.[21] It is the concept of structure changing and structure building, and relates to the adult's evolving life structure. The concept can be helpful in grasping the nature of change throughout adulthood. Structure building is a period in which the main tasks are to build a life structure, to make choices, to commit oneself to a life structure, and then to enrich one's life and pursue one's goals. Structure changing is a transitional period in which the main tasks are to modify the existing structure, to reappraise it, and to consider its value for oneself and others. Structure changing also includes attempts by the person to bring about certain changes in order to create the basis for a new structure, so that when the transitional period ends and the next structure building period begins the person will be able to make choices and begin to live within the new structure. The process of structure building and structure changing is one of continually making and reassessing decisions. A purposeful programmer can use this concept of adult change behavior when designing or facilitating programs by realizing that adults are continually in the process of reassessing life structures.

In summary, change does occur during the decades that comprise adulthood. In particular, change appears to occur in the social sphere according to the nature and degree of involvement with one's community, family, and work; the emphasis on oneself in terms of definitions or redefinitions of identity, needs, and values; and one's insight into oneself and the environment. As we explore the particular stages of adult development, we will also note the psychological and biological changes that occur.

Adult Personality Development. Traditionally, personality has fallen in the domain of psychology and the roles that we addressed earlier have fallen in the province of sociology. The presumed consequences of these two aspects of human behavior interact in determining complex social behavior, including adult growth and development. Personality has been thought of as representing the stable, persistent, internal organization of a person as it exists within the constraints of the roles held by the individual, whereas the roles, representing certain characteristics of social position, exist within the bounds of the personality of the individual who occupies them. Thus there is an interplay between the roles we discussed in the previous section of this chapter and personality. This interplay takes place within the context of a changing organism—the adult human being. While an apparent stability may be evident from year to year in the adult personality, there is evidence of substantial change in and modification to aspects of adult personality from decade to decade.[22]

Bernice L. Neugarten indicates that there is an apparent lack of consensus among developmental psychologists about personality and it follows that there is no general consensus about a theory of personality. According to Neugarten, developmental psychology by definition is concerned with issues of continuity and change. Adult life-cycle shifts or role changes that interact with personality can be related to changes in self-concept and attitudes, decisions that have been made, moral development, and adaptation to life.[23] Knox discusses these phenomena extensively.[24] The following summarizes parts of his and others' work in this area, and draws upon some of our own interactionist thinking as well.

A central theme of adult personality development is the evolution of the psychological self or self-concept. This involves asking (or re-asking) the question, "Who am I?" A positive sense of self for North American adults is associated with self-actualization and effective occupational performance and reflects high self-esteem and self-confidence. The developing sense of self is influenced by the individual's own perceptions and feelings and through experiences with friends, coworkers, and family members. The process of making choices or decisions is related to the adult's personality. Decision making requires assertiveness, goal setting, accommodation, and self-directedness.

Attitudes interact with personality throughout adulthood. Internal and external influences on attitudes generate felt needs that become especially important aspects of personality. While needs affect adult behavior, they also tend to follow some predictable shifts in the life course. Changing needs serve to motivate adults toward affiliation, achievement, expansion, and adjustments in their orientation to time. Affiliation needs are reflected in interactions with friends, family, and colleagues. The degree to which the adult fulfills achievement needs is related to personal characteristics, such as ability and amount of energy available to invest in achievement, and to societal characteristics, such as the value one's social group or setting places upon achievement. The need to make time-oriented adjustments emerges as the adult realizes that "the future is now." As the individual grows older, his or her perspective shifts and decisions are made in light of the perceived amount of time the person feels he or she has left to live.

Another recurring theme related to personality is moral development. The experience of maturing appears to be a requirement for moving to higher levels of moral development following the periodic reconsideration of the way one thinks or feels about previously accepted beliefs and values. The individual, for example, may reconsider beliefs related to the importance of leisure, work, or family.

Adaptation is also related to adult personality development. Making adjustments throughout life is inevitable in interpersonal relations, work, and life style. An indication of success in adaptation is reflected in individual perceptions of life satisfaction and happiness. Adults become unsatisfied and unhappy when they perceive a discrepancy between their expectations and their achievement. More specifically, satisfaction is a function of aspiration and expectation and accomplishment, and happiness is related to feelings of personal security, acceptance of others, ability to affect outcomes in one's life (personal efficacy), and a belief that life has meaning. These ideas and others are elaborated on further in our discussion of stages of adult life.

Adulthood Stages.   Up to now, we have examined some general concepts related to life changes and personality during the adult years. Each topic suggests the importance of psychological tasks and social roles during adulthood. Further, as we highlighted childhood and adolescence, we noted that leisure needs and activities differ during the earlier part of the life course. The same holds true for the various stages of the adult life course which encompass a three decade span of time. In viewing the developmental tasks that must be mastered during adulthood, the importance of psychological tasks and social roles will emerge again. This will provide us with a background for our discussion of adult leisure patterns and engagements.

Buhler, Erikson, and Jung, mentioned in Chapter 1, are among the early social scientists from whom modern authors glean the theoretical frameworks for their investigations and writings. In this section we will emphasize the major stages of adulthood suggested by Levinson,[25] Sheehy,[26] and others. Peter I. Rose states that although Levinson's research work emphasizes men, "much of what is discussed applies to adult women as well.''[27] Sheehy focuses on both men and women. Much of the literature, however, is limited to white middle-class men. Let's turn to a classic.

Levinson completed an extensive longitudinal study of the lives of forty men over a ten-year period, using intensive biographical interviewing techniques. His findings show evidence of transitional periods or stages, which he calls "seasons," within the adult life cycle. While these seasons have a certain shape and form, and some degree of stability, Levinson adds: "To say that a season is relatively stable, however, does not mean that it is stationary or static. Change goes on within each, and a transition is required for the shift from one season to the next.''[28]

Levinson's theory of developmental periods is a way of thinking about the life structure of an individual, which encompasses personality, occupational career, family, and other aspects of a person's life. He found that at any one time in an individual's life the life structure is made up of these components, of which the central ones are occupation and family (or various equivalents of family); more specifically, life structure is "the underlying pattern or design of a person's life.''[29] (The two basic kinds of developmental periods within the life structure, structure building and structure changing, were discussed earlier in this chapter.)

The first three seasons, Early Adult Transition (structure changing), Entering the Adult World (structure building), and Age Thirty Transition (structure changing), are considered to be the "novice" phase of adulthood. During this period of time, the young person is involved in a developmental process that allows him or her to acquire adult interests and values and to make important choices related to work, marriage, and family. It begins as early as age 17 and continues until approximately age 33 (see Figure 2-1). During this time, the individual is engaged in exploring the adult world and creating a provisional life structure. Developmental tasks that were found to be most important during this period of time include forming a dream and

Early Adult Transition	Age 17–22
Entering the Adult World	Age 22–28
Age Thirty Transition	Age 28–33
Settling Down	Age 33–40
Mid-Life Transition	Age 40–45
Entering Middle Adulthood	Age 45–50
Age 50 Transition	Age 50–55

Figure 2-1 Developmental Periods in Early and Middle Adulthood*

From Daniel J. Levinson, *The Seasons of a Man's Life* (New York: Alfred A. Knopf, Inc., 1978), p. 57.

*While there is an average or most frequent age when a developmental period begins, there is also a range of variation that spans about two years above and below the average, with five or six years being the maximum period of time for completing any given developmental period.

giving it a place in one's life structure, forming a mentor relationship, forming an occupation, and forming love relationships that include marriage and family.

The Age Thirty Transition period, like all transitional periods, "serves to terminate one structure and to initiate another."[30] A person arrives at this transition with the life structure that was created during earlier adulthood. The main developmental task during this period is to reappraise that first life structure. Levinson points out that this transition is important because the first life structure created during the twenties has to be imperfect. According to the research findings, all persons make some changes during the Age Thirty Transition period. Sometimes this transition proceeds smoothly, with continuity and without disruption. Levinson notes that for most people this is a painful and stressful transition.[31] The individual has to reexamine prior choices that were related to the developmental tasks of earlier adulthood.

The shift from the Age Thirty Transition period to the Settling Down period (structure building) is one of the crucial steps in adult development.[32] The researchers found that people make important new choices or reaffirm old choices during this time. "If these choices are congruent with his [or her] dreams, talents, and external possibilities, they provide the basis for a relatively satisfactory life structure. If the choices are poorly made and the new structure seriously flawed, he [or she] will pay a heavy price in the next period."[33]

The Settling Down period presents two major developmental tasks to be accomplished: establishing one's niche in society and working at advancement. The first task includes stabilizing the components of one's life structure (family, occupation, and community) and achieving a greater sense of self. According to Kleiber and Kelly,[34] the development of careers and families have a constraining effect upon leisure at this time.

In summary, during these first four seasons of the adult life cycle we see the dynamics, the "fits and starts," of adult growth. We find that the young adult is occupied with testing out selected roles in terms of an occupation and direction in life and with testing out intimacy in interpersonal relationships. In the late twenties to early thirties, the individual further develops selected roles and intimacy with significant others, including offspring. Affirmation of earlier commitments or new directions may take place, as some questioning goes on during the Age Thirty Transition.

The novice phase as a whole might be characterized as self-developmental, whereas the fourth season, Settling Down, might be characterized as more self-expressive. Thus, the adult moves from anticipating roles, through developing and maintaining relationships and establishing roles, to defining a life structure in which primacy is given to work, the community, and to some extent the family, depending on the intensity of commitment to work or the constraints that work places upon the individual's time. At this point, for most working people, their *primary* means of self-expression is probably through their occupation.

Psychologically, the young adult's establishment of autonomy from parents is very important to him or her. Later, the need to be socially competent assumes priority. Finally, we see the society's work ethic being internalized by the employed person during the Settling Down period. Age related biological changes do not assume a great significance until the next era.

What occurs with a person's leisure as he or she moves through the transitions of adult life? During the three seasons of the novice phase of adulthood, leisure relates both to forming an occupation and to forming love relationships. The demands and expectations of employment can modify leisure pursuits and social goals and become a factor in determining leisure choices.[35] As the individual becomes involved in time-consuming efforts directed toward seeking, beginning, and continuing full-time employment, the availability of free time in which to engage in leisure can be lessened. Love relationships are sought, initiated, developed, and reinforced during this phase by using the freedom found in leisure. Thus the young adult's leisure centers around parties, social clubs and gatherings, bars, fitness centers, and other courting environments, as well as sports and other bond-building activities that offer arenas in which to find companionship and friendship or to strengthen existing relationships.[36]

Owing to the reduction in sex-role stereotyping, delays in marriage and having children, and the greatly increased numbers of women working on a full-time basis, occupation is assuming a new meaning for today's women with regard to leisure. Nancy J. Osgood and Christine Z. Howe write:

> The social role of primary bread winner (that has been traditionally the domain of the male member of the couple) also influences one's leisure pursuits. This occurs for the female member, too, if she has an achievement orientation to her work and perceives herself as an upwardly mobile professional in a long term career. As one assumes greater job responsibilities, work related leisure experiences occur. They may include socializing with work colleagues and generally 'playing on the company team.'[37]

The importance of work in relation to leisure is thus very clear for persons up to their early thirties. Initially, leisure may be highly social, then more intimate and other-oriented, and finally highly work-related, especially for males. For both men and women, marriage changes the social context of leisure. The persons involved are definitely "coupled." Later, as children enter the scene, if the female is the primary care provider her leisure becomes sharply differentiated from her "career woman" counterpart—it assumes a family focus. For both parents, the advent of children will define and constrain leisure in terms of time, energy, and money. But all freedom is not totally lost. Kleiber and Kelly find that juggling careers and families can provide the potential of "organizing time and social involvement in such a way that leisure, however limited, is incorporated."[38] Further, more leisure takes place in the home as one's family becomes established.

For persons in the Settling Down period, a major developmental task involves "building a better life, improving and using one's skills, becoming more creative, contributing to society and being affirmed by it, according to one's values."[39] Voluntary involvement in community and service-oriented groups, and leadership roles assumed with youth programs and organizations, may occupy one's leisure. Major developmental tasks during the

Settling Down period are related to building a life around initial choices, establishing oneself as an adult in society, and "the effort to be more fully one's own person."[40] Leisure may be a primary vehicle by which the adult enhances his or her sense of self in a self-directed manner.

The next season we're going to examine is the Mid-Life Transition. This period is one of structure changing in which a person comes to terms with the past and prepares for the future. There are three major tasks that have to be worked out during the Mid-Life Transition. The first is to terminate the era of early adulthood by making a far-reaching reappraisal of the life structure of the Settling Down period. This intense examination of the meaning of one's life up to that time and setting of directions (some of which may be new) for the remainder of one's life is popularly referred to as the "mid-life crisis."

The second developmental task requires the individual to take the first steps toward the initiation of middle adulthood. Levinson's research points to the external and internal aspects of the person's life structure that become apparent when significant changes are made. Visible external changes can involve divorce, remarriage, major shifts in occupation and life study, marked decline in level of functioning, and notable progress in creativity or in upward social mobility. Internally, a person "may change appreciably in social outlook, in personal values, in what he [or she] wants to give the world, in what he [or she] wants to be for himself [or herself]."[41] These changes can be subtle and hidden, or they may become visible, as indicated by the external changes.

A third task is dealing with the polarities of the person's relationship to self and to the external world. The four polarities whose resolution become the principal task of mid-life individuation are: (1) Young/Old; (2) Destruction/Creation; (3) Masculine/Feminine: and (4) Attachment/Separateness.[42]

Each of these polarities exists during the entire life course, and while they are not considered to be specific to the Mid-Life Transition, they do operate during this period with a special force. The Young/Old polarity is central to developmental change at mid-life because the individual must adjust to the biological and social aspects of aging. At this point the person becomes keenly aware of biological changes; the fear of biological decline; the growing recognition of her or his own mortality; and society's lack of appreciation for the value of middle age.

So the Mid-Life Transition may be summarized as a period in which one's authenticity is questioned and new directions may be taken, but from which a keener sense of self and of caring for others (both personally and professionally) emerges. There are bodily changes that reflect the aging process; psychological changes, with some of the differences between men and women becoming less pronounced (men continue to be more self-expressive, while women find a more instrumental side to themselves); and a changing sense of time. Finding and being content with the meaning of life is an important element of this period, as one acknowledges that half one's days have been spent.

The next period of adult development, Entering Middle Adulthood (or

Restabilization), is a time of structure building that provides a basis for living in middle adulthood. Levinson considers this to be the initial outcome of the Mid-Life Transition. During this period, a person may or may not continue to experience anxiety, depending on the individual's ability to adjust to more and more indicators of his or her own mortality—launching children, having aging parents, possibly coping with a change in marital, health, or job status, and finding new sources of satisfaction or achievement outside of work (for example, in community or social life). If the individual has indeed built a comfortable and secure identity by this time, then he or she may be more inner-directed, inclined to help others, and more concerned with questions of ultimate value, as opposed to looking for the quickest solution to problems from a short-term perspective. So the main tasks for Entering Middle Adulthood are to make crucial choices, to give these choices meaning and commitment, and to build a life structure around them. Levinson felt that this newly developed life structure will be needed to carry the individual through the remainder of the middle years.

Levinson's theory and other contemporary views of adult stage development have received wide media coverage. Many people today accept predictable transitions as a part of life. While leisure programmers can and should use much of the emerging information regarding adulthood life stages, you should also be aware of some of the cautions against specific age stereotyping.

Neugarten has suggested that stage theories imply a fixed, one-way progression of issues and conflicts that occurs at chronological intervals. They are appealing because they seem logical and orderly amidst the complex changes the individual experiences.[43] To base leisure programs entirely on· age would be utterly incorrect! The past two decades have brought about vast changes in what Neugarten calls "our social time clocks" and "our biological time clocks,"[44] not to mention all the other kinds of changes that have occurred in North America since the 1950s. Neugarten believes that what gives adults the feeling that they are experiencing life crises during adulthood is not the events of adulthood themselves but the fact that the events can no longer be keyed to their biological and social clocks. Further, there are newer and emerging adult life-styles that have only begun to be systematically studied and reported on. The programmer working with a clientele made up of families, for example, will increasingly experience nontraditional family units. Changes in the family and the growth of "new" special groups are elaborated on in Chapters 3 and 5.

Kimmel speaks of the "historical time line," and this notion also has relevance to adult stage theories.[45] Adult development theorists have integrated biological, psychological, and social age-relevant influences in identifying life-span changes that typically take place in the lives of white middle-class males, or changes in the life-styles of this group. What must also be taken into consideration by leisure programmers is that individuals are "products" of a specific historical period. For example, an individual who was 40 in 1950 may have experienced psychosocial influences very different from those experienced by someone who will be 40 in the year 2000.

Leisure programmers must continually remain cognizant of participants' individuality when they are planning programs. While stage theorists
note general tendencies among middle-aged adult populations, there are
always exceptions to the rule, and these "minority" groupings are becoming
larger as adult life-styles keep diversifying. Successful programmers will rely
heavily on needs assessment when designing programs geared toward adult
populations, or all populations for that matter.

With these cautions in mind, let us turn to some of the information that
has been found about leisure for persons in the establishment phase of adult
life. Leisure can have tremendous importance during this period in the
processes demanded by the serious reappraisal of one's life structure. In
leisure, one has the freedom either to contemplate these issues personally in a
self-directed fashion or to seek socializing experiences with others through
organizations that provide programs for people who want to consider these
issues mutually. Leisure counseling can be used for exploring the role of
leisure in one's life. According to Iso-Ahola, "There is some evidence to
suggest that leisure participation plays an important role in solving
problems which appear during transition from one stage to another."[46]

One may develop one's creativity through exploring career options or
resuming a career, participating in civic, social, or religious organizations,
or developing new hobbies and areas of talent and skill,[47] thereby opening
up additional leisure experiences. You, as a programmer, can and should
assume an active stance in developing programs and services that address
these issues. As Kleiber and Kelly note: "Leisure may take on great
significance in replacing parental tasks and opportunities. It may also be, for
some, a social space in which old identities are reestablished and new ones
tried out. Leisure may thus involve both consolidation and exploration
during this period."[48] Iso-Ahola states: "Furthermore, people change their
leisure activity patterns throughout the several life stages, not necessarily by
acquiring new forms of recreation but by substituting within the familiar
activities."[49]

Regarding biological changes, programs emphasizing physical fitness
and bodily enhancement can take on special meaning. Biological factors
limit or predispose people to certain leisure patterns.[50] The upsurge in the
popularity of body building, for example, indicates one way people in
middle age react to anxiety about biological changes. Resort areas that
feature spa, diet, and exercise programs also address this concern about body
image.

In leisure as well as in parenting and work, early mid-life adults may
seek some demonstration of "performance." They want to achieve and
receive some acknowledgement of success or vicarious success. Some
individuals may seek such success through their children, who are urged to
do well in school, sports, or the arts. Others may develop their own latent
skills if they have the opportunity or the motivation. In later mid-life, leisure
may become more sedentary and/or intellectual. For health purposes,
persons in mid-life must be encouraged to be physically active. This is also a
time for the introduction of new activities or for reinforcing involvement in

familiar ones. Leisure at this time of life can be vigorous and stimulating—physically, socially, and mentally.

Application Section.   Below are several examples of leisure programs. The men and women who established these programs believe that their selection of leisure activities and services speaks directly to the special needs of persons in middle age. Which of Levinson's transitions (it could be more than one) do you think the program participants are most likely to be experiencing? In what ways can the program address the developmental concerns of individual participants, as discussed in this chapter? Finally, what are some ways in which the leisure programmer could encourage adults to experience change and variety in their leisure activities? Attempt to generate other program ideas that would address the leisure needs, interests, and preferences of persons in middle age.

- The San Jose, California YWCA's Career Outreach Program focuses on displaced homemakers: women who are recently divorced or widowed and those desiring to work for the first time. This program offers group counseling, social interaction, networking and support groups, career identification, and career development.

- Both community-based and institution-based therapeutic recreation specialists are actively involved in providing for the leisure needs and interests of adults. By routinely using leisure assessment instruments aimed at identifying the leisure skills, preferences, and attitudes of clients, the therapeutic recreator facilitates recreational experiences designed to encourage change and enhance personal development and independent leisure functioning.

- Commercial and private recreation enterprises have created a number of recreation opportunities designed for the adult population. The availability of spas, resort vacations, racquetball clubs, movie theaters, recreational sports equipment, leisure consulting, travel packages, tour excursions, and more, has provided a wide variety of leisure pursuits for adults with time and discretionary dollars to spend.

Review.   As can be seen by reviewing adulthood stages, leisure is altered and conditioned by differing life experiences and the priorities that individuals place upon leisure. While leisure patterns and engagements are as varied as individual characteristics, similarities in the experience of aging are reflected in the literature. Osgood and Howe have delineated the broad age-based stages of the traditional North American adult life cycle, relating changing activities, values, motivations, and meanings of leisure participation to various biological, psychological, and social-developmental changes that appear to occur in particular life stages.[51] Their work is depicted in Figures 2-2 and 2-3. Figure 2-2 synthesizes the various roles and changes that occur over the adult life course. Figure 2-3 focuses on selected leisure activities, values, motivations, and meanings. This information can

Figure 2-2 Roles and Changes Over the Adult Life Course: The Traditional Pattern

Young Adulthood[1] (age 20–35)	Mid-Life (age 35–55)	Late Life (age 55 →)
+ Development of attitudes, beliefs, values	+ Realization of mortality	+ Integrity/integration vs. despair
+ Establish autonomy	+ Settling down	+ Time consciousness
+ Establish intimacy or isolation	+ Creativity	+ Late adult transition
+ "Catch 30 Transition" occurs	+ Authenticity crisis	+ Flowering
+ Structure a dream	+ Self-reflection	+ Fulfill or fail at goals
+ Culmination of self-determined goals	+ Self-assessment of goals	+ Search for meaning of aging
+ Make the 30's transition	+ Fulfilling the dream	+ Concern with unmet needs of self
•+ Build life structure	+ Inward focus	*+ Self-concept crisis
+• Urge to merge	+ Adjustment to aging parents	*+ Physiological decline
+• Seeker self emerges	+ Mid-life transition (m)	
	+ Generation or stagnation	
	+ Restabilization of the sexes	
	+ "Deadline decade"	
	+• Productivity, societal affirmation	
	+* Male mid-life crisis (m)	
	+* Adjust to physiological changes	
	+* Menopause (f)	
	+* Physical decline	
• Complete formal schooling	• Job promotion	• Assume grandparent role
• First job, getting into the world	• Launch children from home	• Retirement
• First marriage	• Civic/social responsibilities	• Maintain independence, self-direction
• Buying a house	• Divorce	• Cope with loss, widowhood
• Managing a home	• Mid-career change (m)	• Assume role of mentor
• First child born	• Return to work (f)	• Maintain self-esteem and self-concept

Figure 2-2 (*Continued*)

Young Adulthood[1] (age 20–35)	Mid-Life (age 35–55)	Late Life (age 55 →)
● Assume civic, social, and community responsibilities	● Care for aging parents	● Financial losses
	● "Empty nest"	+ Deal with issue of death
	● Teach, train teenage children	+ Life review, introspection
	● Culture bearers; support norms and values of culture	+ Peace, security, comfort
	●+ Socializing over sexualizing	+ Personal autonomy
	+ Changing time sense	+ Meaningful integration
	+ Develop mental flexibility	+ Shift concern from body to intellect
		+ Decreased ego strength, change from active to passive mastery
		* Physical losses
# Intimate-other related leisure	# New experiences	# Reemergence of intimate other-related leisure
# Work-related leisure (m)	# Flexible emotional investments	# Social reintegration
# Family-related leisure (f if care provider for children)	# Intellectual pursuits	# Enrichment and extension of mental and spiritual activities
# Instrumental activities (m)	# Sex-free social interaction	# More time for leisure
# Expressive activities (f)	# Reappraisement of self through leisure	# Relaxation and solitude
# Sensate-focused activities	# Identity consolidation and/or exploration	
# Role-related		
# Social leisure		
# Sensual transcendence		
# Goal-directed		

[1]Generally accepted chronological age ranges for adulthood

Adapted from Nancy J. Osgood and Christine Z. Howe, "Psychological Aspects of Leisure: A Life Cycle Developmental Perspective" *Society and Leisure*, 7, no. 1 (1984), at press.

KEY
+ = Psychological Tasks
● = Social Roles/Tasks (work, family, & community)
= Leisure Experiences
* = Biological Milestones
m = Males Especially Involved
f = Females Especially Involved

Figure 2-3 General Leisure Patterns Over the Traditional Adult Life Course

	Young Adulthood (age 20-35)	Mid-Life (age 35-55)	Late Life (age 55→)
Selected Activities	Vigorous physical recreation (m) Entertainment, spectator sports Home-centered and family-oriented activities Going to bars (m) Courting, dating Outdoor recreation	Spectating, home-centered activities Organizations, clubs, visiting Reading, radio, shopping Entertainment, TV Volunteering, new experiences Relaxing, bars, restaurants Civic/community-centered activities Work-related activities	Contemplation, introspection, life review Group participation, travel, socializing Relaxation, meditation Spectator sports, TV watching Reading, gardening, resting Fishing, walking, picnics, sightseeing Handicrafts, church-related activities
Values	Success (m) Career (m), upward mobility (m) Home & family (f)	Career, success, productivity Performance, family, community	Family
Motivations and Meanings	Extrinsic achievement, accomplishment Competence, arousal, power Affiliation, social bonding (f) Relationship building & strengthening Excitement and adventure Social role-related Instrumental (m), expressive (f) Novelty Autonomy Prestige, status, identity Sensual transcendence Fun	Extrinsic arousal, novelty Achievement Productivity, creative expansion Retain health and vigor Recuperation (compensation from work) Order, continuity Service Status, prestige Role-related Change from work, escape Instrumental	Intrinsic arousal, personal satisfaction Pleasure, creativity Peace, comfort, security Association, socializing, affiliation Self-esteem, integration Retain health, maintain social functioning Passing and structuring time Service to others Unconditional Expressive

Adapted from Osgood and Howe, "Psychological Aspects of Leisure."

KEY

m = males especially involved
f = females especially involved

27

help the leisure programmer to quickly identify the key transitional points and general leisure patterns during adulthood.

LATER ADULTHOOD

Aging is an inevitable part of life for everyone. The major theories of aging are derived from research and observation. They represent attempts to integrate the known facts about older people. Biological theories are founded in the medical sciences. They present explanations of the physical changes associated with aging. Sociological theories explain age-related changes in terms of interpersonal or social dimensions, stressing role changes as major developmental tasks of the aging person. Psychological theories describe personal coping behaviors and reactions to loss and change. All these theories can be used to help define successful aging and the key attributes of life satisfaction during the later years. We believe that healthy leisure functioning is among those keys.

We concluded the previous section with a statement regarding the importance of programming for individual differences. The importance of this point is reinforced by Kaluger and Kaluger, who suggest that individual differences are greater during later adulthood than at any other age.[52] Accounting for these differences would include the years of accumulated individual reactions to life events and social influences that individuals have experienced. At this age, older people begin to experience the loss of loved ones and friends. Many are ill-prepared for retirement. Because their bodies are in decline, "they may have less strength, vigor, and speed of reaction, but they learn to compensate for this change."[53] In fact, *compensating for change* becomes a guidepost for adjustment during later adulthood.

Iso-Ahola encourages leisure service providers to facilitate "opportunities for changing leisure encounters within the sphere of familiar activities"[54] by developing leisure experiences that are familiar to participants and will meet their need to feel competent during the activity. "The need for novelty does not disappear in later years; it merely assumes different forms and appears within a much more limited leisure repertoire."[55] You need to strike a balance between novelty and stability in order to create leisure experiences that are optimally arousing for older persons as well as all other people.

Kleiber and Kelly[56] and Iso-Ahola[57] stress that emphasis should be placed on leisure programs that encourage social relatedness and social interaction. Many programs operating today do address this issue. It is an important one, particularly when the older adult may be experiencing so many losses through death. Also, moving into late life may be quite anxiety-producing, owing to the loss of previously held social roles.[58] The leisure programmer's role in assisting the individual to establish new and ongoing social encounters and social identities is an important one indeed.

Several developmental tasks are required during later adulthood. The following are taken from the work of Kaluger and Kaluger[59] and encompass generalizations made by others. Remember that most older persons have been strongly imbued with the work ethic and may therefore be uncomfortable with "nonproductive" use of time; they may have minimal leisure skills and may lack role definition, especially upon retirement and widowhood. Developmental tasks during later adulthood call for the individual to: reevaluate self-concept and personal identity in light of his or her new role in life; create a workable, personal philosophy of life that includes a view about death and eternity; accept physical changes and limitations by learning to conserve strength and resources; find satisfactory housing on retirement income; maintain interest in people outside the family; maintain some degree of family ties with children and grandchildren; take care of elderly relatives; cope with bereavement and widowhood; and continue meeting social and civic responsibilities by being involved in society and its affairs.

The three most significant adjustive tasks in later life are adaptation to loss, the life review process, and remaining active in order to retain function.[60] Leisure programmers can help to minimize the severity of such adjustments and facilitate accomplishment of developmental tasks through the creative application of leisure programs that address these issues.

It also appears, contrary to some of the popular myths and stereotypes about aging, that older persons experience changes in the way they view and react to their surroundings. These changes are in four areas: valuing wisdom over physical prowess; valuing socializing over sexualizing in human relationships; increasing emotional flexibility; and increasing mental flexibility.[61]

This era might be called the reintegration period, when people attempt to put things all together. Generally, sometime after 55 years of age, employed persons retire and have time free from their previous jobs. Older adulthood is just as diverse as earlier stages, with subdivisions into the "young old," the "old," and the "old old." The "young old" are likely to be healthy, active, and financially solvent, open to new leisure experiences and a rediscovery of and with their spouses or partners.

At the same time, continuing health concerns may lead some older adults to renew moderate or vigorous physical activity. As the years pass, home-based leisure becomes more important. This includes television, gardening, reading, informal social interaction, cards, hobbies, and games for the "old old." In many cases, women find themselves without a marriage partner for some period of their later years. The contribution of leisure programs to rebuilding social contacts and to supplying a network of cohorts or friends is critical. For older persons, organized leisure experiences may be central to expressive identities, feelings of competence, and social integration. In the later years, there are undoubtedly age-group differences in leisure preferences related to early socialization experiences, educational levels, mores, and the individual's historical time frame. The "young old" (ages 55 to 60) may view leisure in general as more meaningful and may be receptive to a wider variety of leisure pursuits than the "old" or the "old old."

Thus we can see that older adulthood is a time for renewing intimacy between adult partners; for being more expressive; for consolidating a number of "loose ends"; for accepting yet another newly-defined self (most likely due to retirement or widowhood); for remaining involved in family and/or community; and for staying healthy in the face of physiological decline. As with younger persons, older people are not alike, static, or predictable. Their leisure interests change, as well as the demands and meaning of their work, family, and social systems.

SUMMARY

It is not only what people do that changes over the years, but what they seek from their leisure. For some, leisure experiences are primarily a vehicle for social interaction and for forming new relationships. There are individuals who find their identity, autonomy, mastery, and self-expression through leisure engagements. Some persons desire relaxation rather than risk in their leisure. As people move through the course of their lives, the meanings of leisure change. Without resorting to any kind of stereotypes, we must design leisure experiences in a manner consistent with the developmental needs and capabilities of our participants. An understanding of both leisure and the human life course is critical. We must be able to apply programming principles to the changes that occur in leisure perceptions held by individuals whose needs, interests, and preferences also change throughout the life-span. If we have an understanding of human development, we may be equipped to address the leisure interests and preferences of individuals engaged in a lifelong dynamic process of building and changing their life structures. We will find that actual implementation of leisure programs requires using differing leadership modes and that no one professional role fits all situations or all program participants. Diversity remains the key for understanding yourself as a professional as well as for understanding your participants.

FOOTNOTES

1. Douglas A. Kleiber and John R. Kelly, "Leisure Socialization and the Life Cycle," in *Social Psychological Perspectives on Leisure and Recreation*, ed. Seppo E. Iso-Ahola (Springfield, Ill.: Charles C Thomas, Publisher, 1980), p. 94.
2. Seppo E. Iso-Ahola, *The Social Psychology of Leisure and Recreation* (Dubuque, Iowa: William C. Brown Company, Publishers, 1980), p. 82.
3. Kleiber and Kelly, "Leisure Socialization," p. 96.
4. Iso-Ahola, *Social Psychology of Leisure*, p. 81.
5. Kleiber and Kelly, "Leisure Socialization," p. 99.
6. Iso-Ahola, *Social Psychology of Leisure*, p. 163.
7. Ibid., p. 88.
8. George Kaluger and Meriem Fair Kaluger, *Human Development: The Span of Life*, 3rd ed. (St. Louis: Times Mirror/Mosby College Publishing, 1984) p. 349.
9. Ibid., p. 367.
10. Geoffrey Godbey, *Leisure in Your Life* (Philadelphia: Saunders College Publishing Company, 1981), p. 174.
11. Kaluger and Kaluger, *Human Development*, p. 370.

12. Kleiber and Kelly, "Leisure Socialization," p. 108.

13. Kaluger and Kaluger, *Human Development*, p. 369.

14. Kleiber and Kelly, "Leisure Socialization," p. 108.

15. Ibid., p. 109.

16. Nancy J. Osgood and Christine Z. Howe, "Psychological Aspects of Leisure: A Life Cycle Developmental Perspective" *Society and Leisure*, 7, no. 1 (1984), in press.

17. Alan B. Knox, *Adult Development and Learning* (San Francisco: Jossey-Bass, Inc., Publishers, 1977), pp. 513-50.

18. Ibid., p. 551.

19. Osgood and Howe, "Psychological Aspects of Leisure."

20. Ibid.

21. Daniel J. Levinson, *The Seasons of a Man's Life* (New York: Alfred A. Knopf, Inc., 1978), pp. 41-56.

22. Knox, *Adult Development*, p. 397.

23. Bernice L. Neugarten, "Personality and Aging," in *Handbook of the Psychology of Aging*, ed. J. E. Birren and K. W. Schaie (New York: Van Nostrand Reinhold Company, 1977), p. 627.

24. Knox, *Adult Development*, pp. 316-404.

25. Levinson, *Seasons*,

26. Gail Sheehy, *Passages: Predictable Crises of Adult Life* (New York: E. P. Dutton and Co., Inc., 1976).

27. Peter I. Rose, ed., *Socialization and the Life Cycle* (New York: St. Martin's Press, 1979), p. 279.

28. Levinson, *Seasons*, p. 7.

29. Ibid., p. 41.

30. Ibid., p. 84.

31. Ibid., p. 86.

32. Ibid., p. 59.

33. Ibid., p. 39.

34. Kleiber and Kelly, "Leisure Socialization," p. 118.

35. Ibid., p. 114.

36. Osgood and Howe, "Psychological Aspects of Leisure."

37. Ibid.

38. Kleiber and Kelly, "Leisure Socialization," p. 116.

39. Levinson, *Seasons*, p. 140.

40. Ibid., p. 192.

41. Ibid., p. 194.

42. Ibid., p. 197.

43. Bernice L. Neugarten, "Must Everything Be a Midlife Crisis?," in *Human Development 82/83*, ed. Hiram E. Fitzgerald and Thomas H. Carr (Guilford, Conn.: The Dushkin Publishing Group, Inc., 1982), p. 260.

44. Ibid., p. 261.

45. Douglas C. Kimmel, *Adulthood and Aging* (New York: John Wiley and Sons, Inc., 1980), pp. 20-21. Reprinted by permission of John Wiley and Sons, Inc.

46. Iso-Ahola, *Social Psychology of Leisure*, p. 181.

47. Kaluger and Kaluger, *Human Development*, p. 523.

48. Kleiber and Kelly, "Leisure Socialization," p. 118.

49. Iso-Ahola, *Social Psychology of Leisure*, p. 181.

50. Ibid., p. 163.

51. Osgood and Howe, "Psychological Aspects of Leisure,"

52. Kaluger and Kaluger, *Human Development*, p. 567.

53. Ibid., p. 567.

54. Iso-Ahola, *Social Psychology of Leisure*, p. 177.

55. Ibid., p. 177.

56. Kleiber and Kelly, "Leisure Socialization," p. 124.

57. Iso-Ahola, *Social Psychology of Leisure*, p. 181.

58. Osgood and Howe, "Psychological Aspects of Leisure,"

59. Kaluger and Kaluger, *Human Development*, p. 577.

60. Ibid., p. 577.

61. Roger Peck, "Psychological Development in the Second Half of Life," in *Middle Age and Aging*, ed. Bernice L. Neugarten (Chicago: University of Chicago Press, 1968). p. 89.

chapter 3

Trends and Issues Relevant to Programming

INTRODUCTION

The programming of leisure experiences occurs within the context of some type of leisure service delivery system. A leisure service delivery system is an agency or organization or a combination of several agencies or organizations that is responsible for the organization, administration, or facilitation of leisure experiences, opportunities, or supplies. Leisure service delivery systems include, but are not limited to, public park and recreation departments, clinical therapeutic recreation divisions of hospitals and institutions, trip and tour outfitters, residential camps, youth agencies, fitness and exercise centers, resorts, theme and amusement parks, and activities departments of residential living facilities and developments. Within these types of delivery systems, the programming of leisure experiences is a primary focus.

Why should programmers who are (or soon will be) involved with leisure service delivery systems be concerned about trends and issues? It is common knowledge that no one is able to *predict* the future with absolute certainty. However, if programmers systematically consider the "probables" or the alternative possibilities that exist for the future and choose from among them, then to some extent they can define their future. If they objectively examine issues and study trends, then as a profession they are better prepared to take a leadership role in society instead of being caught in a reactive or defensive position. As it was started in 1980 in an editorial in *Parks & Recreation,* the future's outlook reflects today's responses.[1]

The profession's movement into the decade of the 1980s seems to have inspired both reflection and prognostication. Perhaps that is because the year 2000 looms so close. The challenge of assessing the future of recreation was discussed in a 1983 editorial in *Parks & Recreation.*

> There is always a certain cynicism associated with attempts to assess the future of any given issue. Surely some who describe themselves as "futurists" frequently talk in lofty, almost pontifical terms. And all of this is so much hogwash to the recreation person toiling in the trenches day and night and keeping one step ahead of the commission meeting.
>
> Still others extoll both the philosophical and practical aspects of stretching the mind and looking to the future. The secret, they argue, is to keep one foot planted firmly in the practical politics and demands of the present, while the other probes the uncertainties of the next decade or two.
>
> The National Recreation and Park Association has ventured forth with the latter group of individuals believing that we, as a civilized and for the most part high technology society, cannot be satisfied with the status quo. We cannot presume that the laws, public policies and programs, and even the institutional arrangements of the past or present are appropriate for tomorrow and the future.
>
> Our first public call for a comprehensive reassessment of our collective approach to recreation and parks in America occurred in January, 1981. . . .
>
> There are, of course, many uncertainties—even risks—associated with "taking the lid off" and looking, in some respects, at our own performance. Clearly, overt, unchecked political actions could sway the parameters and results of this or any inquiry.
>
> We believe the benefits are worth the risk. The United States and much of the world is on the crest of a new frontier of thought and action involving discretionary time. For the committed professional and civic leader, it is an exciting time.[2]

Before addressing some of the trends and issues that are relevant to leisure programming, let's take a look at the nature of the profession as a human service.

Leisure as a Human Service.   We believe that the primary mission of the parks, recreation, and leisure profession is to serve people. Park, recreation, and leisure service, as a profession, therefore falls under the umbrella of human services professions. In recent years, the profession has heeded calls from personnel in allied fields, as well as encouragement from its own clients and leaders, to broaden its role in human development and improvement of the quality of life and to use multiservice delivery approaches. Public agencies in particular are moving toward an emphasis on human dignity, the welfare of the people, social development, community cohesion, racial harmony, and responsible social action. The fundamental thrust of leisure programming, under a human services perspective, is to emphasize the human side of the leisure experience, not the activity itself, the facility, or the site. What happens to the participant is of central concern.

E. William Niepoth states that a human service philosophy is based on the belief that people have a right to grow, to experience satisfaction, and to be self-determining. He also believes that people are to be understood in their totality. Thus, humanism and holism go hand in hand.[3] Further, these premises are most compatible with what you have already learned in Chapters 1 and 2 about the meaning of leisure, freedom, and individual integrity. Niepoth continues:

> At the basic level, all personnel positions in the field are justified in terms of their contributions, direct or indirect, to creation of opportunities for people to engage in leisure behavior. We have many other related objectives, and we are concerned about the quality of the opportunities and the nature of the behavior encouraged. But fundamentally, we want to create the conditions that lead to satisfying leisure experiences. . . .
>
> It would be fairly safe to assume that we wish to promote the growth and self-sufficiency of the people we serve, though we probably differ in our ideas of how to accomplish this. . . .
>
> Regardless of how we feel about the question of recreation and park agencies providing a variety of other human services, or taking the lead in coordinating the efforts of other human service agencies, most of us would probably support the idea of cooperating with other agencies. . . .
>
> The field of recreation and parks does attempt to change people . . . by teaching skills, by attempting to develop appropriate attitudes, by encouraging activity that leads to improved functioning, etc. To accomplish some of these purposes, we often process people—through class registrations, fitness screening, skill testing, etc. In the largest sense, we engage in functions of making things easier. We do those things that help people to enjoy and benefit from satisfying leisure experiences.
>
> It seems clear that we do use methods and processes which basically are the same as those used by various other fields that work with people—other human service fields.
>
> At the broadest level, we seek the same objectives as these other agencies, to promote the ability of individuals to become well-integrated persons. At a somewhat more specific level, this means, for recreation and park persons, that we attempt to facilitate people's opportunities and capacities for engaging in recreational behavior that will enrich their lives.[4]

So it appears that the benefits that are known to be derived from leisure engagement are consistent with the human service philosophy, and that the practices of the leisure profession are congruent with human service methods. Niepoth concludes:

> Whatever the differences, and whatever our past shortcomings, there seems to be no argument that the field exists to serve people. A greater willingness to capitalize on professional processes that are consistent with human service methods should enhance our abilities to help people lead fuller, more satisfying lives.[5]

TRENDS AND ISSUES

The writings of numerous "futurists"—among them Alvin Toffler, Edward Cornish, Herman Kahn, Buckminster Fuller, John Naisbitt, and Daniel Bell—have entered the popular literature. We have examined their works as well as others in the field of recreation and leisure in searching out trends and issues that we believe will affect leisure now and in the future. Issues are phenomena that are of concern to leisure professionals and over which there may be conflicting points of view. Trends are grass-roots movements that catch on and endure over a lengthy period of time. Fads may also emerge at the grass-roots level, but they are relatively short-lived. In an article on studying the future, Bernie Ward offers the following quote from the well-known science-fiction writer Isaac Asimov:

> The important thing to predict is not the automobile, but the parking problem; not the television, but the soap opera; not income tax, but the expense account; not the bomb, but the arms race.
>
> In other words, the important thing to forecast is not what new technologies will be developed, but what will happen to people because of the technology. What changes in people's activities, values, cultural rituals, social processes and learning patterns will spring from changes in communications. . . .
>
> Today's decisions are building tomorrow's worlds.[6]

Meg Maguire and Dana R. Younger make some very interesting points in their article about the forecasting that the Heritage Conservation and Recreation Service was involved in during the Carter Administration.

> One of the best ways of discerning meaningful trends in recreation is through futures research. Trend analysis specifically and futures research generally help policymakers to be aware of change and ultimately help us deal creatively with it. However, the value to recreation of a futures perspective will depend on the degree to which it is possible to anticipate future events and the extent to which it is possible to respond to new circumstances. If a society clearly maps out the future but fails to plan for or react to that future's environment, then it is doubtful that information about the future is of much value.[7]

Clearly, they too suggest assuming an active posture, especially when the rate of societal change is rapid. They feel that recreation and leisure is a rapidly changing profession whose future patterns will be even more varied than they are now. They suggest that social and institutional innovation will be the keys to living successfully with change. From a planning point of view;

> In order for futures research in parks and recreation to have any impact, it must succeed in reorienting decision makers from short-term, reactive planning. Most decision makers place highest priority on those factors which relate to the immediate consequences of their actions while ignoring long-term consequences. Futures forecasting is valuable not for its accuracy as much as for its role in sensitizing planners and policymakers to the ranges of possibilities that await them just beyond the horizon of what can be predicted or foreseen. Although accuracy in terms of timing and magnitude of events is desirable, the prime objective of long-range forecasting is to reveal the full spectrum of possibilities that might be realities in five, ten, 20, or 30 years.[8]

Planning is a primary responsibility of leisure programmers. Therefore, we'd like to reflect on a few things in the hope that leisure programmers may develop a keener sense of what is going on around them and of whether those things will continue in the future.

In the next several sections, we take the luxury of conjecturing—that is, presenting our opinions about the trends and issues affecting leisure now and in the future, based on our understanding of the data that are available for us to examine. In the course of our work and teaching experiences, along with our research efforts, we have come across numerous ideas and findings about leisure and human life. What we're going to do is share with you our interpretation or synthesis of this information in relation to selected aspects of styles of life in North America. We are going to discuss what appears to be occurring in technology, economics, politics, values, and so on as they interact with leisure. We hope that you will find this to be as thought-provoking as we have.

A POSTINDUSTRIAL SOCIETY

It was in the early 1970s that the popular media began to refer to the "leisure boom." The leisure boom consisted of a tremendous increase in leisure participation and in personal and governmental leisure expenditures. General factors that contributed to the leisure boom included more widespread affluence, earlier retirement, an increase in individuals' free time, and an increase in the number of nonworking holidays, which created larger blocks of free time through three-day weekends. The leisure boom was viewed as a major signal that the old industrial society was ending and the beginnings of a new postindustrial society were at hand. In the post-industrial society, the leisure ethic would replace the work ethic and technology would continue to be "labor-saving," thus freeing people from the obligations of work.

Under the work ethic, people derive much of their self-concept, sense of identity, and well-being from their work. This ethic has its roots in the 1600s with the influx of Puritans into North America. The proper combination of Protestantism and capitalism was championed as the basis of salvation and righteousness. To a great extent, the Puritans' focus on success in work as *the* measure of a person's value has persisted in the United States over the past several centuries and into the present.

We believe that North American society has taken the first steps into the postindustrial era and that it is moving toward a leisure ethic. Under the leisure ethic, people derive much of their sense of identity and well-being through their leisure engagements. One's work productivity is not the primary measure of one's societal worth; instead, society values happiness, health, and fulfillment. It is not what the individual does, but who he or she is, that is of importance under the leisure ethic. Adoption of this ethic would be the most positive outcome of the leisure boom.

Some authors have suggested that in its move from the work ethic toward the leisure ethic, the United States has stopped at the "consumption ethic." People who live by a consumption ethic wallow in materialism, narcissism, and sensation-focused hedonism. This is reflected in the prevalence of the "me" attitude, in which the individual *always* comes first, even at the expense of others. If consumption gets out of control and a massive, compulsive "buy now, pay later" mentality overtakes American society, then Americans will not find the kind of long-term personal satisfaction that underlies the definition of leisure given in Chapter 1. To be caught in a consumption ethic would result in people's personal and social bankruptcy, in terms of finances and values.

Although we can currently see much consumption *activity*, we are not sure that this is a full-fledged consumption *ethic*—at least not yet. Still, if an ethic is defined as a moral principle or choice, or as a principle of right or good conduct, such consumerism clearly cannot be perceived as a virtue. There is evidence of the emergence of a leisure ethic, mediated by economic constraints, in which free time and the quality of life are assuming an increasingly important role. Many of the satisfactions once derived from work—autonomy of effort, intrinsically motivated behavior, and optimum stress[9] in spite of economic uncertainty—are now being derived from leisure. The following trends are indicative of this move toward a postindustrial leisure ethic.

Economic Trends. The affluence (or perceived affluence) of the 1960s is gone, although the taste for the good life, of which leisure is a central part, remains. Our synthesis of available information leads us to believe that between now and the year 2000, the economy of the United States will continue to be in an inflationary state, with moderate to high unemployment, especially among the unskilled, youths, members of minorities, and the technologically displaced. This is an uneven distribution of unemployment. Underemployment of college-educated people and of women will be a persistent problem. As the specter of recession continues to hang over the country, there will be further cutbacks in state and federal government services and a general decline in the standard of living of both the new and the chronic poor. Nevertheless, people will continue their leisure expenditures, if for no other reason than to escape from the unhappiness of hard times. Local public and charitable services will be called on even more to ameliorate the problems of those who are truly impoverished and in a situation of enforced leisure, including boredom, the nonconstructive use of leisure time, and leisure illiteracy.

Some people will continue to acquire costly material goods and as a result will have large debts. There will be an increase in two-income households as more and more people seek to maintain a high or "comfortable" standard of living. Expenditures will go for the traditional necessities as well as for the "new necessities"—the "luxuries" of the past. New necessities include such leisure-related items as personal fitness equipment, high-risk or adventure-oriented vehicles and devices, designer-label leisure attire, high-tech games, high-tech audiovisual equipment and supplies, and trips abroad.

Many have referred to our present economic condition, especially in the public sector, as an era of limits. Fiscal crises have occurred in major cities and in several states. People are keenly aware that the cost of running the United States and servicing the national debt has reached the trillion-dollar level. The energy crises of the 1970s did their share in contributing to an inflationary and recessionary climate. This has left a legacy of bare-bones survival and "cut-back management" for public leisure services. Yet the demand for leisure experiences, opportunities, and supplies is increasing, despite the decline in real purchasing power. In essence, people are spending more on leisure even though they are earning less. Participation has also remained high, taking on new forms and occurring in new spaces. So it can be seen that leisure is playing an expanding role in the lives of people and that people are allocating scarce resources (time and money) to it.[10] This enigma will persist.

Technological Trends.   Part of the country's emergence as a post-industrial society is related to continued technological advancement. Whether as a result of technological revolution or technological evolution, innovations in automation and cybernation are making real the possibility of meeting the subsistence needs of the population of the United States with severely reduced human labor in terms of hours and years of employment. Those who do work will be employed in the information, communication, and service fields.

Further, with the decreasing competitiveness of the "smokestack" industries, there is already an increase in the numbers of the technologically unemployed—persons in their middle years who are entering a state of forced leisure (through layoff or early retirement) because their knowledge, skills, training, and experience do not meet the demands of today's employers. Because the general population is aging—the "graying of America" phenomenon—the workforce of the "information society" is made up of a smaller number of younger persons who have the required analytical and technical skills. But the numbers of baby boomers who are now between 25 and 45 years of age, and the numbers of persons over 65, are swelling. Certainly, technological change has given these people time free from work. But has it given them leisure?

On the other hand, those persons who are presently caught up in the prevailing work ethic, as managers, salespersons, or entrepreneurs, may suffer from a time famine.[11] A time famine is a shortage of time. It is a problem not only for persons who continue to function according to the work ethic, but also for those whom technology has *not* freed from obligations of work and/or daily living. Although mechanization may save human labor or energy, it is not necessarily true that an overall savings in *time* results. Stanley Parker elaborates on this as follows:

> With little or no reduction in work and self-maintenance time, and an increase in goods-maintenance time, there is less time for leisure. Furthermore, the same attitude which seeks to save time in work and non-work obligations spills over into an attempt to save time in leisure. Speeding up physical and mental operations in work leads logically to speeding up non-work obligations: food is thawed and heated rather than cooked, some people eat their lunch standing up, and many cannot spare the time for exercise to keep themselves healthy. Children are farmed out to nurseries; parents purchase exemption from giving them personal attention by pressing coins into their hands. At the other end of the life-cycle, only a few people will sacrifice the time needed to care adequately for the old and infirm.

The quality of leisure, too, is affected by the need to save time. Many forms of pleasure take time to enjoy properly, but increasingly attempts are made to skimp on them. A love affair takes time, as does learning to play a musical instrument or writing a poem.[12]

But technological advancements are received positively by the majority of citizens who are employed, and they are quite willing to adapt to such changes. For example, changes in health technology are helping people to live longer and better. Transportation advances have sent Spacelab out and back several times. Microwave ovens can bake an individual a nutritious potato in minutes. Communications technology has indeed turned the world into a "global village" where we can instantaneously hear and see things happening on the other side of the world. Cable television has greatly expanded our entertainment alternatives. Technology has also given us other sources of power, ranging from nuclear to solar.

That leads us to the third category of trends resulting from the shift to a postindustrial society—value trends.

Value Trends.   Changes in values go hand in hand with a changing economy and technology as the society moves toward a postindustrial era and a leisure ethic. Gray is almost poetic in his discussion of this matter.

The 1980s may be a watershed decade in human events, a period manifesting profound changes in conditions at home and in our position abroad. Americans are reappraising the basic assumptions that have guided our nation since the end of World War II, a reappraisal based in pervasive ambiguity and the realization that never again will the quality of American life be the same. In this context, we are now beginning our own reappraisal of the recreation and park movement and its future.

Social, economic, and political trends are relatively easy to identify. What is difficult is to synthesize a comprehensive view and to predict, not the trends but the turn. . . .

Developments now under way all argue for impending massive change in American life. The recreation and park field, therefore, will need to look beyond itself at the environment in which it operates in order to identify directions for the future. We will be unable to take an aloof position with respect to the forces reshaping the surrounding world. As a movement we would prefer the status quo, but in the bewildering array of currents, counter-currents, and cross-currents marking contemporary life, maintenance of the status quo is no real option. Social, political, and economic forces are remaking our environment and we must adapt lest we become but a footnote in the social history of our time.[13]

What are some of the ways in which basic assumptions and values are changing? On one end of the continuum, there are people who appear to be living only for today. Perhaps it is because many of them have grown up with the threat of nuclear war; thinking that total, utter devastation is imminent, they think it is useless to care about tomorrow. Whatever the reason, a segment of the population exists in a sensate, hedonistic, antiauthoritarian, present-oriented life-style. These values are reflected in what they wear, whom they listen to, and how they spend their time. On the other end of the continuum, but just as extreme in their own way, are the conservative "new rightists" who typically embrace religious fundamentalism and believe that they will be among the select few who make it to heaven. Their emphasis on the importance of the "other world," and on who should go there and how to get there, may be made at the expense of living reasonably in the here and now. Between these two extremes is the middle ground—people who may be liberal, moderate, or conservative, ethical and/or religious, but who fall between those who are blindly obedient and those who are loyal to no one.

These are the people who would still like to buy a house if the interest rates ever go down, who want to send their children to college someday, and who give generously to the United Way. These folks don't trust government as much as they used to, yet they really want the democratic system to work. They're willing to pay for this if and only if they can be assured that their dollars will indeed have some positive effect. Accountability is a critical element to them—in terms of others and of themselves. They are the new "do-it-yourself" people, whether in home repairs or personal health.

What these brief descriptions show is that the United States has developed a multidimensional, pluralistic value system. Think for a moment about the cultural "melting pot." All the diverse peoples who had come to settle in this new land were to become integrated and develop a common heritage. History demonstrated that persons who were not too different were fairly easily assimilated. So, from the melting pot emerged a rather bland soup whose flavor was dominated by one ingredient—the WASPs, the group that has traditionally held most of the power in the United States.

But in the 1960s the bubbling melting pot simmered and boiled over! Well-intentioned attempts to assimilate Jews, blacks, women, Hispanics, the poor and so on did not result in the same old soup. What has come from the melting pot is a new stew, one that is rich and flavorful, spiced with the distinctiveness that the nonassimilated groups have brought to the hearth. Not only do we have a more flavorful broth, but we have the special taste of each of the elements of the stew. This mixture is a little spicier, giving those who preferred the bland soup an occasional touch of heartburn or an upset stomach. But for those who can appreciate the fuller flavor, the meal is a satisfying and enriching one.

So it appears that we are headed toward a postindustrial society. But what other trends are contributing to the transition to a leisure ethic?

THE LEISURE ETHIC REVISITED

James Glover believes that the fundamental doctrine that people believe in today is that in order to live the good life, one must consume. That is, one must purchase more equipment, travel farther and faster, do more in less time (time deepening) and, above all else, look beautiful while doing it. If this means holding two jobs in order to pay for these pleasures, so what? If one works hard, then one can play hard.[14] This is a bit more frenzied than the type of leisure ethic we spoke of earlier, which might be characterized as a state of mind or being in which people are fulfilled through a recreative existence and/or recreative experience(s). We believe that this is an optimum condition to which people should aspire. But unlike the consumption trend or the omnipresent work ethic, the leisure ethic produces no tangible "result."

Frank Benest and Gail Hershberger address this in another way:

> There is a problem with emphasizing that recreation departments continue to provide life-enriching activities. We assume *a priori*, without any evidence, that recreation programs do, of course, enhance our lives. For us to gain the support of community groups and policy makers, we must *demonstrate*, through program evaluation and marketing efforts, that particular recreation activities do, in fact, have life enrichment *outcomes*.[15]

They suggest that the human consequences of leisure engagement must be demonstrated in tangible ways. Therein lies one of the greatest difficulties in making the transition toward a leisure ethic: How do we know when we've arrived? Further, the move toward a leisure ethic is being shaped by trends that are part of the shift toward a postindustrial society.

Social Trends.   Since the 1970s the populace has been more compliant and more internally focused. People seem to want a constantly improving standard of living. Yet the recognition of the costliness of maintaining or achieving a high standard of living brings disillusionment. This has, perhaps, contributed to the emphasis on meeting the needs of oneself before others. It is as though people are driven by the urge to have it all, even though they know there is not enough. This glorification of the self at the expense of others has led to a merely grudging contribution to the general welfare, either through individual or collective acts of giving. Within a framework of pluralistic values and during a time of diminishing resources, it is no wonder that people are concerned about themselves and in competition with one another, if indeed consumption and acquisition are of paramount importance to them. The disillusionment comes when the costs of this way of life are realized.

Instant gratification appears to be another persisting social trend. Not only do people want the expensive foreign sports car, but they want it right now! Instead of saving, they have multiple credit cards from which to choose in order to make an instant purchase, whether that is a new outfit for the season or a new lover for the night. They want things instantly and effortlessly. Yet this does seem tempered by the kind of self-discipline that manifests itself in working hard or in careerism. Iso-Ahola states that "people prefer activities that are perceived to offer a relatively great amount of challenge, require relatively high-level skills, and provide a strong feeling of control over their actions."[16] If work provides these opportunities, then these needs may be satisfied there. If not, persons may turn to leisure, but their leisure may be work-identified.

It does appear, though, that more and more people are finding a sense of competence, freedom, and optimal challenge through their leisure engagements. But even then, there seems to be an obsession with trade-offs. For example, some people run not to experience the joy of movement or the pleasure in motion, but to lose weight so they'll be "better to look at." The pain of running is traded off for the presumed pleasure of a better appearance.

The emphasis on the "body beautiful" is there, but not in terms of the glorification of the youth culture, as in the past. Rather, greater numbers of older people have more clout with regard to extremely important things: political power and purchasing power. The future is the era of the adult.[17] Those people in the 55-years-of-age-and-older cohort are generally healthier, more educated, and more affluent than the older people of the past.

Demographic Trends.   Declining birth and death rates are producing a bulge in the middle-to-upper end of the age distribution of whites in America. The numbers of older people have been increasing more rapidly than the total population. It is expected that the proportion of older people will continue to rise. More specifically, the most rapid population increase in persons 65 years or older is expected between the years 2010 and 2020, when the baby boom generation reaches that age. This means that by 2000, those 65 and older will represent at least 13.1 percent of the population; that figure will climb to 21.1 percent, or one in five persons, by 2030.[18] To state it another way, by the year 2000, one-half of the population of the United States will be over 35.[19] These persons represent a tremendous new market for leisure experiences oriented to adults.

In addition to population trends, there are immigration and migration factors to be considered. Immigration is a significant factor in U.S. population growth. On some levels, the United States has become a nation of special populations—refugees, freed "political prisoners", non-English-speaking people, and undocumented workers, to name just a few. Immigrants to America, both legal and illegal, especially those who are escaping political oppression, may bring with them orientations to life that are very different from those of assimilated Americans, including tremendous religious and cultural differences and different value systems. These newcomers may also be hampered by language barriers.

Americans will continue to be a mobile population.[20] Migration to the "Sun Belt" regions of the country will continue, but not as rapidly as during the 1970s. The migration to suburbia will diminish. Some major cities will experience a greater amount of growth than the suburbs. In other places, the growth of small towns and rural areas will outpace that of the suburbs.

Family Trends.   Profound social and demographic changes are related to changes in the family, some of which are stressful and/or regrettable. There is a strong dynamic between leisure and the family: The family is usually the first place in which leisure life-styles are formed; it is also the launching pad from which individuals begin to live life and search for meaning in their lives. As they grow, the search for meaning sometimes involves their peers and frequently occurs during leisure.

There is no question that the definition of family is changing. The divorce rate is high, nearing 50 percent. Even though many divorced persons remarry, unfortunately many of them end up with a second or a third divorce. This creates a very stressful complex of emotions, finances, and kinship. People are also delaying marriage and childbearing, with many women working longer prior to having children. Some—the "never nesters"—delay marriage indefinitely. In contrast, there are many women—predominantly young, less educated, poor, and members of minority groups—who are having children out of wedlock, without the stigmatization that previously faced unwed mothers. There are more single-parent households, more female heads of households, more cohabitating heterosexual couples, and more openly gay people. The proportion of children under 18 living with one parent will continue to increase, reaching 25 percent in 1990, compared with 20 percent in 1980.[21]

Sex roles are changing, especially in families where there are two full-time breadwinners and among childless couples. There are also noticeable attitudinal changes among fathers with daughters of high-school age or younger. If the daughters are bright or athletic and are perceived to be discriminated against solely because of their sex—whether in organized or competitive athletics, on debate teams, in enrollment in preengineering, industrial arts, or automechanics classes, or in any other way—then these fathers become surprisingly activist!

The search for meaning, along with the search for intimacy, typically begins in the home, with parental and sibling relationships. But the stability of the home—and hence the psychological well-being of family members—may be threatened by some of the changes that are occurring. If both parents are working from 8:00 A.M. to 5:00 P.M., who takes care of the children when school ends and/or the playgroup takes a holiday? Since families are highly mobile, grandma and grandpa probably do not live within babysitting distance, and with the decline in numbers of younger persons, paid babysitters at inexpensive rates are getting harder and harder to find.

What about single-parent families? They have the same problems and more. Which parent is going to have the kids on Christmas Eve and Christmas Day? What about New Year's Eve and New Year's Day? If the divorced parents live far apart, the holidays could be very costly in travel time and transportation. The multiple sets of gifts can be confusing, and feelings that one must provide many presents can run rampant.

Finally, what about the families of remarriages, which may include step-parents, step-siblings, and step-grandparents? What are the ground rules for the merger of these units of people? Certainly the trend is toward a much more complex inter- and intrafamilial network. There are strains and ambiguities under these conditions. Much has been written about the psychological effects of divorce on children. We expect that there will be more "pathological" families in both the single-parent and the remarriage types of households. But we also foresee an increase in intergenerational kinship between blood relatives and relatives by marriage (or second marriage). These forms will reflect the diversity that is already with us today.[22]

How do these social, demographic, and family trends relate to the leisure ethic and to leisure programming as a human service profession in a postindustrial society? It is of ultimate importance that programmers study the trends that are associated with population shifts and the characteristics of each subgroup within the population. Prior to providing a service, programmers must assess the population to be served. Failure to study social trends is disastrous for individual clients as well as for the profession itself. To us, these trends suggest new ways to practice the profession.

FUTURE DIRECTIONS IN PROGRAMMING

In the future, people's leisure interests may not necessarily coincide with what we currently believe are the most positive expressions of leisure involvement. Perhaps, in reaction to workplaces that are more automated and more boring, people will want greater risk and challenge in their leisure engagements. We expect to see more people able to afford and a continued rise in legal and illegal gambling of all types; in high-risk sports such as hang gliding and parachute jumping; and in multisensory, mood-modifying experiences achieved through the use of drugs, audiovisual media, or other stimuli. Advances in computers and electronics will provide more entertainment and communication alternatives. People will be able to put on headphones and hear marvelous symphonies, as well as be able to synthesize their own music on home computers. They will have big screens on which images can surround them and little screens on which they can carry video images with them. They will be entertained, free to tune in and turn on (or off) at will.

Not all leisure programming will be high-risk or high-tech. Some persons will prefer more traditional types of experiences—those that keep them in touch with their own past, with a national or ethnic heritage, or simply with an earlier time. Folk festivals, celebrations of earlier eras, pageants, and so on will continue to attract performers and participants as well as onlookers. Arts, crafts, and handiworks will continue to flourish as hobbies and in consumer sales as people demand the feel of "homemade" goods. Other creative outlets will include the cultural and performing arts for people who want to practice their crafts, entertain others, and be entertained themselves.

Sports involvement and spectating will continue to grow, but certain sports will be more in vogue to watch and play than others. The current interest in fitness-oriented activities, after continuing to increase for a time, will level off at a rate of participation that is higher than today's. The same phenomenon will occur with trips to theme parks and full-service resorts.

More ominously, it appears as though the trend in overuse and underfinancing of public outdoor pleasure grounds will continue as the year 2000 approaches. Public recreation areas are in great demand, yet they are deteriorating owing to lack of funds. The tension between development, preservation, and controlled interpretation and access will persist. In general, environmental problems will remain with us. Citizens will continue to have to express their points of view about the handling of toxic wastes in our oceans, streams, and land; air-quality and pollution standards will have to be enforced; supplies of groundwater must remain pure; acid rain must cease to fall; and fewer chemicals must enter the atmosphere.

Related to this is the matter of energy. Since the oil embargos of the 1970s, energy—access, price, amount, and form—has remained a controversial issue. Is there indeed a limited amount of fossil fuel? Can North America be independent of "foreign oil"? Are certain people hiding vast holdings of fuel somewhere in order to keep the price of a gallon of gasoline well over a dollar? Should the country pursue the development of alternative forms of power such as solar and nuclear energy?

This is a major issue on which the public will remain most skeptical and most concerned. The consumption of inexpensive energy has been a major part of the American way of life for at least three generations. This is most easily observable in the national love affair with the automobile. We believe that now and in the future, Americans will continue to expect affordable energy for personal use, whether in the home, for the car, at work, or in public places.

These are just a few of the types of activities in which, we suggest, people are likely to be involved in the future. Seymour M. Gold captures our thinking when he writes: "A new generation of activities will become common . . . [requiring] new spaces, management techniques, and sophisticated program leadership. Many of these activities will be self-directed, noncompetitive, and energy conserving. . . . They will symbolize dramatic changes in lifestyle, ethics, or attitudes toward people and the environment."[23]

The programming of the future, under a human services perspective, will include leisure information services and referral; leisure education, counseling, self-help, and literacy or training; advocacy, access, transportation, and support services such as day care; dining opportunities; and companionship. Some of this will be available commercially. Some will be publicly subsidized. Agencies will provide recreation services for the new special populations—after-school opportunities for the children of working parents; daily opportunities for retired persons to interact socially and to enjoy the fellowship of other human beings; coping and survival skills workshops for the unemployed, recently disabled, displaced homemakers, and newly arrived immigrants; expressive opportunities for the deinstitutionalized; and programs to enhance community and familial cohesion. This implies a multiservice program approach in which the changing needs and interests of very different individuals are recognized. Iso-Ahola would call this facilitating the management of intrinsic leisure motivation.[24]

Gray states that human nature has remained unchanged. People need and desire participation in recreation and leisure as respite from the tension and turmoil of the rapid economic, social, technological, and political changes of recent years.[25] How best to do this remains as yet an unanswered question. But programmers can think of some ways to be forward-looking in their vision, to be responsive to their clientele, to be dynamic and innovative in their service delivery, to be respectful of individual and group differences, to encourage meaningful and independent leisure functioning, to preserve the environment, and to aid in human development. We will touch upon these points in the chapters that follow. But let us conclude now with some comments on the sociopolitical system under under which the United States presently operates.

THE SYSTEM

The kind of interplay that exists among previously mentioned trends also exists for sociopolitical trends. Each interacts with the others and none exists in isolation. It is our observation that political involvement will become more vigorous as citizens from coalitions around single issues or special interests. There will be a slowly increasing skepticism toward authority as symbolized by the major political parties. There will be a greater amount of lobbying and advocacy for special interests or special groups. This will parallel the continuing move toward "states' rights," that is, the shift of powers and responsibilities to the state and local levels. The crucial act to watch for is the transfer of funds to state and local government bodies to carry out these responsibilities. A shifting of influence to different geographic regions is already apparent: The southeastern, southwestern, and western states will persist in making gains. At the national level, reductions in social spending will occur, as well as agitation to balance the national budget.

On the other hand, defense spending will increase as sporadic conflicts throughout the world continue. Increasingly, the country will be faced with the dilemma of greater international interdependence along with greater international competition. West Germany and Japan will make technological advances while the United States and the Soviet Union will not be as dominant as in the past. Third World countries, including countries in Africa, will see more strife over land, human rights, and natural resources.

What do these concerns mean for persons in the parks, recreation, and leisure field? David E. Gray and Seymour Greben write of certain ideals on which the United States is based. Among these are the beliefs that a positive social, physical, and psychological environment is essential to human welfare, that leisure is critical to human development and a life of quality and fulfillment, and that each person has a responsibility to other human beings and must live a life that recognizes that responsibility.[26]

Leisure is one vehicle through which people demonstrate their concern for individuals, for the quality of their lives, and for the realization of their potential. It is also a vehicle for the development and expression of values that may be the one countervailing force against the emerging "technocracy," in which, some writers warn, there will be little humanity. Gray and Greben suggest that there is yet another question to answer: "Shall the government be used as an instrument of social and economic policy as well as political policy?"[27] They continue by stating their tremendous concern for the vitality of the parks and recreation movement specifically and for the meaning and vitality of social progress generally. They also feel that the question of what kind of America we want to live in and what the American dream shall be is at stake.[28] Gray and Greben conclude: "As a discipline and a philosophy, recreation is concerned with human beings and human fulfillment. We exist; we have validity, primarily in the kind of world in which human values—and service to human beings—are paramount."[29]

SUMMARY

Scenarios are images of the way things may materialize. They are orderly collections of assumptions about the future based on expectations of the way selected key events will occur in light of certain developments or trends. We have attempted to highlight for you the trends and issues that we find to be relevant to the future of leisure and leisure programming. We have not prepared a scenario per se, but have tried to do a bit of forecasting within trend areas, leaving you to draw your own conclusions. Social, economic, political, and technological influences must be considered in the delivery of leisure services, both now and over the next fifteen years. We have tried to suggest (without prescribing too much) how these trends may impact upon leisure and what you need to think about in response to or in anticipation of them.

Application Section. Thinking in terms of the possible as well as the probable, what is your opinion of the future of leisure and leisure programming over the next fifteen years in light of the trends and issues that have been raised in this chapter?

FOOTNOTES

1. "The Future's Outlook Reflects Today's Responses," *Parks & Recreation*, July 1980, p. 20. Reprinted by special permission of the National Recreation and Park Association.
2. "The Challenge of Assessing Future Recreation," *Parks & Recreation*, January 1983, p. 38. Reprinted by special permission of the National Recreation and Park Association.
3. E. William Niepoth, "Human Service Methods in the Field of Recreation and Parks," in *Special Report on Human Services,* ed. Frank Benest and Gail Hershberger (Sacramento, Calif.: California Department of Parks and Recreation, 1981), p. 18.
4. Ibid., pp. 22-24.
5. Ibid., p. 28.
6. Bernie Ward, "Thoughts for Our Tomorrows," *Sky,* January 1983, p. 49. Reprinted through the courtesy of Halsey Publishing Co., publishers of *Sky* magazine.
7. Meg Maguire and Dana R. Younger, "HCRS Sheds Light on Recreation Trends with Futures Forecasting," *Parks & Recreation,* May 1980, p. 60. Reprinted by special permission of the National Recreation and Park Association.
8. Ibid., p. 60.
9. Joseph Levy, "A Recreation Renaissance," *Parks & Recreation,* December 1977, p. 18. Reprinted by special permission of the National Recreation and Park Association.
10. Theodore R. Deppe and Daniel Sharpless, "Financial Outlook," *Parks &*

Recreation, July 1980, pp. 51–57. Reprinted by special permission of the National Recreation and Park Association.

11. Stanley Parker, *The Sociology of Leisure* (London: George Allen and Unwin, 1976), pp. 34–35.

12. Ibid., p. 35.

13. David E. Gray, "State of the Art . . . Future Challenge," *Parks & Recreation,* July 1980, pp. 22–23. Reprinted by special permission of the National Recreation and Park Association.

14. James Glover, "In Defense of Simplicity," *Journal of Physical Education, Recreation, and Dance,* February 1983, p. 62. Reprinted with permission from The Journal of Physical Education, Recreation, and Dance, February 1983, p. 62. The Journal is a publication of the American Alliance for Health, Physical Education, Recreation and Dance, 1900 Association Drive, Reston, VA 22091.

15. Frank Benest and Gail Hershberger, "Human Services & Recreation in the 1980s," *California Parks & Recreation,* December/January 1980/81, p. 19.

16. Seppo E. Iso-Ahola, "People Today: Withdrawing, Coping, Adapting," *Parks & Recreation,* May 1982, p. 65. Reprinted by special permission of the National Recreation and Park Association.

17. Gray, "State of the Art," p. 24.

18. "A Profile of Older Americans" (Washington, D.C.: American Association of Retired Persons, n.d.), p. 1.

19. "Over 55: Growth Market of the '80s," *Nation's Business,* April 1981, p. 27.

20. "U.S. by 2000: A Nation That Won't Sit Still," *U.S. News & World Report,* April 25, 1983, p. 60.

21. Andrew Cherlin and Frank F. Furstenberg, Jr., "The American Family in the Year 2000," *The Futurist,* June 1983, pp. 7–10.

22. Ibid., p. 8.

23. Seymour M. Gold, "Urban Leisure Environments to Come," *Parks & Recreation,* May 1979, p. 56. Reprinted by special permission of the National Recreation and Park Association.

24. Iso-Ahola, "People Today," p. 66.

25. Gray, "State of the Art," p. 28.

26. David E. Gray and Seymour Greben, "Future Perspectives II: The 1980s and Beyond," *Parks & Recreation,* May 1982, pp. 52–56. Reprinted by special permission of the National Recreation and Park Association.

27. Ibid., p. 54.

28. Ibid., pp. 55–56.

29. Ibid., p. 56.

chapter 4

Comprehensive Program Development in Recreation and Leisure Services

INTRODUCTION

Sometimes the terminology found in the literature of our field is confusing. Thus we are beginning this chapter by clarifying our usage of some words. In Chapter 1, we defined a program as a singular phenomenon: an activity, event, or experience that occurs specifically for its own purpose. When we speak of leisure program development here in Chapter 4, however, we are referring to *comprehensive* program development. This is the organization and administration of the *full set* of leisure experiences that an agency oversees. Program development here refers to the entire comprehensive set of programs that an agency offers and not just to one specific leisure experience.

We noted in Chapter 2 that human development involves change. *Comprehensive* program development also involves change. You must be prepared to both initiate and respond to program changes. Certain factors affect human beings and cause changes throughout their development; similarly, certain factors affect sets of programs and cause changes throughout their development. We noted earlier that changes in people's lives are the result of internal and external factors, such as life events, social influences, and personal reassessment of values and earlier decisions. The kinds of changes that occur in comprehensive program development result from such internal and external factors as individual, organizational, and community needs and organizational goals, purposes, and constraints.

To help us understand change in relation to comprehensive program development, let's apply Levinson's concept, introduced earlier, of structure changing and structure building in human development.[1] Think of the entire leisure program as a multifaceted organism capable of change, and of yourself, the leisure programmer, as a technician capable of facilitating change.

Something triggers a need within the organism to change, such as declining participation. At this point, you decide to examine the present structure of the agency's overall program and reappraise previous decisions, especially those that relate to client participation. Thus, the program is at a transitional (structure-changing) point, and you are the agent actively engaged in the process of facilitating change. In this process, you may reaffirm earlier decisions, make new decisions, alter or terminate elements of the program, or add new ones. Following this, you build a new program structure by making choices and commitments that support the changes you have made. A different program structure is put in place to serve clients until the needs of the organism (program) change again.

Clearly, this metaphor can also illustrate the application of evaluative techniques so important in programming and comprehensive program development. We do not wish to confuse the issue of evaluation at this point. Rather, we want to suggest that both human and program developmental concepts have close similarities because in both cases the individual is compelled to deal with change within an organism. Without change, development would not occur and the organism (program or person) would become static. Leisure programmers charged with the responsibility of maintaining viable programs and services must understand and accept the inherent dynamics that operate at full force during comprehensive program development.

COMPREHENSIVE PROGRAM DEVELOPMENT STRATEGIES

There are numerous program development strategies and approaches that you can draw on that have been proven successful over the years. Simply stated, these strategies are suggested ways to do large-scale leisure programming. Some leisure programmers use very traditional modes, while others use some of the newer approaches. Still others combine the two by using a traditional approach as a keystone to support nontraditional or newer approaches to leisure programming.

The strategy used depends upon four primary factors. The first is the kind of agency or organization you are part of and its mission, goals, purposes, and needs. The second factor is your knowledge of and ability to apply concepts related to human development in leisure programming. The third factor is your ability to identify individuals' leisure needs, interests, and inclinations, and then to create the leisure experiences that encourage independent leisure functioning. The fourth factor is your ability to identify and orchestrate community, special-interest, and individual needs that may be in opposition and/or competition.

APPROACHES TO COMPREHENSIVE PROGRAM DEVELOPMENT

It is also important to realize what programming options exist. Leisure programmers who are committed to professional growth and development will experiment with many of the known strategies as they develop and refine their own modes of comprehensive program development.

Many authors agree that today's leisure programmers blend or mix several approaches to form the best possible combination of options necessary to ensure a successful set of leisure programs and services. Achieving this success often depends upon the fit between the particular organization's mission and your unique skills, abilities, and experiences. This fit can be affected by your own programming preferences, which may have come about as a result of working in a variety of leisure settings or with a variety of programming approaches. As you gain more experience, you are more likely to know which types of agencies and which programming approaches are best suited to your personal and professional values, philosophies, goals, and needs.

A number of authors have articulated approaches, models, plans, strategies, and theories regarding the ways in which leisure experiences are developed and delivered. These various approaches can and are being used as comprehensive program development takes place. Each approach requires differing amounts of programmer intervention and supervision. All the approaches discussed in this chapter have been reviewed and summarized by others (see, for example, Richard G. Kraus[2] and Christopher R. Edginton, David M. Compton, and Carole J. Hanson[3]). To avoid reexplaining the approaches, we touch upon each only briefly, and encourage you to seek out other authors for additional information. We feel that the title of an approach often adequately conveys its focus. Thus, each approach is presented by source and title. To clarify them further, we have added to each a hypothetical quote that a leisure programmer might make about it.

Howard Danford and Max Shirley suggest four approaches for leisure programmers to consider.[4] Their approaches have received much attention from other authors writing about programming. Even though these approaches were originally offered as *unsound* approaches to programming, many discussions have occurred over the years regarding their benefits as well.

Traditional Approach	"we've always done it this way; what's worked in the past will work now, so I'll stick with what has been successful"
Current Practice Approach	"if it's new it's got to be good . . . let's go with it"
Expressed Desires Approach	"we'll do whatever our public wants us to do, the squeaking wheel gets the oil"
Authoritarian Approach	"I am the leisure programmer; I'm a trained professional and know what these people want"

To the four approaches above, Kraus added a fifth:[5]

Sociopolitical Approach	"We must be especially sensitive to these political or special interest groups . . . after all, they have the ear of city hall"

Three other approaches, called plans, are offered by Albert Tillman:[6]

Reaction Plan	"the loudest voice gets the action around here"

Investigation Plan — "we must do a survey to find out what our program participants want"

Creative Plan (merges the Reaction and Investigation plans) — "we use both peoples' demands and interest inventories when deciding what to offer"

James F. Murphy identified other approaches that have some similarities to those mentioned above.[7] Murphy's approaches are derived from the mission of the organization and serve to operationalize its philosophy.

Direct Service Approach — "we're committed to providing leadership, facilities, and equipment (leisure opportunity) and this will encourage direct and immediate participation from people"

Enabling Service Approach — "as a programmer, I am a catalyst—my job is to help people implement their leisure desires and interests"

Cafeteria Service Approach — "our program consists of a number and variety of leisure opportunities for people of all ages, interests and abilities to select from"

Prescriptive Approach — "leisure programs are social instruments and should be provided in a manner that ensures that the social and personal needs of participants are met"

Instrumental Goal Approach — "the programs planned are a means to an end—gratification from participation may not be immediate, but accomplishment will be felt"

Expressive Activity Goal Approach — "the programs provided are ends in themselves—I only want to see participants experience"

The last approach Murphy offers combines both the instrumental and expressive approaches:

Interactionist Service Approach — "our programs embrace the holistic concept of leisure—they allow the participant to experience spontaneity, expressiveness, and further development of personally sought-after individual potential"

Christopher R. Edginton and Carole J. Hanson developed several program planning "theories" that they feel underlie programming practice.[8]

Trickle Down Theory — "if this is what the administration wants us to offer, this is what we will offer"

Educated Guess Theory	"we've got a feeling that our clients would like this leisure program—let's do it"
Community Leadership Input Theory	"since the advisory board represents the leisure needs of our participants, we'll do what they suggest we should do in our programs"
Identification of Need Theory	"our programs result from the systematic review and analysis of the needs of our leisure consumers"
Offer What People Want Theory	"after talking to our clientele, we offer whatever they want"
Indigenous Development Theory	"we go straight to the people in their own neighborhoods, at the grass-roots level, encouraging them to plan their own leisure programs"
Interactive Discovery Theory	"we meet face-to-face on an equal basis with our program participants and decide together what we will offer"

We spoke earlier of the fit between the desires of the agency you work for and your programming abilities. Institutional goals and purposes exert an influence over the leisure programmer's approach to comprehensive program development. Edginton, Compton, and Hanson speak of a continuum along which their seven theories can fall (see Figure 4-1). Two organizational stances or foci are depicted along either side of the continuum.

SOCIAL PLANNING ← → COMMUNITY DEVELOPMENT
• DIRECT SERVICE DELIVERY ········· • INDIRECT SERVICE DELIVERY
• TASK-ORIENTED ········· • PROCESS-ORIENTED
• PROFESSIONALLY CONTROLLED ········· • CONTROLLED BY THE PARTICIPANT
• RELATIONSHIP OF DEPENDENCY ········· • INDEPENDENCE
• SERVES INSTRUMENTAL AND ········· • SERVES EXPRESSIVE NEEDS UTILITARIAN NEEDS
• ROUTINIZED PROGRAM SERVICES ········· • INDIVIDUALIZED PROGRAM SERVICES
• PARTICIPANT VIEWED AS ········· • PARTICIPANT VIEWED AS A CONSUMER AN ACTIVATOR
• OUTER-DIRECTED ········· • INNER-DIRECTED PARTICIPANT GRATIFICATION PARTICIPANT GRATIFICATION
• PROFESSIONAL VIEWED AS EXPERT ········· • PROFESSIONAL VIEWED AS COLLABORATOR

TRICKLE DOWN	EDUCATED GUESS	COMMUNITY LEADERSHIP	IDENTIFICATION OF NEED	OFFER WHAT PEOPLE WANT	INDIGENOUS DEVELOPMENT	INTERACTIVE DISCOVERY

Figure 4-1 The Program Continuum

Adapted from Christopher R. Edginton, David M. Compton, and Carole J. Hanson, *Recreation and Leisure Programming: A Guide for the Professional* (Philadelphia: Saunders College Publishing Company, 1980), p. 47, 49.

The authors show how their program planning theories can be placed within an organizational focus that emphasizes either social planning or community development. Additionally, other factors affecting the delivery of leisure programs and services are suggested. If you work for an agency that emphasizes social planning, you would need to develop the comprehensive program in a way that stresses direct service delivery, task orientation, and so on. On the other hand, a programmer working in an agency that stresses community development would need to develop his or her program in an opposite manner. This programmer would assume less direct input into service delivery, stress process rather than task orientation, and so on.

Understanding the many dimensions of the organization-programmer relationship is extremely important because programmers do not exist in a vacuum. Either they are part of a larger organization that has certain goals and purposes, or they function independently as their own organization with their own set of goals and purposes. Further, the programmer has to consider the individual needs of participants and the needs characteristic of the community in which the programs take place. Thus there are many factors to consider during the process of developing a program.

Application Section.   A number of approaches to comprehensive program development have been offered so far in this chapter, each accompanied by a hypothetical quote that a leisure programmer using that approach might make. Reread the quotes and select eight with which you feel you can identify. Rank these from first through eighth according to their congruence with your leisure programming philosophy. Discuss your rankings with others and reevaluate your selections if necessary.

CONSIDERING NEEDS IN COMPREHENSIVE PROGRAM DEVELOPMENT

In discussing the process of translating needs into program objectives, Malcolm Knowles elaborates on what he calls the "pool of needs."[9] The pool includes individual needs, organizational needs, and community needs. These needs are filtered through a process in which needs are assessed in terms of institutional purposes, feasibility, and interests of clients. Following this screening process, objectives are determined and prioritized (see Figure 4-2). Program objectives result from the process of combining and screening need areas. Determining program objectives is a critical part of comprehensive program development.

The leisure program is an extension of the sponsoring organization. The leisure program represents the larger entity and reflects the organization's needs. Today, organizational needs are as diverse as organizational purposes. An example of an organizational need is enhancement of the agency's financial base. A teen travel program to the Summer Olympics could have components that would generate money for the sponsoring organization.

At the same time that a leisure program reflects organizational needs, it can also reflect individual needs. Staying with the Summer Olympics example, let's see how the successful leisure programmer considers individual needs in program development. To do this, we must first have an overview of needs.

Essentially, needs are experienced by the individual as being either basic,

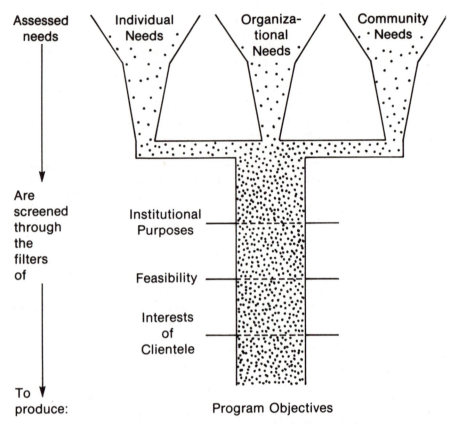

Figure 4-2 The Process of Translating Needs into Objectives

Reproduced from *The Modern Practice of Adult Education*, copyright 1980 by Malcolm S. Knowles. Published by Cambridge, The Adult Education Company, 888 Seventh Avenue, New York, New York 10106. Reproduced with the permission of the publisher.

ascribed, or felt. *Basic needs* include physical needs (to maintain one's body); personal growth needs (such as self-fulfillment); security needs (both for physical and for psychological comfort); new experience needs (for adventure, novelty, or risk); affection needs (to share and care); recognition needs (to receive attention or respect); and learning needs (to gain competencies or master skills).

Ascribed needs, though felt by individuals, initially come from sources outside them. For example, if someone suggests to you that you should go to the Olympics and you accept that as a need of yours, then it is an ascribed need. Organizations are often masters at convincing individuals that they need one particular leisure experience or another. An agency may create a demand for the Olympics by subtly suggesting that people need to see them. Later, after you become interested, you may be motivated to go to the Olympics because it is a new experience. Now the ascribed need has become a basic need. Ascribed needs often become basic or felt needs. The demand may be created elsewhere, but after a time the need is internalized and becomes real for you.

This leads us to *felt needs*. Some individuals seek particular leisure programs because they have been told that they need the experience. Ideally, they will have agreed that they do need the experience. It is critical to note that if the individual participant does not feel perceived freedom to engage, he or she may not become engaged in the leisure experience. Felt needs come from inside the person. They are intrinsic motivators.

Finally, community needs are filtered through organizations and do have an influence on program objectives and program development. Some community needs that might be operating in the Olympics example are (1) your community's sister city is near the Olympic site, so the city council supports a youth exchange; (2) the local school district supports a very active athletic program for teenagers and encourages the trip so that students can view role models; or (3) the local Chamber of Commerce is promoting travel and the Olympics provides it with a distinct marketing focus.

We have spent quite a bit of time on needs because as a strategy for leisure programming our cycle begins with the systematic assessment of individual needs. We feel that it is important that you have a full understanding of needs. We also feel that it is important for you to be aware of the realities under which you will work.

JUGGLING NEEDS AND REALITIES

Within the pool of needs, neither organizational needs, individual needs, nor community needs can consistently be treated equally. All these needs are screened through institutional purposes, criteria for program feasibility, and the specific interests of clients. Because organizations, individuals, and communities are continuously changing, needs and the realities surrounding them are dynamic rather than static. Institutional purposes, for example, vary as organizations set new priorities for operating. The organizational philosophy and goals (organizational needs) may not change that greatly, but priorities (institutional purposes) might. Stated another way, the organization's goal of improving the quality of participants' lives through leisure activities (organizational need) may be realized by creating leisure experiences for a specific population during a particular program year (institutional purpose). In another case, because there is an increasing number of retirees in a given town (community need), your agency establishes programs for older adults (institutional purpose).

As filtering occurs, program development strategies are altered and take on unusual characteristics. The strategies that are discussed next are not wrong; rather, they reflect reality. Actual leisure programming is rarely textbook tidy. Often, organizational needs are considered to have greater programmatic relevance than community needs or individual needs. At other times, clientele interests may be considered to have greater importance than organizational needs.

There are innumerable combinations of these factors. What you should keep in mind is that the needs of organizations, individuals, and communities are dynamic and that the filters we are discussing here are also subject to change. Also, other screening factors may be added to your situation. As a result, the act of program development, as it is done day by day in the real world, may be very unsystematic and unscientific as programmers yield to these influences. The following programming strategies reflect the author's own experiences as well as those of our colleagues. In the long run, these strategies have led to failure.

REAL-WORLD PROGRAMMING STRATEGIES

Some programmers have been known to develop programs by the "seat of their pants" through the process of "winging it." That usually happens when they have been caught unprepared. Perhaps this is excusable if they are in a crisis situation, which happens, though rarely. But to program continuously in a haphazard, catch-as-catch-can manner can prove to be a most inefficient and ineffective practice. The proper way to establish a program is through thoughtful and careful planning that occurs over a specific period of time.

Programmers have also maintained programs long after they should have been put to sleep. This happens when a program has become a tradition and has entered into the "folklore" of the organization, so that no one is willing to put an end to the saga. We expect that you have observed some of these dinosaur leisure programs and have asked yourselves why they still exist.

At other times, programmers have wallowed in blissful ignorance, perpetuating programs in which their clients really have no interest. They boost the programs up to keep them going without consulting the people they're supposed to be serving. Programmers would be better off if they asked their clients what they wanted and attempted to facilitate it. They must avoid the pitfall of putting their heads in the sand.

Many programmers have felt that they've had no other choice but to follow the dictates of their superiors. Programming by dogma is not uncommon. A director or chief executive officer, by virtue of his or her position, requires that programmers do what they're told. They may feel compelled to obey even though they know that the tasks reflect the input of only one person—the boss.

There are times when programmers succumb to external pressures, too. There may be a particularly powerful special-interest group that uses programmers for its own ends. Thus the needs of others may go unmet, or a leisure program may get used as a vehicle through which the special-interest group advances its own agenda. This tends to occur most often in public leisure service settings.

Finally, there is the smorgasbord approach: Programmers try to provide a potpourri of activities, hoping that everyone will find something to choose and will be satisfied. But with today's operating costs, they'd probably be better off going with a limited menu that encompasses the tastes of their clients in order to meet their preferences optimally. This is especially important in a fee-based or profit-making enterprise.

Application Section. We do not advocate these approaches. But they do occur with regularity in the real world of leisure programming. Take the illustrations above and go back to the various components within the Knowles model of translating needs into objectives. Think about how manipulating and altering those components might improve these practices. Persons who currently are or anticipate becoming leisure programmers may want to further stimulate their thinking by imagining other programming realities and then deciding which components could receive greater or lesser priority in comprehensive program development in the context of the Knowles model and good programming strategy.

STRATEGIES FOR USE DURING TIMES OF CHANGE

Now that we've reviewed the programming strategies that others have employed, we turn to the approaches that we feel are the best ones to use in changing times or under changing conditions. Most of these strategies have been developed as a result of programmers' attempts to work within a context of change. These are the most recent approaches to comprehensive program development and they allow the leisure programmer to function as a change agent, in an active manner.

As an experience maker, you have the opportunity to facilitate or create programs that will change participants' leisure behavior by altering their leisure repertoire. This gives you direct input. You become active, and you plan changes after specific objectives have been determined through careful needs assessment. These objectives are then carried out through the application of successful programming approaches. This stance allows you to function as a change agent and to retain some element of control.

The opposite can be true as well. You may function in such a manner that you exert little or no control over change. The program is unplanned, and changes in leisure behavior (desirable or not) are disorderly. Between planned (active) and unplanned change there is reactive change. Here, you respond rather than initiate. You do not actively encourage the development and enhancement of leisure experiences for participants; rather, you function reactively, providing experiences that will be viewed as limited at best.

To conclude this chapter and our discussion of comprehensive program development, we are going to explore the approaches that we feel have particular application to today's leisure programming. Each of these approaches addresses change, which, we have argued, is inherent in comprehensive program development in today's world. They emphasize the role of the leisure programmer as an active one, and as one in which the programmer is concerned with the development of programs and experiences that will encourage growth and independent leisure functioning for participants.

SYNERGETIC APPROACH

The concept of synergy became popular in the early 1970s, as more and more park, recreation, and leisure professionals played a game called "Lost on the Moon." The game is designed to engage participants in a group problem-solving exercise. Participants are asked to rank fifteen items in the order of their importance to a space crew that is experiencing mechanical difficulties in rendezvousing with the mother ship. Next, they are asked to do the ranking again, this time with a group, using group consensus to arrive at decisions. The decisions of the group as a whole are consistently judged better than the decisions of any one individual in the same group. This exercise helped popularize the concept of synergy, which, generally speaking, states that the whole is greater than the sum of its parts.

Transferred to leisure programming, the concept of synergy implies that several organizations and agencies working together can offer better leisure experiences to a community or a large group of people than any one organization or agency. To take this idea a step further, several professional staff members working together within an organization can produce better leisure experiences than one person working alone.

Synergetic programming, according to Diana R. Dunn and Lamarr A. Phillips, is the process of combining the unique resources of two or more agencies to produce leisure services that could not be offered successfully by one agency acting alone. During the mid-1970s, Dunn and Phillips studied the synergetic programming efforts of more than one hundred American cities with populations of more than one hundred thousand. They found what they felt was an impressive and diverse collection of program examples. "Today, isolationism by urban public recreation agencies is not only unjustifiable philosophically, it is untenable at the practical level. In addition to diminishing municipal budgets, growing operation and maintenance costs, and rising inflation, federal revenue sharing is compelling all local services to demonstrate their respective contributions to the quality of urban life."[10]

This point remains compelling today. Let's think about it.

Application Section.   It has been estimated that by 1990 the number of American households made up of single persons (never married, divorced, separated, and widowed) will nearly equal the number of households of married people.[11] We'd like you to think *synergetically,* together with some other leisure programmers representing other agencies, about this population and their leisure needs and preferences. Appoint yourselves to represent four leisure service providers: (1) a local park and recreation department; (2) a YMCA, YWCA, YMHA, or YWHA; a synagogue- or church-based adult group; (3) the local adult education service; and (4) a private travel agency. Now, do some imagining.

Begin by considering the pool of needs: the population's individual needs, each of your agencies' organizational needs, and the needs of your community. Of course these are hypothetical, but try to make them close to a real situation. Can you and your fellow programmers work together, or are you competing with each other? How might your synergetic program ideas be changed as they are filtered through institutional purposes, feasibility criteria, and interests of clientele? Identify the possible benefits and drawbacks in programming for singles in this fashion. Are these strengths and weaknesses the same ones you would expect if you were programming for another population?

It is our feeling that synergetic program development practices enhance the quality of programs and services because of the cooperative way in which expertise is mixed and shared. We feel that this is particularly beneficial during an era of technological and social change as described in Chapter 3, in which it is almost impossible for one person or unit acting alone to know of all the alternatives that may be available. This leads us to our second contemporary strategy, the facilitative approach to programming.

FACILITATIVE APPROACH

This mode of comprehensive program development places you in the role of facilitator. It assumes that programmers have the ability to work closely with program participants and that the program participants have a desire to increase or renew their leisure functioning in a self-directed fashion.

As a group, the program participants and the programmer share the responsibility for making decisions regarding leisure choices. Therefore, you must be able to manage the program planning process in a way that encourages clientele input. Figure 4-3, which depicts a seven-step process of *andragogy,* provides a good illustration of what we mean. Andragogy is the body of theory and practice on which self-directed learning is based. It is defined as the art and science of helping adults and/or maturing human beings learn.[12] In this case, we are interested in applying the andragogical process to leisure program participants who desire to increase or renew their independent, self-directed leisure functioning.

Viewing leisure learning in a problem-identification/problem-solving context means that you must approach facilitative program development by making sure that the self-directed process elements are carried out. Figure 4-4 adapts the work of andragogists to a leisure learning model.

In addition to guiding this process, you must be creative in finding ways to draw program participants into leisure decision making; must value the information and resources that program participants possess; must obtain expectations from clientele; must actively seek feedback from participants; and must be a willing source of information and referral regarding leisure opportunities. The facilitative leisure programmer must be willing to give up control, to help the participant assume more and more

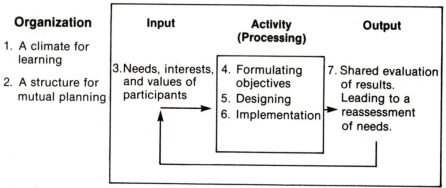

Figure 4-3 Andragogical Process

From J. D. Ingalls, *A Trainers Guide to Andragogy* (Washington, D.C.: U.S. Government Printing Office, 1973), p. 11.

Process Elements	Facilitative Approach	
Climate	Informal Mutually respectful Consensual Collaborative	Problem Finding
Planning	By participative decision making Mutual planning	
Diagnosis of leisure needs	By mutual assessment	
Setting goals	By mutual negotiation	Problem Solving
Designing the leisure experience	Shared Sequenced Developmental	
Leisure activities	Multifaceted Independent Experiential Self-directed	
Evaluation	By mutual assessment or self-collected evidence	Problem Finding

Figure 4-4   Leisure Learning Process Elements in the Facilitative Program Development Approach

Adapted from Malcolm Knowles, *Self-Directed Learning* (New York: Association Press, 1975), and J. D. Ingalls, *Human Energy: The Critical Factor for Individuals and Organizations* (Reading, Mass.: Addison-Wesley Publishing Co., Inc., 1976), pp. 147-150.

responsibility for his or her own leisure. Essentially, the programmer must want to launch the ready participant successfully out of the nest.

Application Section. How might this work in reality? For a moment, assume that you are a coordinator of student activities at a college or university. You have direct responsibility for a number of student organizations, including the Native American Student Council. The council president has just commissioned a program committee with responsibility for planning and conducting the annual week of festivities, events, and activities aimed at educating the general campus population about contemporary needs and issues related to Native American people. Additionally, the program would have entertainment value for spectators through the sharing of traditional songs, lore, crafts, foods, and dances. As coordinator of student activities, you are responsible for working with this program committee. Using the facilitative approach outline, how would you proceed to aid in the development of this program?

The idea behind this strategy is to help participants to become self-directed in their leisure. In order to do this, they must first be taught how to function in this manner, especially if they are members of groups that have traditionally been told what to do (for example, children, patients, and enlisted personnel). If the facilitative programmer is successful, indigenous leaders should emerge from the group, and the group should become more and more able to function on its own.

CONSULTATIVE OR CONTRACTUAL APPROACH

Under this strategy, you are an independent contractor hired by a park, recreation, or leisure agency to manage leisure programs for its constituents. Contracting for services is not unusual in private or public agencies anymore. Agencies typically make formal agreements for the design and construction of recreation facilities; the operation of special facilities (for example, tennis courts or golf courses); the joint use of school or other community facilities; and special services such as repair of motor vehicles.

Contracting for leisure programs and services is becoming more common because financially constrained agencies are unable to hire their own full-time leisure programming staffs. However, even when a programming staff does exist, an agency will often contract with someone to provide a specific program or service (for instance, a recreation program for a military base, a therapeutic recreation program, or even a course in break dancing. These contracts are typically obtained when the skills or abilities required to operate an activity cannot be supplied by the personnel on the full-time program staff.

There are also instances of an agency contracting with a private firm of leisure programming professionals exclusively for the purpose of planning and administrating the agency's comprehensive leisure program. One such firm is Leisure Pro, Inc., of Fair Oaks, California. This private corporation has been serving the community Recreation and Park District since 1979. Under the agreement, Leisure Pro has full responsibility for all recreation activities, while the district continues to provide facilities and maintenance.

Experienced leisure program consultants point out that a key advantage of using contractors in this way is the reduction in overall agency costs. Wayne Lowery finds that this is due to the greater flexibility contractors have because they operate under fewer organizational constraints, must comply with fewer regulations, and have lower personnel costs. Also, because they usually perform specific functions, leisure program contractors can "fine tune" their products in such a way that they are cost-effective and have general application to a number of agencies.[13]

As aspiring programmers look ahead to professional opportunities, they tend to visualize themselves as being affiliated with one particular park, recreation, or leisure agency. This has been the usual pattern, and indeed is an entry-level goal directed toward professional development. It is conceivable, however, that in the future, contracting for leisure programs and services could become the rule rather than the exception. Consider for a few moments your reaction to that possibility. Do you feel you would rather be associated with a private firm that contracts with leisure agencies to provide or facilitate leisure experiences for their clienteles? Or would you rather be more directly associated with an agency as a member of its leisure programming staff? Discuss the pros and cons of your thinking with others.

MULTIPLE-OPTION APPROACH

Based on research about learning, Lyn Sheffield proposes a multiple-option approach to leisure programming that includes three goal structures: competition, individualization, and cooperation.[14] Competitive goal structures are characterized by only one person or group winning and all others losing. Individualistic goal structures occur when a person or a group successfully attains a goal (wins) independently of the performance of others. In cooperative goal structures, participants are mutually dependent on each other for success.[15] Sheffield suggests using these goal structures to expand the diversity and variety of leisure program offerings to allow the participant more choices or options. Examples of selected leisure activities in each of the goal structure categories are given in Figure 4-5.

This approach enables programmers to consider how a particular activity may meet different needs or how different activities may be used to meet the same need. In the past, most programs have emphasized competitive goal structures. How might that affect participants as a shift towards individualistic or cooperative goal structures are made? What are some other pros and cons to using this type of programming approach?

Examples of Multiple-Option Programming			
Activity	*Competitive Goal Structure*	*Individualist Goal Structure*	*Cooperative Goal Structure*
Swimming	Swim meets or water polo leagues	WSI/Life saving course or aquacise	Synchronized swim or water games water ballet
Aerobics	Best original routine contest	Aerobic fitness class	Cumulative job or partner aerobics
Cooking	Chili cook-off	Cookbook of "my best" recipes	Clam bake or fish fry
Birdwatching	Christmas bird count	Hunting with a camera outing	Establishing a bird sanctuary
Needlecraft	Needlecraft show with prizes	Folk art technique class	Commemorative or "city" quilt
Tennis	Challenge ladder	Practice board for solo usage	Tennis marathon
Cycling	BMX racing	Bike care class	May Day bike ride
Orienteering	Orienteering meet	Wilderness survival skills clinic	Partner/team orienteering
Creative Writing	Short story contest	Open workshop on creative writing	City history project
Flower arranging	African violet show	Plant care classes	Garden club
Woodworking	Pipe carving contest	Auction "find a treasure" trips	Carve a totem pole
Painting	Juried show	Face painting at art festival	Town hall mural
Social Dance	Break dance contest	Aerobic fitness	World record/fund-raising dance-a-thon
Choral Group	All-city chorus tryouts	Musicians' hotline program	Community sing-a-longs
Basketball	HotShot tournament	Weekend coaching clinic	All touch/no scoring/no standing

Figure 4-5 Activities and Goal Structures

From Lyn Sheffield, "Are You Providing Multiple-Option Programming?" *Parks & Recreation*, May 1984, p. 57. Reprinted by special permission of the National Recreation and Park Association.

Application Section.   This application section takes the form of a case study. You have been hired as Director of Leisure Programs and Services for a military installation in the Great Lakes area of the United States. You have a small budget that will allow you to hire on-base activity specialists or other personnel to facilitate leisure experiences for soldiers assigned to the base and their spouses and dependents. The facilities available for your use include a lakefront beach and small marina; an eighteen-hole golf course; an open club or mess; a gymnasium with two basketball courts, an indoor pool, a weight room, and three racquetball/handball courts; four outdoor tennis courts; one baseball diamond; and one football field circled by a cinder track. You have some used physical education equipment and supplies (volleyballs, badminton racquets, and the like) and an equipment/supply room attendant. You also have a small auditorium in which movies and stage entertainments may be shown.

Your job is to establish an entire set of leisure opportunities for the persons at the base. What strategy or combination of strategies will you employ to best meet this responsibility?

SUMMARY

In this chapter, we have examined comprehensive program development, with particular attention to approaches and strategies that have been and continue to be used in park, recreation, and leisure settings where leisure programs and services are being offered. Rather than make judgments in favor of any one mode of operation, we suggest that you choose an approach by combining a careful consideration of your skills and abilities with a careful consideration of individual, organizational, and community needs. The successful leisure programmer is apt to create a unique strategy that incorporates the strengths of a variety of approaches, allows for change in clientele, organizational, and community needs, and assumes continued development of skills and abilities on the part of the programmer.

FOOTNOTES

1. Daniel J. Levinson, *The Seasons of a Man's Life* (New York: Alfred A. Knopf, Inc., 1978).
2. Richard G. Kraus, *Recreation Today: Program Planning and Leadership*, 2nd ed. (Santa Monica, Calif.: Goodyear Publishing Co., Inc., 1977).
3. Christopher R. Edginton, David M. Compton, and Carole J. Hanson, *Recreational and Leisure Programming: A Guide for the Professional* (Philadelphia: Saunders College Publishing Company, 1980), pp. 47, 49.
4. Howard Danford and Max Shirley, *Creative Leadership in Recreation*, 2nd ed. (Boston: Allyn and Bacon, Inc., 1970), pp. 110–11.
5. Kraus, *Recreation Today*, p. 83.
6. Albert Tillman, *The Program Book for Recreation Professionals* (Palo Alto, Calif.: Mayfield Publishing Company, 1973), p. 57.
7. James F. Murphy, *Recreation and Leisure Service: A Humanistic Perspective* (Dubuque, Iowa: William C. Brown Company, Publishers, 1975), pp. 93–94.

8. Christopher R. Edginton and Carole J. Hanson, "Appraising Leisure Service Delivery," *Parks & Recreation*, March 1976, pp. 44–45. Reprinted by special permission of the National Recreation and Park Association.

9. Malcolm Knowles, *The Modern Practice of Adult Education*, copyright 1980 by Malcolm S. Knowles, p. 122. Published by Cambridge, The Adult Education Company, 888 Seventh Avenue, New York, New York 10106. Adapted with the permission of the publisher.

10. Diana R. Dunn and Lamarr A. Phillips, "Synergetic Programming or 2+2=5," *Parks & Recreation*, March 1975, p. 37. Reprinted by special permission of the National Recreation and Park Association.

11. Richard G. Kraus, "Singles: A Large (And Largely Ignored) Target Population," *Parks & Recreation*, May 1982, p. 48. Reprinted by special permission of the National Recreation and Park Association.

12. Knowles, *Modern Practice of Adult Education*, p. 43.

13. Wayne Lowery, "Privitization to Cut Costs and Increase Revenues," speech given at the National Recreation and Park Congress, Minneapolis, Minnesota, October 1981.

14. Lyn Sheffield, "Are You Providing Multiple-Option Programming?" *Parks & Recreation*, May 1984, p. 56. Reprinted by special permission of the National Recreation and Park Association.

15. Ibid. p. 56.

chapter 5

Introduction to Leisure Programming and the Programming Cycle

INTRODUCTION TO PROGRAMMING

In the preface to this book, we stated that programming, the process of planning and delivering leisure experiences to an individual or a group of individuals, is a way of managing play without putting constraints upon its joy and spontaneity. We believe that skill in programming, a basic necessity for all contemporary park, recreation, and leisure professionals, is both an art and a science. By accepting play (leisure behavior) as a psychological state, a rationale for programming becomes apparent. To return to Toffler, "experience makers," or professionals who facilitate play, program in order to provide experiences and environments that enhance the leisure awareness, well-being, and quality of life of their participants.[1] These are viewed as psychological phenomena, allowing the four components of the Carol A. Peterson and Scout L. Gunn leisure education content model to be used as a conceptual basis for programming.[2] Programmers program in order to increase their constituents' level of self-awareness and awareness about leisure, to develop their constituents' leisure/play attitudes, and to facilitate their constituents' problem-solving capabilities. Also, they create opportunities for their participants to develop their social skills through cooperation and competition. They facilitate participant competence in leisure activities, both traditional and innovative. Finally, they encourage the growth of knowledge and use of leisure resources within the family, the community, and the society at large. Thus, programmers program in order to meet their constituents' cognitive, affective, social, and psychomotor needs and interests in order to increase their positive and independent leisure functioning, thereby enhancing what can be derived from their *total* life experience. It is an underlying premise of this book that there is a generic process that allows leisure programmers to be the catalysts described above. We call this process the leisure programming cycle.

GENERIC LEISURE PROGRAMMING

Each of the authors of the numerous textbooks that currently exist in leisure programming suggests a programming recipe or formula to follow. Upon examining these "recipes," we can identify some ingredients that are basic to all, even though they may come into the mixture in differing quantities or at different times.

Our cyclical approach to leisure programming implies by its very name that there is indeed a generic and systematic way of identifying and meeting participants' leisure needs and interests. The programming process begins with the assessment of participant needs and interests and moves to the planning of the program. This is followed by the provision or implementation of the program, its evaluation, and its revision. Then the cycle begins again. The cycle is illustrated in Figure 5-1.

It appears that we are best able to understand the leisure programming cycle as a generic process when we discuss it as though it were a sequence of discrete, linear steps. In reality, though, each phase of the leisure

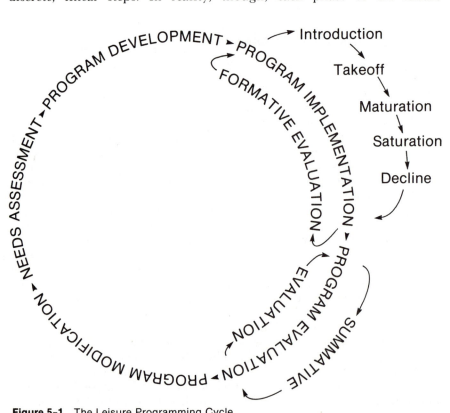

Figure 5-1   The Leisure Programming Cycle

programming cycle overlaps with others in a circular, interdependent manner. We show the phases as a circle in order to reinforce the cyclical nature of the process. Before we explain these generic steps a bit further and describe how they work, we need to consider who the participants are and where the programs occur.

WITH WHOM DO PROGRAMMERS PROGRAM?

It is by design that we use the word "with" as opposed to "for" when we seek to describe leisure programming's clients, participants, constituents, or audience. This is because we adamantly believe that the desirable end product of involvement in the leisure experience is responsible, independent leisure functioning. The most effective way to ensure that this takes place is genuinely to seek and use the input of the identified client group. Among the most successful vehicles for doing this is needs assessment. But first, who are your constituents?

Your constituents are those whom you serve, those who desire to whatever degree to partake in leisure experiences. This includes latch-key children, single adults, refugees, homemakers, unemployed individuals, retirees, long-term institutionalized people, deinstitutionalized people, mid-career persons, incarcerated criminals, one-parent families, working women, immigrants, people in mid-life, military personnel, gays, international visitors, widowers, religious workers, the rural elderly, and migrants. Obviously, some of these people have always been identified as members of the leisure clientele, while others very likely have neither received nor sought leisure programming services, especially as an identified "group." The point is that your constituents are everybody whom you can reach and that "everybody" is less easy to stereotype and more diverse as each day passes. The persons with whom you program are as varied as the cultural, ethnic, racial, class, and age groups of the entire world. But in your enthusiasm about all these many and varied peoples, keep in mind the developmental stages and periods that all people seem to go through, as discussed in Chapters 1 and 2. These phases, as understood today, are common to human beings collectively as they combine to form the one big category called humanity. An awareness of these patterns, used in conjunction with a recognition of individual uniqueness, should lead you to optimal leisure programming. Programmers have much to do as more and more North Americans seek more and more leisure opportunities and fulfillment in all kinds of places and in all kinds of life-styles.

WHERE DO LEISURE PROGRAMS OCCUR?

Census data show that the world's population is increasing and that the population of North America is too, but at a lesser rate. Generally, our population is maturing, and our migration patterns are such that we are clustering together in certain regions as opposed to distributing ourselves evenly across the continent.[3] As a result, the people that we serve tend to be mobile, moving from one high-density area to another and tending to migrate toward the "sunbelt" areas of the United States.[4] With this and other population demographics in mind, it becomes apparent that leisure programs are shifting from the traditional playgrounds and public parks to urban corridors, hallways, and empty lots. Programs are happening in neighborhood elementary schools that have closed, warehouses, community rooms of high-rise apartment buildings, storefronts, church basements, stoops, alleys, and beachfronts. Some programs are based in mobile units that move from place to place, taking leisure experiences to potential participants, as opposed to having the participants come to an established program site. This kind of flexibility, especially, allows the leisure programmer to gain access to the hard-to-reach or home-centered individual.

Thus the locales for programming, like the participants, are many and varied. Traditional locales have a sense of history and continuity working in their favor, whereas the new locales have developed in response to the emerging needs of constituents. Both have their place in the delivery of a comprehensive set of leisure programs. Gold emphasizes the interrelatedness of open space, leisure opportunities, and traditional and nontraditional environments in terms of the quality and the quantity of leisure experiences. At the very least, the places where programs take place should reflect constituent needs and leisure behavior. A concern for human development and stewardship of land and water go hand in hand. Program locales should help relate people to their environment and to each other. Gold calls this an emerging emphasis within recreational planning and suggests that the future holds in store the recycling of developed land into open spaces and malleable play areas in which noncompetitive, self-determined activities occur. He also foresees the integration of cultural programs and performing arts, adult and child day-care programs, and adult education services with traditional park, recreation, and leisure services.[5]

It is already mandated through P.L. 94-142, Equal Education for All Handicapped Children Act; P.L. 90-480, Architectural Barriers Act of 1968; and P.L. 93-112, Vocational Rehabilitation Act, Section 502 that the places in which leisure programs occur be accessible to all. Attitudinal barriers are to be removed along with physical ones, so that no one may be prohibited from entering and using leisure spaces. So the mission of leisure programmers is broadening. To supplement the traditional pastoral parks and large athletic playfields, leisure programmers are also working on rooftops, in rehabilitated buildings, in cemeteries, and in homes.

Application Section. Assume that you are responsible for planning and operating a new urban downtown recreation center to be opened in two years. Your supervisor has stated that she doesn't want you to meet this responsibility based on either the application of "national standards" or the past practices of the agency. What are the important elements for you to consider as you begin to work on this project? How will you use citizen input regarding the planning and design process? Why might you want to assess the social impact of the new center? How can you ensure that the particular space or facility that you advocate will meet the needs of those to be served? How might the answers to these questions differ if your task were to develop a rural recreation center?

OVERVIEW OF THE PROGRAMMING CYCLE

We are now ready to return to the programming cycle and its generic steps. Programming is the process of assessing needs and interests, generating ideas through planning and development, implementing the program, evaluating it, and finally modifying it. In the context of leisure programming, a program is an activity, event, or experience that occurs specifically for its own purpose. It is an experience for either an individual or a group of people. It is the vehicle through which the participant achieves a leisure state of mind.

The leisure programming cycle commences with the *needs assessment* phase—the assessment of constituent needs and interests. Preliminary information collection may take several forms. Some agencies conduct formal participant surveys through face-to-face interviews, telephone interviews, or mailed questionnaires. Other organizations merely ask participants for informal information at the end of a program. Others rely on the observations, intuition, and experience of the professional staff, while some use citizens' advisory boards to get "representative" opinions about programs. Without regard to what means or combination of means is used to determine the needs and interests of clients, the important thing is that the determination is indeed made! The key to needs assessment is systematically to collect and record information about the constituents' leisure awareness, attitudes, needs, patterns, and interests—and to use, not shelve, the results! Using such data will help programmers to broaden the base of support for leisure programs that is so very much needed today.

The second phase of the cycle is the planning or *development* of the program. If leisure opportunities are unavailable elsewhere, or are few, a responsive agency will plan and market new or additional programs to meet the expressed desires of its constituency. In reality, this will mostly be done by reallocating already existing resources or limiting new programs to those that are likely to be economically self-sufficient. There are operational aspects of the program development phase that can be assisted by sound program planning and evaluation techniques. These aspects include gathering and storing demographic and attitudinal information about the participants; reading past evaluations and reports made by the agency; counting participants; making personnel time budgets and reports; and accounting for income and expenditures for each program. This information clearly allows for factually based decision making, as opposed to guesswork.

In terms of the marketing aspect of the planning phase, it is essential to know who the audience (or target market) is and how to reach its members. This necessitates using a strong advertising and public-relations program to carry the desired message to the identified audience. At the very least, publicity must include the "who, what, where, when, and how much" of the program. Media ranging from print to film to tape are all available for use today.

Following the development of the leisure program is its *implementation*. This third phase of the cycle is the actual provision of the leisure experience to the participants. John L. Crompton suggests that leisure programs have life cycles much like human beings, with general periods of ascent, maturity, and decline. More specifically, when a program is delivered it goes through five stages: It is introduced, "takes off," matures, saturates the market, and finally declines. Crompton calls these the five stages of the product life cycle for leisure programs (see Figure 5-2).

These five stages all happen during the program implementation phase of the leisure program cycle. Stage one, the introduction stage, serves to generate acceptance and support for the program; it involves promotion, testing, and finalization. In a sense, it's like the tryout that a theatrical play is given prior to opening on Broadway. During stage two, the takeoff stage, a number of persons are actually participating in the program, and if it is a good one it is likely to show enrollment growth. During the third stage, maturity, the program may still be growing, but at a slower rate. The program peaks, and if it is particularly successful, competitors may enter. The focus of the leisure programmer changes from generating public awareness of the program to getting participants to prefer it to competitors' programs. The degree to which satisfaction is derived from the leisure experience impacts on the program's continued existence.

The fourth stage, saturation, is the time when the leisure programmer can alter the shape or duration of the life cycle of the program in the implementation phase. In terms of participation, the program basically relies on repeat business and is vulnerable to those who drop out. However, the program may be revitalized by infusing it with "new blood," if indeed the program merits being continued (that is, is still doing a good job of meeting participant needs and interests). "New blood" may include a change

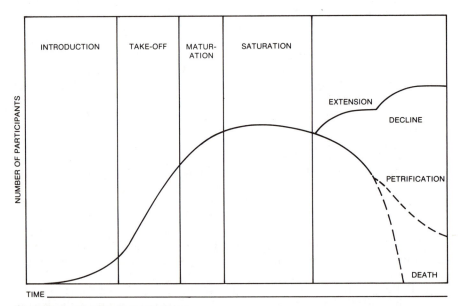

Figure 5-2 The Product Life Cycle

From John L. Crompton, "Programs Have Life Cycles, Too," *Parks & Recreation*, October 1979, p. 53. Reprinted by special permission of the National Recreation and Park Association.

in program structure or format, new leadership, a different time or place, and/or alternative equipment and supplies.

If the program cannot or should not be regenerated, then it enters into the decline stage. You should not fear this fifth part of the life cycle, for decline is natural and ultimately inevitable. People's needs, interests, and behaviors change. That fact underlies the very definitions of leisure that we use in this book, and it is nothing to be anxious about. Decline is not always a negative stage. Within the decline stage there are several phenomena that may occur. One of these is petrification.[6]

During petrification, decline arrests itself and participation levels off, as opposed to totally disappearing. Crompton states that "a small number of enthusiastic participants remain in the program, which may then run itself with no social or economic reason for abolishing it."[7] If, during the decline stage, the program does not petrify, then it dies, meaning that the decision is made to terminate the program.

Crompton further suggests that programs in the decline stage of their life cycle should be reviewed and evaluated yearly. If a program is to be stopped, he believes that it should be phased out over time in order to maintain good will and to minimize any inconveniences for the remaining participants. To end a program when its time has come allows the resources used to support the declining program to be allocated elsewhere.[8] Even so, leisure programmers can have a terrible time "pulling the plug." Dennis R. Howard and John L. Crompton discuss two reasons why programs often are not allowed to die. They believe that programs are permitted to continue because of personal or political considerations and lack of information: "Established programs or services have a tendency to become sacrosanct. They are retained because of inertia, management sentiment, or the influence of vested interests."[9]

Leisure programmers who are cognizant of these factors can do much to minimize their effect by encouraging an open dialogue about program termination. The political overtones involved in dealing with subjective and personal biases and persons with vested interests can be awesome to the programmer. Dealing with organizational politics is a difficult task. But it will help if you understand and are willing to articulate the program life-cycle concept and other ongoing information to your peers and others who influence the implementation of programs.

PROGRAM EVALUATION AND MODIFICATION

Let us pause for a moment to summarize what we have done thus far. First, we have stated that the leisure programming cycle consists of five phases. We have discussed the first three: needs assessment, program planning or development, and program implementation. Within the third phase of the programming process, program implementation, we have described five stages in the life cycle of a program: introduction, takeoff, maturation, saturation, and decline, which may lead to either program petrification or termination. If, during the decline stage, the decision is made to modify the program (with termination being the most extreme form of modification), formative evaluation[10] may be called for. Formative evaluation is an evaluation of program worth that is made while the program is actually happening. It allows the leisure programmer to make adjustments to a program as the program is being implemented.

Consider for a moment a current-events discussion club that is sponsored by the therapeutic recreation staff of a psychiatric care facility. The program was initiated based on the results of a formally conducted needs assessment of the entire client population *and* in response to the wishes of several clients, expressed during informal interactions. It was developed by the staff in conjunction with the clients, was based on the developmental status of the clients, was well publicized and promoted, and was grounded in the resources of the facility (library magazines, newspapers, television news shows, and radio). There were also some therapeutic benefits to be derived from the program, such as enhanced social interaction with peers, greater awareness of the world outside the hospital, and independent involvement in collection, distribution, and evaluation of information.

The program appears to have been done in a sound manner. It proceeded through the initial stages of the program life cycle: introduction and takeoff. However, during maturation the program experienced a drastic and unexpected decline in both the actual numbers of clients participating and in the quality of involvement of those who remained. The staff judged that this was happening prematurely, before the program had peaked. They decided that some type of adjustment needed to be made. So the staff began a formative evaluation procedure that was designed to seek out the cause of this unanticipated turn of events and to suggest possible remedies.

What was discovered was that there had been a change in the medication schedules of many of the participants. Clients were coming to the discussion group shortly after ingesting their prescribed drugs. In response to this, the therapeutic recreation staff rescheduled the club meeting to a time when the clients were not so recently medicated, and found that participation returned to its previous rate and level of quality. In this case, formative evaluation led to a simple adjustment during the implementation phase of the programming cycle—a change in the time that the program was offered.

This illustration leads us to the fourth phase of the leisure programming cycle, program *evaluation*. This evaluation, which occurs *after* a program has been implemented and has gone through its life cycle through the stage of decline, is known as summative evaluation.[11] It is the final judgment of the merit or worth of a program. This is in contrast to formative evaluation, which is done to revise and/or improve a program while it is still happening. Generally, when leisure programmers refer to evaluation, they mean summative evaluation.

Whether formative or summative evaluation is used depends on the leisure programmer's purpose—revision or final judgment—and the time frame in which the evaluation occurs. When the programmer has a special concern for accountability, then it is wise to evaluate both formatively and summatively. Formative evaluation allows for greater and immediate responsiveness to the constituents served, whereas summative evaluation is useful to external bodies that have an interest in the justification of programs and program expenditures. Used together, the two kinds of evaluation provide increased depth of information for decision making.

The fifth and final phase of the leisure programming cycle is program modification. This is when any changes that are suggested through the summative evaluation are made. It is the point of departure for the new version of the program, which begins the entire cycle again.

SUMMARY

This chapter has served to introduce briefly the five major phases of the leisure programming cycle and the stages that exist within one of the phases. In the chapters that follow, each phase is discussed in detail.

Programming is the process of planning and delivering leisure services to people in order to enhance their leisure awareness, functioning, and quality of life. It is important for programmers to recognize the diversity of those with whom they plan programs (that is, the participants), to remember the commonalities of the life courses of human beings, and to be aware of the new environments in which leisure programs are taking place. An awareness of the developmental stages that all people go through, combined with a sensitivity to our changing environment and population, can enable you as a leisure programmer to use the cyclical programming approach in order to facilitate optimal leisure experiences systematically. In the next chapter, we will closely examine needs assessment as the first phase of the leisure programming cycle and as a means of being responsive to the wishes of leisure clientele.

Application Section. In this exercise, we'd like you to think of a community that you know well—your hometown, the city in which your school is located, or the town in which you work. Answer the following series of questions about your chosen community.

1. How do you think that leisure is "defined" by the people who reside in the community?
2. How has the complexion of the community changed since the 1960s? the 1970s? Has there been a population change? If so, is it due to immigration or emigration? What sociodemographic characteristics must be considered in answering this question?
3. How have the recreational spaces in the community changed?
4. Find a friend and, in your own words, explain Figure 5-1 to him or her. Tell this person how using this approach to leisure programming can help you to be a more effective professional.

FOOTNOTES

1. Alvin Toffler, *Future Shock* (New York: Random House, Inc. 1970), pp. 226-227.
2. Carol A. Peterson and Scout L. Gunn, *Therapeutic Recreation Program Design: Principles and Procedures*, 2nd Ed. (Englewood Cliffs, N.J.: Prentice-Hall, Inc.,

1984). Copyright 1984. Reprinted by permission of Prentice-Hall, Inc., Englewood Cliffs, N.J.

3. A. H. Underhill, "Population Dynamics and Demography," *Leisure Today: Population Dynamics—The Changing Face of America*, October 1981, pp. 33-34. Reprinted with permission from The Journal of Physical Education, Recreation, and Dance. The Journal is a publication of the American Alliance for Health, Physical Education, Recreation and Dance, 1900 Association Drive, Reston, VA 22091.

4. Hilmi Ibrahim, "Immigrants and Leisure," *Leisure Today: Population Dynamics—The Changing Face of America*, October 1981, pp. 36-37. Reprinted with permission from The Journal of Physical Education, Recreation, and Dance. The Journal is a publication of the American Alliance for Health, Physical Education, Recreation and Dance, 1900 Association Drive, Reston, VA 22091.

5. Seymour M. Gold, *Recreation Planning and Design* (New York: McGraw-Hill Book Company, 1980), pp. 29-44.

6. John L. Crompton, "Recreation Programs Have Life Cycles, Too," *Parks & Recreation,* October 1979, pp. 52-57.

7. Ibid., p. 54.

8. Ibid., p. 55.

9. Dennis R. Howard and John L. Crompton, *Financing, Managing and Marketing Recreation and Park Resources* (Dubuque, Iowa: William C. Brown Company, Publishers, 1980), p. 400.

10. Michael Scriven, "The Methodology of Evaluation," in *Perspectives of Curriculum Evaluation*, ed. Ralph Tyler, Robert M. Gagne, and Michael Scriven (Chicago: Rand McNally and Company, AERA Monograph Series on Curriculum Evaluation, no. 1, 1967), pp. 39-83.

11. Ibid., pp. 39-83.

chapter 6

Needs Assessment
Phase One of the Leisure Programming Cycle

INTRODUCTION

Needs assessment, the first step in the leisure programming cycle, is extremely important, as it sets the tone for the rest of the programming process. In leisure programming, needs assessment performs two major functions: the generation of program ideas and the facilitation of input from constituents and responsiveness to constituents by service providers. In order to carry out an assessment, the leisure programmer must have a basic understanding of the developmental stages that are thought to be common to all people (see Chapters 1 and 2); an understanding of the meaning of leisure, as deduced from his or her training and experience (see Chapter 1); and an understanding of systematic information collection and analysis techniques and instruments (elaborated on in this chapter and Chapter 9).

But first, what are these needs with which leisure programmers are concerned? Peter A. Witt and Rhonda Groom offer a succinct description: Needs are ingrained, innate characteristics that are found among people.[1] These characteristics are inherent in individuals without regard to time or place, and their satisfaction is crucial in maintaining psychological, physical, social, and/or spiritual stability. Needs must be both identified and met. Here we are specifically interested in the identification and satisfaction of leisure needs. For a further discussion, please refer back to Chapter 4.

If we accept leisure as a psychological state, then satisfaction through leisure occurs when participants perceive themselves to be competent, in control, relaxed, aroused, experiencing novelty, relieved, and/or socially involved. When people feel free to pursue whatever experiences they believe will give them these feelings, then they are intrinsically motivated; Iso-Ahola suggests that they are more likely to find themselves more deeply into a leisure state.[2] This implies that when leisure programmers are conducting assessments, they are well advised to use instruments that probe beyond simple interest inventories into the identification of intrinsic needs, leisure attitudes and behaviors, and leisure styles. Leisure is a complex phenomenon, and assessment is one means of helping programmers along the path of improving or enhancing the meaning of the leisure experiences of their constituents.[3] Assessment may be a first step toward initiating and measuring changes in leisure behavior as a consequence of services delivered.[4]

WHAT IS NEEDS ASSESSMENT?

There are a variety of ways to define needs assessment, depending on whether the leisure programmer's conception of it is narrow or broad. For our purposes, needs assessment is broadly defined as a process of identifying and discovering constituents' leisure needs, attitudes, values, and behaviors, as well as areas in which clarification, improvement, or reinforcement of leisure functioning is desired. This information is used as a guide in the provision, development, or facilitation of leisure experiences for the constituent, based on the changes, clarifications, improvements, or reinforcements indicated. Needs assessment is an integral part of the total leisure programming process and helps professionals to make informed decisions with and about their constituents.[5,6]

Needs assessment also allows programmers to amass fairly large amounts of information that is both current and accurate in a relatively short period of time. There is a growing body of knowledge about needs assessment and needs assessment instrumentation to be tapped. We are using the phrase "needs assessment" within the context of leisure behavior; this colors the needs assessment instrumentation that we have elected to include in this chapter. More specifically, much of the recent activity in leisure needs assessment has been the product of therapeutic recreators. This is reflected in our overview of instrumentation.

DIFFERENTIATING AMONG CONCEPTS

Before we examine leisure needs assessment and specific current instrumentation, a clarification of the concepts (or constructs) of need, attitude, interest, behavior, and style, in lay terms, is in order. Terms such as reliability and validity are also explained as an aid to understanding the next couple of sections in this chapter.

As stated earlier, a *need* is an innate characteristic that persons are driven or motivated to satisfy. It is a longing. An *attitude* is a statement of readiness or an emotional feeling that influences a person's response to objects, situations, or persons with whom the attitude is associated or to whom it is related. *Interest* is an attraction to, or an identification or involvement with, some type of activity or experience. *Behaviors* are the observable acts that people perform. *Style* is the meaning that is attached to a person's leisure experiences and the psychological satisfactions that are drawn from them, without regard to the actual leisure activity participated in.

Reliability is the degree of consistency that a needs assessment instrument or procedure demonstrates over time and use. *Validity* is the quality that allows the needs assessment instrument or procedure to discover what it is intended to discover. Since these two concepts are so critical to an understanding of the next sections, they must be elaborated on.

Reliability reflects the dependability of an instrument. When a person scores similarly on an instrument over a period of time and under comparable circumstances, then the instrument is considered to be reliable. Comparisons between different administrations of an instrument can be expressed in statistical terms as a coefficient of correlation on a scale ranging from -1 to $+1$. The greater the value of the coefficient, the more consistent or reliable the instrument is thought to be. There are four ways in which reliability may be estimated: the test-retest method; the use of alternate or parallel forms of the same instrument; the split-halves method (comparing the instrument by dividing it into two halves); and the internal consistency method (using statistical formulas to test the instrument's homogeneity).

Reliability is important because assessment instruments should be accurate each time they are used. But accuracy is not enough, for you must be sure that you are measuring what you think you're measuring. That is where validity enters in. Validity is the extent to which the instrument or procedure determines the concepts or constructs that it is supposed to determine. Validity may be expressed through expert judgment or, for numerical data, it may be expressed as a correlation coefficient. There are three major types of validity: content validity, criterion-related validity, and construct validity.

In determining *content validity*, the question is: Do the items included in the instrument truly represent the concept that the instrument is supposed to be measuring? Content validity is often determined by subjecting an instrument to the evaluation of a group of experts.

Criterion-related validity has two subtypes: concurrent validity and predictive validity. Criterion-related validity is generally found by correlating the results from the use of one instrument with an external criterion, yielding a validity coefficient. To determine concurrent validity, the instrument and the criterion are used at the same time and the results are compared with each other. Predictive validity is the instrument's capacity to predict what is likely to happen on the criterion measure when it is taken at a later time.

Construct validity evaluates the extent to which a particular instrument measures the theoretical phenomena that are being assessed. For example, leisure attitude theory involves constructs (or attributes) such as perceived freedom, control, choice, and time. Do these items, as they appear on a leisure assessment instrument, represent leisure attitude? If so, the instrument demonstrates construct validity.

Reliability and validity are very complex concepts. To aid you in understanding the information later in this chapter, we encourage you to examine some introductory statistics or research methodology texts that go into the subject in much greater detail.

Finally, let us reiterate that we are following a psychological definition of leisure as a subjective experience or state of mind. Particularly from a therapeutic recreation or leisure counseling perspective (and our instrumentation framework is drawn from that), the desired end result of using the instrumentation should be the facilitation of clientele movement toward a leisure state of mind.

Each of these concepts is of concern to the leisure programmer, as they are all related to understanding the role and function of leisure for those whom the programmer serves. The process of needs assessment enables programmers to collect information about each of these aspects of peoples' lives so that they may program accordingly. One of the primary ways in which leisure needs information is collected is through the use of leisure assessment instruments.

GENERAL COMMENTS ON INSTRUMENTATION

Larry C. Loesch,[7] Witt, Connolly, and Compton,[8] Loesch and Wheeler,[9] Paul Wehman and Stuart J. Schlein,[10] and Howe[11] are among the authors who have systematically examined the status of leisure assessment instruments. Loesch had some disappointing results from a 1980 computer-assisted literature search.

> Fewer than ten leisure assessment instruments are commonly mentioned in the professional literature, and two of these are no longer available. . . . only one . . . is published by a major publishing company; the others typically are available only from their respective authors. In sum, even the few available assessment instruments directly relevant to leisure counseling are hard to obtain.[12]

In addition to the inaccessibility of the instruments, Loesch and Wheeler and Witt and his associates expressed concern about the low quality of the instruments regarding validity, reliability, and level of sophistication. The instruments tend to be underdeveloped in terms of having a substantive base of research support. Rarely have they been subjected to standardization using large and representative samples.[13,14]

These concerns and criticisms lead to the challenge to improve the quality of leisure assessment instruments so that they may be confidently used in the leisure programming process. By using assessment instruments that are reliable, valid, standardized, and practical, leisure programmers will be able to better identify and meet their constituents' needs.

A second challenge is to develop or modify the existing instruments so that the results are useful for social aggregate groups. Many of the currently available assessment instruments that we are going to review have primarily been used in leisure counseling situations on a small, one-to-one basis. Most are not representative of full-scale community surveys, which are typically mailed to masses of people. These instruments have been used in a much more individualistic manner and often as a means to assess the respondents for therapeutic intervention purposes. Please be reminded that we have limited our discussion to these kinds of instruments because they are the ones

Category	Instrument/Developer	Reliability	Validity	Comments
Leisure Attitudes	Leisure Orientation Scale (Burdge, 1961)	Deteriorated	Deteriorated	Historical value
	Study of Leisure (Neulinger, 1974)	Currently unreported	Stated	Credible reputation
	Leisure Ethic Scale (Slivken & Crandall, 1978)	Stated	Stated	Narrow emphasis
	Leisure Attitude Scale (Ragheb, 1980)	Stated	Stated	Stepping stone to later work
	Leisure Diagnostic Battery (Ellis & Witt, 1982)	Stated	Stated	Version A only for "community settings"
Leisure States	Walshe Temperament Survey (Walshe, 1977)	Currently unreported	Currently unreported	Initial phase of development
	Leisure Well-Being Inventory (McDowell, 1979)	Currently unreported	Currently unreported	
Leisure Behavior	Mundy Recreation Inventory for the Trainable Mentally Retarded (Mundy, 1966)	Stated	Stated	For use with TMR clientele, emphasizing physical functioning and the cognitive domain
	Joswiak's Leisure Counseling Assessment Instruments (Joswiak, 1975)	Currently unreported	Stated	Emphasizing the affective domain
	Comprehensive Evaluation in Recreation Therapy Scale (Parker & Assc., 1975)	Stated	Currently unreported	For use with short-term psychiatric care clientele emphasizing the affective domain
	Recreation Behavioral Inventory (Berryman & Lefebvre, 1979)	Stated	Stated	For use with psychiatric and geriatric clientele emphasizing the cognitive domain and sensory and perceptual motor skills
Leisure Satisfaction	Milwaukee Avocational Satisfaction Questionnaire (Overs, Taylor, & Adkins, 1977)	Stated for field test only	Stated for field test only	Community survey

Figure 6-1 Selected Leisure Assessment Instruments

Category	Instrument/Developer	Reliability	Validity	Comments
	Leisure Satisfaction Inventory (Rimmer, 1979)	Stated	Stated	
	Leisure Satisfaction Scale (Beard & Ragheb, 1980)	Stated	Stated	Heuristic Device
Leisure Interests	Leisure Interest Inventory (Hubert, 1969)	Stated	Stated	
	Self-Leisure Interest Profile (McDowell, 1973)	Currently unreported	Currently unreported	
	Mirenda Leisure Interest Finder (Mirenda, 1975)	Currently unreported	Stated	
	Leisure Activity Blank (McKechnie, 1975)	Stated	Stated	Well-known
	Avocational Activities Inventory (Overs, Taylor, & Adkins, 1977)	Currently unreported	Currently unreported	For use with members of special populations
	Constructive Leisure Activities Survey (rev. ed.) (Edwards, 1980)	Currently unreported	Currently unreported	Psychometric limitations
	State Technical Institute Leisure Activities Project (Navar, 1979)	Currently unreported	Stated	For use with adults who may be members of special populations

Figure 6-1 *(Continued)*

that are most readily available and have been subjected to at least preliminary scientific testing procedures. Never-the-less, the problem of developing new instruments or modifying the existing ones for programming use with large groups remains unsolved.

Some additional words of caution are in order. In Figure 6-1, we have conformed to judgments that others have made in categorizing which aspect of leisure the instruments measure: attitudes, values, states, behaviors, satisfaction, and interests. What we do not have are measures of the reliability and validity of each and every instrument. We were able to obtain some statistical indices of reliability and criterion-related validity from some of the developers of the instruments. We were also able to find opinions from users regarding content validity. We elected not to report numbers, but to express our interpretation of coefficients for you. Persons in need of further details are urged to consult the original sources.

Keeping in mind our mention of leisure styles, remember to look not only at what people do as leisure, but how they do it and why.[15] Leisure is a very complex phenomenon in and of itself. When one begins to consider things that influence leisure (such as environment, developmental stage, and opportunity), it becomes even more apparent that one must be extremely vigilant about not oversimplifying leisure as one tries to understand it.

CURRENT LEISURE ASSESSMENT INSTRUMENTS

Wehman and Schlein's,[16] Loesch and Wheeler's[17] Julia K. Dunn,[18] and Howe's[19,20] work forms the basis for Figure 6-1, which presents an overview of instrumentation. Their reviews describe the categories under which the instruments fall and provide additional evaluative information about the instruments themselves.

This figure includes only those instruments that are easily available from publishers or that are cited in journals or textbooks. In-house or agency-specific materials are not included in order to keep the listing reasonably accessible. Each programmer, based on his or her philosophy, education, and experience, develops criteria for use in selecting among the various instruments that are available. To some extent a programmer's selection criteria may be tempered by the purpose of the assessment, how it will actually be implemented, and, by whom the assessment will be conducted and the results used.[21]

Beyond this, the programmer probably further considers whether the instrument is norm-referenced or criterion-referenced, easily administered and readministered, and designed for the population with which he or she intends to use it. The programmer may also be concerned with the mode of response and the validity and reliability of the instrument.[22, 23]

The following discussion of the assessment instruments illustrated in Figure 6-1 takes into account the aforementioned criteria. But the discussion is just that; it is neither a comprehensive nor a definitive evaluation of instrumentation. It is expected that the programmer will be the final judge of the utility of a specific instrument for a particular situation or constituent. In addition, the evolutionary and/or sketchy status of many of the instruments prohibits a summative, detailed evaluation. However, there are some data that should be helpful in at least making some formative judgments about these instruments.[24]

Leisure Attitudes. Programmers assess clients' attitudes toward leisure in order to help them clarify their feelings about leisure. Knowing what clients believe about leisure helps programmers to address any negative feelings and to enhance positive attitudes by helping people to select rewarding and pleasurable activities.[25]

We commence our review of attitude assessment instruments with Rabel J. Burdge's Leisure Orientation Scale (LOS)[26] because of its historical importance. Burdge is credited with being the first person to recognize the need for a scale to specifically measure leisure attitudes.[28] In his master's thesis, Burdge presented evidence of the unidimensionality, internal consistency, and validity of the LOS. However, in 1976, Dean R. Yoesting and Burdge reviewed reports on the use of the LOS and found that the original scale had undergone numerous modifications. The "changed" scales do not have measures of validity and reliability reported with their trials. Thus, Yoesting and Burdge felt that the scale had "deteriorated" over time.[28]

Neulinger's Study of Leisure (SOL) was published in 1974. In his book *The Psychology of Leisure,* Neulinger outlines the development of his instrumentation and presents data about the standardization procedures and the factor analyses used with the SOL. There are no quantitative data on its reliability.[29] However, Loesch and Wheeler judge the SOL to be reliable and a psychometrically credible leisure assessment instrument.[30] This is in part due to the factor analyses to which the various forms of the SOL were subjected. They cautiously recommend using the SOL in leisure assessment situations when a large amount of information is desired and it is anticipated that the client will be able to respond to a self-administered closed-ended questionnaire of approximately 150 items. Neulinger's book provides complete directions for the administration and scoring of the SOL in Appendix A.

In her master's thesis, Karla Slivken and her advisor, Rick Crandall, reduced their Leisure Ethic Scale (LES) to ten items to unidimensionally measure affinity toward leisure. They report the development and refinement of the LES in terms of validity, reliability, and standardization procedures. Slivken presents detailed results of various tests of her instruments that support the validity and reliability of the LES as an indicator of affinity towards leisure.[31]

The LES is certainly more narrowly focused than the SOL, inasmuch as the selected aspect of leisure stems from one of the SOL's *five* factors. Slivken thought that Neulinger's affinity factor was the most important one, and that is what the LES measures. However, Loesch and Wheeler are concerned about the brevity of the self-administered scale from a psychometric viewpoint and find the LES to be basically a gross indicator of leisure attitude.[32] This implies that the SOL could give a finer indication of leisure attitude, but at the expense of greater effort and time consumed.[33] Both instruments must be judged within the context of their utility as leisure programming aids. The determination of clients' attitudes toward leisure is only one of the many questions that must be answered.

Mounir G. Ragheb's Leisure Attitude Scale (LAS) is another instrument that has undergone extensive analysis. It, too, is a relatively brief, self-administered instrument. Ragheb assesses the cognitive, affective, and behavioral components of attitude. His instrument uses six original closed-ended items that assess the cognitive component in the form of views of and beliefs about leisure. He employs a modification of Neulinger's Question 15, Form 0769, to assess the affective component[34] and uses H. Triandis's Behavioral Differential Scale to determine the respondents' intentions toward leisure.[35] The LAS is not specifically designed to serve as a leisure assessment tool, but as a means of investigating the interrelationships among leisure participation, satisfaction, and attitudes. It now seems that the LAS is better used as a valid and reliable heuristic device for purposes of inquiry. The LAS seems to have formed the basis for Jacob G. Beard and Ragheb's later work with their leisure satisfaction index.[36]

The Leisure Diagnostic Battery (LDB) is the last entry in this category. It entered the published literature in 1982 through a manual by Gary Ellis and Peter A. Witt.[37] We have arbitrarily placed their instrumentation in this category since their definition of leisure functioning is based on perceived freedom and barriers to it. Thus it is attitudinally focused.

It measures the leisure functioning of normal, physically disabled, and higher-functioning educable mentally retarded children and youths through five primary diagnostic scales. The LDB is grounded in sociopsychological and leisure theory and consists of group-administered self-response to a series of questions. Extensive reliability and validity data are available for the LDB.[38] The authors recommend using their instrument cautiously, even though factor-analytic and path analysis procedures have been used to establish validity and are extensively discussed and documented.[39] Along with a twenty-five item short form test that can be used with children or adults, the LDB has been rigorously analyzed and provides a valuable aid to those who want information about client leisure functioning based on psychological indicators of competence, control, needs, involvement, and playfulness. These factors provide insight into readiness for leisure behavior through assessment of the client's ability to use reaction to attain leisure.[40]

Leisure Values. The single entry in the Leisure Values category is the Survey of Leisure Values (SLV) developed by Loesch in 1980, as reported in Loesch and Wheeler's original categorical system. This instrument still needs further testing. Because the SLV is still in the trial stage, it is not yet recommended for actual use in assessing leisure values. However, the category in itself is interesting. Knowing what a client holds dear in leisure enables programmers to better suggest meaningful leisure options.[41]

Leisure States. Instruments in the category of Leisure States attempt to assess the totality of one's personality as it relates to leisure. This category might be more broadly labeled Psychological States. Willoughby A. Walshe sees personality as a blend of four temperaments: melancholic, phlegmatic, sanguine, and choleric, with one or two tending to dominate. Her Walshe Temperament Survey (WTS) assesses which temperaments are dominant, allowing the programmer to help participants to select leisure experiences in light of their dominant temperament.[42]

Walshe's discussion does not report any standardization, validity, or reliability data. Efforts are, however, being made regarding these psychometric characteristics. The WTS consists of forty-eight items for each of the four temperaments, requiring about half an hour of response time.[43] Assuming that programmers accept Walshe's concept of personality and temperament, once traditional measures of reliability and validity become available the WTS will join the ranks of leisure assessment instrumentation.[44]

C. Forrest McDowell's Leisure Well-Being Inventory (LWBI)[45] also falls into the category of Leisure States. Unfortunately, traditional indices of validity and reliability are not available. The LWBI determines how prepared and able the client is to maintain leisure well-being based on McDowell's four aspects of psychological health: coping, awareness/understanding, knowledge, and assertion. One hundred twenty-five closed-ended items are distributed through four subscales that measure these attributes. There are ranges of scores that McDowell interprets to show leisure well-being. But without psychometric data to examine, this instrument, too, must be used cautiously. Thus, the LWBI is a further attempt at gleaning additional information from clients to aid in discussions relevant to their leisure needs.[46]

Systematically collected data about a client's personality or psychological health can aid programmers in understanding the client's day-to-day existence as well as his or her expressions and demeanor. Once the programmer has tapped into the client's personality as an extension of his or her self, a better "fit" between the person and the leisure experience may be possible.[47]

Leisure Behavior. Underlying the category of Leisure Behavior is the programmer's desire to know what the participant, by his or her own account, *actually* does within the context of leisure. Ideally, a more accurate indication of actual leisure behavior would be found through extensive and probably unobtrusive observations occurring within the participants' natural environment. But that type of opportunity is rarely available. Thus the instruments in this category seek to discover, through self-reported data, what clients do.[48]

All of the available instruments in this category are specifically designed for use by therapeutic recreators with members of special populations. Dunn[49] discusses Jean Mundy's Recreation Inventory for the Trainable Mentally Retarded; Doris Berryman and Claudette B. Lefebore's Recreation Behavior Inventory; and R.A. Parker, C.H. Ellison, T.F. Kirby, and M.J. Short's Comprehensive Evaluation in Recreation Therapy Scale. Those who expect to work in clinical settings with individuals with disabilities are referred to Dunn's work. We have included the instruments in Figure 6-1 because they do have some indicators of validity and reliability.

Kenneth F. Joswiak's[50] Leisure Counseling Assessment Instruments (LCAI) focus on the affective domain, have demonstrated content validity, and have been subjected to standardization procedures throughout their development. They stem from Joswiak's master's thesis and have been used for leisure counseling purposes by persons in the field of therapeutic recreation. Reliability information is not available, but the instruments appear to be generally credible, again as a vehicle for collecting information for discussion purposes.

Leisure Satisfaction. The category of Leisure Satisfaction contains some of the better-known assessment instrumentation. Pioneering work in the field was done by Robert Overs, Sharon Taylor, and Catherine Adkins with the Milwaukee Avocational Satisfaction Questionnaire (MASQ).[51] Reliability, validity, and standardization information is limited to what was found during field testing with the Milwaukee Avocational Counseling Project. The instrument has twenty-four closed-ended items to which the client responds. It is of practical value in forming the basis for discussion in an idea-generating session.[52]

Susan M. Rimmer's Leisure Satisfaction Inventory (LSI)[53] demonstrates reliability and validity and was initially standardized with persons of high-school age. The instrument consists of forty closed-ended items that examine leisure satisfaction through intrinsic and extrinsic dimensions including self-fulfillment, self-improvement, catharis, social interaction, and psychological confidence.

Satisfaction is an important feeling that is expressed by persons when they report that they have had a positive leisure experience.[54] As with attitude, satisfaction is a key element in assessing the totality of client leisure experiences for programming purposes. Joseph G. Beard and Mounir G. Ragheb's Leisure Satisfaction Scale (LSS) is another contribution to this category.[55]

The original LSS has fifty-one closed-ended items; the revised form is reduced to twenty-four items. The original questionnaire has six factors or components: psychological, educational, social, relaxational, physiological, and environmental/aesthetic. The instrument is reliable and valid as judged by a group of experts, and was standardized using a wide variety of subjects. Most respondents complete the instrument in 20 minutes.[56] The authors suggest:

> The LSS could be used in a counseling situation as a vehicle for examining the use of an individual's free time, and for discussing ways in which leisure activities could be altered to better serve one's needs. At the least, minimal discussion of the LSS results should cause an individual to develop an awareness of, and interest in, the time available for leisure activities, and to develop priorities among competing leisure activity choices.[57]

They also suggest that the LSS should be used as a heuristic device to explore various constructs, relationships, and items on the scale in terms of leisure satisfaction theory.[58] The psychometric data available on this instrument allows its use in real-world situations.

Leisure Interests.   The instruments in this category are leisure interest finders—devices that allow individuals to check off activities that they are curious about, are already involved in, are skilled at, or enjoy, depending on the exact focus of the instrument. Some are used to determine leisure preferences. But all are framed in terms of recreational activity selection. They are useful in determining activities that the client may be aware of, interested in, or already engaged in, or that he or she might want to pursue in the future. They do not afford insight into the meaning of the activity for the client.[59]

The Leisure Interest Inventory (LII) was developed in 1969 by Edwina E. Hubert.[60] As described in her dissertation, the LII has a sound theoretical base, demonstrating both concurrent validity through correlations with other instruments and content validity through a jury process. Reliability data for subscales and standardization data for college youths are also available. The LII has eighty closed-ended items, ranging from "most liked" to "least liked," that are taken from the work of Max Kaplan.[61] If programmers agree with the typologies—sociability, games, art, mobility, and immobility—as being an adequate indication of leisure interests, then the LII is an acceptable inventory to use.

The Self-Leisure Interest Profile (SLIP)[62] came about in 1973 as a result of McDowell's master's thesis. It was designed for self-administration by the general public and is criterion-referenced; thus it may be used to examine changes in a single individual's self-reported leisure interests. SLIP must be used cautiously because of the lack of information about its psychometric characteristics.[63]

The Mirenda Leisure Interest Finder (MLIF), developed by Joseph Mirenda and reported in 1975 by Mirenda and George T. Wilson, is another self-administered instrument that uses closed-ended items. According to Wehman and Schlein, the MLIF is norm-referenced and designed for use by the general public.[64] It is quickly administered and demonstrates validity. Thus it would seem to be a credible instrument for use in assessing interests and in making comparisons with others who have completed it.[65] As with many of the other categories, leisure interests are one of several elements worthy of assessment. The information derived from leisure interest devices should be used in concert with other data about the clientele.

That brings us to one of the most widely distributed and applied leisure interest inventories, George E. McKechnie's Leisure Activities Blank (LAB). The LAB manual was published in 1975. The LAB consists of 120 closed-ended items that elicit information from persons age 15 and above about past and future involvement with selected activities. It is a self-administered and easy-to-complete checklist. Reliability data are available, along with guidelines on interpreting various subscale score patterns.[66] Loesch and Wheeler state that the LAB can be used with confidence in its validity.[67] It serves well as a basis for discussion about self-reported leisure activity, and because of the rigorous standards used in its development, the LAB is a good resource for both practical and theoretical purposes.

The Avocational Activities Inventory (AAI) is yet another product of the Milwaukee Project.[68] The AAI lists more than eight hundred leisure activities and was intended to be used to classify avocational activities. This classification system uses the card sort technique and formed the foundation for the MASQ, described earlier in this chapter. The AAI is directed towards special populations. The AAI might best be used to stimulate conversation about the breadth of activities that may be available to the participant in order to enhance his or her leisure awareness. It may serve as a starting point for the person who has little knowledge of the range of leisure experiences that exist.[69]

A revised edition of Patsy B. Edwards's Constructive Leisure Activities Survey (CLAS-2), as discussed by Edwards and P. A. Bloland,[70] is subject to psychometric limitations in terms of validity and reliability information. However, the CLAS-2 is criterion-referenced and designed to determine the clients' past, present, and future leisure activities and interests, along with their needs and preferences. The instrument is an interview schedule that typically takes twenty minutes to complete. It includes five categories: physical and outdoor activities; social activities; arts and crafts; learning; and general welfare and personal satisfaction. CLAS-2 is not focused solely on leisure interests; thus it may provide broader insight into the respondents. With additional testing and development, this instrument could prove to be a valuable asset to standardized leisure needs assessment.[71]

The State Technical Institute Leisure Activities Project (STILAP) was published in 1979 by Nancy Navar.[72] STILAP is an activities checklist to obtain information on the leisure participation patterns and interests of adult clients by inquiring about fourteen areas of competency. STILAP also measures how often leisure skills are used and what skills the respondents are interested in developing further. STILAP demonstrates construct and face validity. At this time there is no evidence available regarding reliability or standardization procedures. The fourteen competencies were drawn from the literature on investigating adult leisure behavior. The competencies range from physical to mental to social, with skills perceived as the means to an end: responsible independent leisure functioning. STILAP provides direction for the involvement of the clientele in leisure experiences.[73] Although traditional psychometric information is available only on a limited basis, this particular instrument has been used extensively by therapeutic recreators in the field. This leads us to believe that it has some practical utility.

This recounting of selected assessment instruments has by no means exhausted them. Upon deeper examination, it can be seen that the instruments can easily cross categories. Thus the categories in Figure 6-1 should not be considered mutually exclusive. There is duplication and overlap among the instruments that fall within them.

It is good to review systematically from time to time the tools of the trade. Programmers are bound to continually monitor their practices and the tools that they use to aid the decisions they make. That particular responsibility is of the utmost importance at this particular stage of development in the profession of parks, recreation, and leisure services. Programmers must endeavor to be responsive to the people they serve. Using valid and reliable assessment instruments is one means of doing this. These concerns are equally applicable to evaluation, as shall be seen in Chapter 9.

Up to this point we have presented many of the needs assessment instruments that are focused on the individual. Most of them exist in questionnaire form, with closed-ended or forced-choice response formats. What if these existing instruments are not appropriate for the leisure programmer's purposes? What if the programmer needs a broad-based examination of his or her clientele?

OTHER TECHNIQUES FOR COLLECTING INFORMATION FROM CONSTITUENTS

Rather than limit yourself to the existing questionnaires and interview schedules, it is possible to construct your own. Self-made questionnaires may contain relevant closed-ended items but allow for open-ended questions to which constituents may respond. You can also develop your own attitude rating scales that may be completed by the participants themselves using paper and pencil or that may be administered in interviews.

Interviews can take several forms. They may be done face-to-face or over the telephone. The interview schedule (or question guide-sheet) is similar to a questionnaire in that the questions may be open- and/or closed-ended. A major difference is that the interviewer completes the schedule and is immediately available to clarify or probe further. Interviews are generally thought to be a little less superficial than mailed questionnaires, but they are not as anonymous.

Written reports, documents, and records are often sources of information. These items exist in a variety of forms and are available from a variety of sources: clientele, staff, outside consultants, governing bodies, and so on. These documents may contain self-reported information or they may contain data about something or someone else as reported by an interested other.

That brings us to yet another data collection technique: observation. Observation can range from obtrusive to unobtrusive. It falls on a continuum of detachment; at one extreme the observer is fully detached from the events and simply watches them, at the other the observer is involved in the events as a participant as well as a recorder. The information may be collected through one's own eyes or on videotape or film. What happens is generally written up in the form of field notes. Sociometric instruments are available to determine relationships and perceptions of others in group situations. Most of these are fairly standardized. The following chart displays some of the strengths and weaknesses of the various ways of collecting information. It comes from the work of Blaine R. Worthen and James R. Sanders in evaluation.[74]

The instruments that are used must fit the immediate situation, whether the needs that are being assessed are those of an entire community or a single individual. Further, the method of inquiry must be acceptable to the persons being queried. Some techniques provide hard statistical data about conditions as they exist. Others yield perceptual data from constituents, reflecting their opinions and beliefs about the status, frequency, intensity, and meaning of their leisure experiences, as well as what they feel future conditions should be. Some instruments and data collection approaches require more technical expertise and capabilities than others. It is critical to remember that the instrumentation used is just one part of the needs assessment process, not the end product!

GUIDELINES FOR USING SELECTED TECHNIQUES

At this point, you are aware of many of the published questionnaire and checklist instruments and interview schedules that are available for use in conducting needs assessments. You also have some hints on the strengths and weaknesses of other information-gathering techniques, including those that are self-constructed. But when is it best to choose one technique over another? Ideally, it is most desirable to triangulate[75]—that is, to use several data collection techniques. In reality, most agencies do not have the resources for multiple data collection methods. The most common technique used by large public agencies and commercial ventures is the questionnaire.

Questionnaires. Use questionnaires under the following circumstances: when it is important to assess a large or broadly based population; when the recipients are fully able to respond to the questions accurately

I. DATA COLLECTED BY A MECHANICAL DEVICE (E.G., AUDIO OR VIDEO TAPE, GALVANIC SKIN RESPONSES).

Strengths	Weaknesses
Avoid human errors. Stay on job—avoid fatigue. May capture content missed by written records (e.g., voice inflection).	Cost. Cannot make independent judgment. Complexity can cause problems in operating devices.

II. DATA COLLECTED BY AN INDEPENDENT OBSERVER.

Strengths	Weaknesses
Can be used in natural or experimental settings. Most direct measure of behavior. Most direct measure of behavior. Experienced, trained, or perceptive observers can pick up subtle occurrences or interactions sometimes not available by other techniques.	Observer's presence often causes an artificial situation. Hostility to being observed. Inadequate sampling of observed events. Ambiguities in recording. Frequent observer unreliability.

A. Written accounts.

Strengths	Weaknesses
Can use critical incident technique, eliminating much "chaff."	Hard to be complete. Hard to avoid writing interpretation as factual data (e.g., "Mary kicked John because she was angry with him.").

B. Observation forms (e.g., observation schedules).

Strengths	Weaknesses
Easy to complete; saves time. Can be objectively scored. Standardizes observations.	Not as flexible as written accounts—may lump unlike acts together. Criteria for ratings are often unspecified. May overlook meaningful behavior that is not reflected in instrument.

Figure 6-2 Strengths and Weakness of Data Collection Techniques

From Blaine R. Worthen and James R. Sanders, *Educational Evaluation: Theory and Practice* (Belmont, Calif.: Wadsworth Publishing Co., Inc., 1973), pp. 286-87.

III. DATA PRODUCED BY THE SUBJECT.
   A. Self reports.

Strengths	Weaknesses
Can collect data too *costly* otherwise (e.g., eliminates the endless observation necessary to really get to know a person's philosophy, attitudes, etc.).	Depends on respondent's real awareness of self.
	Depends on respondent's honesty and/or security.
Can collect data not accessible by any other means (private thoughts, feelings, actions; emotion-laden material).	Depends on respondent's "accurate memory" when dealing with past events (selective recall).
	May necessitate anonymous responses where threat is perceived.

   1. Diary—may be difficult to analyze, but can be comprehensive.
   2. Checklists—sometimes force choices between unacceptable responses.
   3. Rating scales (covered earlier)—often tell more about the respondent than about the topic under consideration.
   4. Semantic differential.[a]

Strengths	Weaknesses
Adaptable to varying research demands.	Often tells more about the respondent than about the topic under consideration.
Quick and economical to administer and score.	

   5. Questionnaires.

Strengths	Weaknesses
Self-administered.	Frequent low percentage of returns.
Anonymity can bring about more honest responses.	No assurance that the intended respondent understands the questions.
Economical.	No assurance that the intended respondent actually completed the form himself.

   6. Interviews.

Strengths	Weaknesses
Allow depth and free response.	Costly in time and personnel.
Flexible and adaptable to individual situations.	Require skilled interviewers.
	Often difficult to summarize.

Figure 6-2 *(Continued)*

Allow glimpse of respondent's gestures, tone of voice, etc., that reveal his feelings.

Many biases possible (e.g., interviewer's, respondent's, or situational biases).

7. Sociometry.

Strengths
Easy to analyze.
Naturalistic method.
Clinically insightful.

Weaknesses
Criteria used in making choices are often vague.

8. Projective techniques

Strengths
Clinically insightful.
Allow measurement of variables typically unavailable through other techniques.

Weaknesses
Lack of objectivity in interpretation.
Uncertain reliability and validity.

B. Personal products.
1. Tests

Strengths
Practicality — do away with need for observer to gather similar data.
Most reliable measures we have at present.
Can record products or thought or thought processes themselves.

Weaknesses
Validity is always a problem in work sample sense—i.e., is test representative of criterion?
Lend themselves to "law of the instrument"—we often exclude other techniques.

a. Supplied answer.
i. Essay.

Strengths
Allow students to synthesize their knowledge about a topic.

Weaknesses
Difficult to score objectively.
Sampling of topics is relatively limited.

ii. Completion.

Strengths
Can be quite objective.

Weaknesses
May lend themselves to testing trivia (factual recall only).

iii. Short response

Strengths
Can be quite objective.

Weaknesses
May lend themselves to testing trivia (factual recall only).

iv. Problem-solving.

Figure 6–2 *(Continued)*

Strengths	Weaknesses
Can look at actual processes (diagnostic).	Lend themselves to mechanical drill.
Can look at actual mastery.	

    b. Selected answer tests (multiple-choice, true-false, matching, rank order).

Strengths	Weaknesses
Greater objectivity in scoring.	Problem of validity is always present.
Speed of scoring.	
Potentially higher reliability.	Standardized tests sometimes used in situations requiring specially constructed tests.
Can be item analyzed for improvement.	
Quantity of available standardized tests.	*Apparent* precision often masks very bad items.

    2. Samples of work.

Strengths	Weaknesses
Best measure of ability, mastery, etc.	May be difficult or costly to administer.

IV. DATA COLLECTED BY USE OF UNOBTRUSIVE MEASURES.

Strengths	Weaknesses
Nonreactive.	Hidden measures are considered unethical by some.
Nonconsciously biased.	
Often readily available and easily measurable.	Doubtful validity when used alone.

Figure 6-2 *(Continued)*

without a staff person present; when ease of quantifying results is important; when the questions are prespecified and uniformity of response is desired; and when anonymity is needed.

If a few rules of thumb are followed, the use of questionnaires may help to keep data collection costs to a minimum. First, be economical and specific in your choice of questions. Do not get sidetracked away from the main items that you want to assess. Formulate clear, understandable questions in a logical sequence. Present them in an easy-to-follow format and pretest them—that is, make a trial run of the questionnaire. Then revise the instrument, set your distribution and collection strategy, and analyze and summarize your results.

Checklists and inventories are generally closed-ended variations of questionnaires, and these suggestions apply to them as well. Remember, though, that questionnaires should be used judiciously because they rarely examine the causes or sources of needs; they merely describe them. If there are subtle social, psychological or economic phenomena affecting your constituents, questionnaires may not be valid representations of their true thoughts.

Interviews.   When you desire to assess a smaller number of people and perhaps to probe at greater depth, interviewing becomes the preferred data collection technique, either over the telephone or face-to-face. Interviews are used when the target population is readily accessible (for example, institutionalized persons) or best able to respond orally (for example, illiterates, the visually impaired, and the very young or very old). They are also used when quantifiable responses to predetermined questions are not necessarily of the utmost importance; rather, the interviewer wants to elicit spontaneous information that emerges uniquely from each respondent. Generally, interviews go beyond questionnaires to the extent of determining not only what is said, but *how* it is said. Again, however, the focus is merely descriptive.

To conduct interviews properly, your interviewers must be trained, supervised, able to establish rapport yet remain unbiased and unbiasing. In the interview situation itself, accuracy is enhanced when the trained interviewer has a sense of what the primary focus of the assessment is and how the questions relate to that. One way to help ensure correctness is to record the answers in the respondent's own words and then to analyze and summarize the results as soon as possible after the interview is completed. If the interviewer is trained and well prepared, the interview is an excellent means of communication between programmers and constituents.

Observation.   Intuitively, we all make observations about the events that occur around us and draw some conclusions from them. However, systematic and unbiased observation is both an art and a science for which training and practice are necessary. When done properly, this information collection technique provides a rich and detailed portrayal of the leisure needs and interests of the persons observed. Observation is particularly useful in needs assessment when programmers want to verify, on a firsthand basis, what people actually do—not what they say they do, but their observable leisure behavior and preferences. In order to do this in a valid, reliable, and objective manner, there are several procedures that should be followed.

The site and the subjects for observation must be identified and permission to observe, either overtly or covertly, must be obtained. Whether or not the subjects should be aware that they're being observed, and why, must be determined, as well as the format or structure of the observations themselves. How much is the observer going to be a participant in the observed situation? The observation schedule, note-taking or recording system, and analysis procedures must be decided on in advance. Finally, the results must be summarized and reported.

Preexisting Materials.   Leisure needs may be inferred from the secondary examination or analysis of pre-existing information. This happens when records exist and are accessible and legally obtainable. The examination of previous needs assessments allows you to see changes over time as well as to assess your constituents indirectly. Such records may reflect needs that have emerged naturally from specific groups or individuals and not as an artifact of an intrusive inquiry.

In order to do this, you must locate and organize documents, files, old assessments, notes from forums or meetings, comments or letters from key people, reports of critical incidents, news articles, and minutes from discussions among community, industry, and political leaders, as well as service statistics and social indicators. Relevant items should be reviewed using document analysis, then summarized and collapsed to shed light on trends found across records. This technique is especially helpful in cross-checking and verifying results obtained through other information-gathering techniques.

The desirability of using multiple techniques for collecting needs assessment data cannot be overemphasized. However, limited resources place constraints on techniques of collection and analysis.

TECHNIQUES FOR ANALYZING
CONSTITUENT INFORMATION

Needs assessment is a process that informs and guides the planning and prioritizing of programs by programmers in response to the wishes and desires of those whom they serve. It is an active attempt to achieve an accurate and full understanding of the leisure needs of their constituents. It is an ongoing process that is integral to the systematic leisure programming cycle. Needs assessment consumes resources, especially in terms of the collection and analysis of data. Thus it requires the support of leaders, programmers, and administrators, as well as the cooperation of constituents. This implies that the whole needs assessment endeavor, from beginning to end, should be understandable by all who participate in it. Data must be analyzed in a form that is comprehensible to the potential users, based on the way in which the information was collected initially and the nature of the information itself.

For purposes of analysis, there are generally two types of information collected: quantitative (numerical) and qualitative (verbal). Each type has analytic (reduction and summarization) procedures associated with it. The following discussion of quantitative and qualitative data analysis techniques is intended to introduce you to the manipulation of information. It is neither definitive nor exhaustive, so we urge you to extend your reading in this area beyond this book. However, we do attempt to put these techniques within the context of leisure needs assessment for you.

Quantitative Data Analysis. In order to determine what statistical technique to use for the analysis of numerical data, one must first determine their category. There are several categories under which numerical data may fall. First, the data may be discrete or continuous. *Discrete* data are finite and exact, and can be precisely represented by a number. For example, "The number of households interested in renting cross-country ski equipment is 6,002;" "The number of persons who attended the film festival on the closing day was 567." *Continuous* data have numerical values that are approximate, falling on a continuum and capable of being reported in a meaningful way at various levels of refinement.

Data are also classified by level: nominal, ordinal, interval, or ratio. *Nominal* data are discrete and are used only to identify or differentiate among items. A common example is the assignment of an identifying number to a contestant. Analysis of nominal data is limited to frequency counts, cross-tabulations, and chi-square analyses. Frequency counts are just that—counting up the number of items that fall in some category (for example, taking attendance). Cross-tabulations or chi-square analyses enable the researcher to determine associations or relationships between nominal data, such as between the frequency of participation of college students in a selected intramural sport and the cost of registering a team.

Ordinal data can be ordered or ranked in some way, but there is no precise measure of the *meaning* of the distance between ranks. For example, entrants in a dog show might be ranked first through twentieth, with the top five dogs receiving awards for good behavior. There is a logical relationship between the first and fifth best-behaved dogs, especially in comparison to the dog who ranked twentieth, but it cannot be said that a particular rank is x times better than another rank. Being first is not twice as good as being second, it is just better. With ordinal data, measures of relationship (or rank-order correlation) are used to see how items vary.

Interval scales do have measurable units between points on the scale, thus allowing arithmetic operations. One point is arbitrarily designated zero, and there is equal distance between all points on the scale. Thus, if it is your job as a programmer to monitor the temperature of a room in which aerobic dancing is held, you can be assured that the difference between 68° and 70° and between 74° and 76° is numerically the same—2°. However, you can expect much more sweating by participants at the higher temperature!

Interval data may be reduced and summarized in a variety of ways, including frequency counts, percentages, cross-tabulations, and many other descriptive and inferential statistical techniques. Among descriptive statistics, there are measures of central tendency, including mean, median, and mode—numbers that represent what is typical of a set of data and that are generally located toward the middle of a distribution of values or scores. The mean is the arithmetic average of the scores. The median is that score at which the distribution is divided in half. The mode is the most frequently appearing score in a distribution.

If all individuals (or their attributes, needs, or interests) were alike, then leisure programmers could stop here in the measurement process. However, the more differences they encounter, the less adequate measures of central tendency are for decision-making purposes. So, after selecting a measure of central tendency as an indicator of how people, characteristics, or data vary among themselves, a programmer must also examine the degree to which individuals, characteristics, or data vary *from* the center. This is done using measures of variability, dispersion, or spread, including the range and the standard deviation. The range provides an approximation of the diversity within a set of data or the difference between the highest and lowest scores in a distribution. The standard deviation is a measure of variability that allows the researcher to make comparisons between individual scores and the mean of a distribution, as well as comparisons to different distributions or sets of data. The larger the number indicating the standard deviation, the greater the variability around the mean of a distribution.

Ratio scales, which have absolute zero points, are rarely used in leisure needs assessment. They are much more a part of the physical sciences. A common illustration is the use of a ruler to measure the length of something. If you are building an adapted hockey stick and you want it to be 30 inches long, you know that 0 inches is truly no inches of length. Suppose your ruler is 15 inches long. You know that 30 inches are twice as long as 15 and that the ratio of 30:15 is equal to 2:1.

Data may be parametric or nonparametric. *Parametric* data are presumed to have a normal distribution that follows the shape of the well-known bell curve. *Nonparametric* data are data about whose shape (or distribution) no assumptions can be made. It is important to know the shape or distribution of your needs assessment data in order to choose the appropriate analytical techniques and to compare a single score or observation to the total population. That brings us to the topic of sampling.

In parks, recreation, and leisure services, very rarely do programmers have the resources to assess (or evaluate, for that matter) all the persons whom they would like to serve (their population). Occasionally it is reasonable and efficient for programmers to assess every person they are interested in, if they are concerned about a very small group of people. In therapeutic recreation settings, when information about all individuals in the population is needed, it is usually necessary to assess the entire group. In commercial and public leisure services, the size of the group is often too large to allow programmers to study them all efficiently and accurately. One is left with the alternative of assessing a representative sample of the total population.

Sampling is an important part of any systematic information collection and analysis procedure, including leisure assessment and evaluation. Although sampling may require the programmer to sacrifice the "absolute accuracy" of contacting everyone in the population, there are some techniques that ensure reasonable accuracy in the assessment of a sample or a portion of the population.

After carefully defining the population to be assessed, the programmer establishes a sampling frame—a physical representation of the population from which the sample can be selected (for example, a census list). The ideal sampling frame is one that includes each member of the population without duplicating any members and that contains no one other than the persons in the population. In other words, there should be an exact correspondence between the sampling frame and the population. The next step is to select individuals from the frame. These individuals constitute the assessment sample. They will, in the aggregate, serve to represent the entire population in which the programmer is interested.

There are a number of different methods for drawing a sample. A table of random numbers from statistics textbooks may be used or random numbers may be generated by a computer. The major types of probability samples that can be drawn are *simple random samples, stratified samples, cluster samples,* and *multistage samples.* In a simple random sample, each member of the frame has the same chance of being selected. Simple random sampling is useful since it ensures that differences between the sample and the population are randomly distributed and that the researcher's subjective bias is eliminated. Statistical tests can be applied to determine the probability of differences between the sample and the population as a whole. A simple random sample can thus be said to be representative of the population within a certain degree of probability.

One potential difficulty of simple random sampling is that chance will occasionally produce a sample that is *not* representative of the population. You can improve the chances of accurate representation and increase the precision of your measurement through stratified sampling, which requires you to take into account the characteristics of each person or element in the population. The procedure consists of dividing the population into categories or strata based on special characteristics that have some logical relationship to the persons being assessed. Typically, programmers conducting leisure assessments stratify on the basis of certain demographic characteristics (income, age, sex, and race). There are many more things to be considered in stratified sampling, including proportionate and disproportionate stratified sampling and the nature of the characteristics used to stratify the sample, that go beyond our simple introduction here. Once again, we urge you to consult social science research or statistics texts.

There may be times when you wish to select clusters of population units rather than individual units for your sampling procedure, even when the individual is the unit of analysis. Cluster sampling is often carried out in a multistage sampling design in which clusters are first selected and then individuals are drawn from clusters according to a strategy. Cluster sampling is used for large-scale needs assessments because it is more efficient. But some precision may be sacrificed unless the clusters are carefully chosen.

A multistage sampling procedure involves the successive random sampling of clusters or units within them. This can be done for any sampling unit.

Finally, there are some sampling techniques that we do not recommend, though we find that they are regularly used in our field. They are all examples of nonprobability sampling. In accidental sampling, only those who happen to be available are queried. In purposive sampling, persons or units are selected because they possess the characteristics in which the programmer is interested. This sampling relies on the programmer's judgment and presumptions. Systematic sampling consists of selecting every kth unit from the sampling frame, with k representing some interval selected to cover the entire frame and result in the sample size desired. The problem is to ensure that there is no systematic arrangement of units in the sampling frame that can bias the sample.

The last poor practice, quota sampling, is the attempt to obtain a sample whose characteristics reflect the characteristics of the population in several important dimensions. It is possible to use quota sampling to obtain the requisite number of individuals possessing certain characteristics so that the sample matches the population with regard to these characteristics. But this does not necessarily mean that the sample is *representative* of the population. In selecting the quota, the assessor may make numerous decisions that bias the sample. No matter what sampling technique is used, it is critical to make your best effort to obtain an unbiased, accurate, and thorough assessment of those chosen to represent the population.

Programmers need to know about sampling and probability in order to understand a second type of statistics, inferential statistics, which may be used to analyze interval (and ratio) data. We discuss the conceptual relationship between descriptive and inferential statistics more extensively in Chapter 9, "Program Evaluation," because we believe that it is during the evaluation phase of the leisure programming cycle that you will be more likely to use inferential techniques. Here we will take a brief look at descriptive statistics and inferential techniques.

Descriptive statistics describe the quantified characteristics of a group under study so that the programmer may more easily comprehend the nature of the group. They do so by reducing and summarizing many numbers into fewer numbers that may be more convenient to use and more easily communicated. Inferential statistics generalize this information by allowing the programmer to infer, or draw conclusions from, some kind of evidence. You cannot rely on descriptive statistics alone in drawing inferences from your data. Techniques of inferential statistics, however, do make it possible for you to draw inferences with a certain degree of confidence.

Inferential techniques go beyond description and are built upon the rules of probability. In leisure assessment and program evaluation there are two key applications to be aware of: statistical inference from samples to whole populations, and hypothesis testing.

Probability theory takes descriptive statistics and converts them into a standard form based on the normal curve we mentioned earlier. Statistics that describe a sample are compared with statistics found in probability tables. In order to infer accurately and confidently from a sample to the whole population, you use the probability sampling procedures mentioned earlier, followed by selected formulae.

In addition to helping programmers make estimates of population parameters (characteristics) from sample statistics, inferential statistical techniques provide a means for testing hypotheses (assumptions about population parameters) by evaluating the probability significance of a sample statistic. The sample statistic is compared to the established probability statistic with reference to a particular level of significance (degree of probability). Based on the results of this comparison, inferences (inductive guesses as to whether there is a relationship) can be made. The

Z-test, t-test, chi-square analysis (for nominal data), and analysis of variance are used as inferential tests of hypotheses.

Regression and correlation analyses are more refined techniques for testing the relationship between two continuous variables on an interval scale. Correlation analysis provides an explanation of relationship (how things vary) in the form of a decimal ranging from -1 (negative correlation) through $+1$ (positive correlation). Regression analysis yields an equation by which one can make a prediction about phenomena as they relate to one another (one variable predicts another). In correlation analysis, one looks at the interdependence between two variables. The Pearson Correlation Coefficient is a very well known measure of relationship for interval variables. The Spearman Rank Order Correlation Coefficient is used for ordinal data.

There are other nonparametric and parametric statistics available for use in analyzing quantitative data. Once again, we urge you to consult statistics or research methodology texts to go beyond the brief introduction to techniques for analyzing data presented here.

That leads us to the next means of analysis we must consider—techniques for analyzing qualitative (verbal) data. *All* information is not necessarily best expressed in the form of numbers, and some information by its very nature is incapable of being adequately expressed as a number. Generally, when you use quantitative assessment techniques, you are emphasizing counting, scaling, and abstract reasoning. When your approach is qualitative, you are concerned with personal understanding, common sense, and introspection.

The research literature is filled with comparisons of qualitative versus quantitative research, measurement approaches, and techniques. It is our belief that each can work in support of the other. Therefore we encourage the use of multiple assessment and evaluation techniques and, as appropriate, a combination of methodologies.

Qualitative Data Analysis.   When you attempt to order, categorize, reduce, and summarize qualitative data, you are concerned with accounts of observations that have been recorded as field notes, personal statements that have been taken down in interviews, responses to open-ended questions on questionnaires, case or life histories, and other written documents and artifacts that are relevant to the assessment procedure. Much of this information is *not* numerical in nature, but rather is expressed and recorded in words. Often there are hundreds of pages of words that describe the characteristics of your clientele; the forms, types, and variations of their leisure attitudes and interests; and their own perceptions of the meaning of their leisure engagements. How do you go about integrating, summarizing, and drawing conclusions from all these words?

One technique for analyzing qualitative information is content analysis. It is a formal system for doing something that we all do informally—formulating opinions through an examination of some kind of content. Formally, content analysis is a procedure for the categorization of verbal and/or behavioral data for the purpose of classification, summarization, or tabulation. (Some persons consider it to be an intermediate step between data collection and inference drawing.) Records, documents, testimony, books, newspaper articles, speeches, songs, broadcasts, diaries, letters, and other printed and recorded materials from a particular time and place are systematically examined and their contents classified and evaluated according to established criteria. This enables the investigator to describe the prevailing practices and conditions and to discover people's attitudes toward a specific topic, problem, or phenomenon, such as leisure. The process of content analysis requires the investigator to code the data into sets of categories, using key words or phrases to represent the nature of the verbal information, and then to tally them, that is, to count the frequency with which these indicators appear. The coding of units of communication is the "data processing" element of content analysis. If the coding procedures do result in numbers, they are likely to be either nominal or ordinal. A chi-square analysis may be useful in making comparisons between two sets of data derived from content analysis; a t-test or analysis of variance may be useful if the data are interval, normally distributed, and otherwise appropriate for that technique. But many investigators emphasize categorization over computation in content analysis as being the most useful way to uncover and order information during an assessment process.

Analytic induction involves setting up categories of phenomena or experiences and examining the data to determine relationships among these categories. It also involves searching for "negative cases," those responses that do not corroborate or fit into the mainstream categories. These "negative cases" are used to adapt or modify the initial categories to account for the full range of expression of information. This strategy is very demanding of the assessor's own capacity for logical thinking. The intent is to use the subjects' own words to explain their attitudes or behaviors in the aggregate.

The constant comparative method allows for a cross-comparison of leisure-related phenomena as they are being classified and categorized. Inductive categorical coding occurs simultaneously with comparison of the observations. From this, statements of relationship are generated. This technique builds upon analytic induction and can go beyond description into the construction of theories about human behavior and social phenomena.

As in our discussion of quantitative data analysis, we have only touched upon the techniques available for describing data, making generalizations from them, and drawing conclusions. We have highlighted those techniques that we believe you will be mostly likely to use in your initial needs assessments and evaluations. We urge you to go beyond this book in developing your expertise in this area.

We further urge you to consider the use of both quantitative and qualitative data analysis techniques when appropriate for the data that you have collected. In other words, we suggest that you use multiple instruments and techniques to collect assessment information and multiple techniques to analyze that information. In recent years researchers have consistently reported the advantages of triangulation.[75] There are instances when qualitative evidence enriches simple statistical data; when psychological concerns such as motives, assumptions, or frames of reference may not be quantifiable; or when indirect observation yields a better picture of a complex social situation than direct inquiry. These are just a few of the times when integrating multiple methods, techniques, and analyses can further the programmer's understanding of human behavior and human needs.

REPORTING THE RESULTS OF A NEEDS ASSESSMENT

Now that you have systematically uncovered some information about your clientele, the next thing you need to do is share it. The leisure profession has a unique relationship with lay people, who are the consumers, the beneficiaries, and even, at times, the governors of what we do. Parks, recreation, and leisure professionals are involved with the public on some, if not all, levels of decision making and service provision and delivery, from one-to-one leadership situations to large group policy-making efforts. In communicating the results of needs assessments to their colleagues as well as their constituents and/or clientele, they rely primarily on the spoken or written word.

In verbal presentations they may enhance the impact and retention of what is said by using audiovisual aids. They may give an informal talk, present a prepared speech, appear on a panel, give testimony at a hearing, or participate in a group discussion. All of these are techniques for presenting information orally.

Presentation of the results of a needs assessment usually takes the form of a written report. Typically, a comprehensive description of the results is prepared and an "executive summary" (that is, a brief statement of the most noteworthy results) is made available. The use of figures, graphs, tables, and illustrations in written reports can help to clarify volumes of numerical data. The key is to keep the expression of the results as straightforward and simple as possible.

When complex statistical treatments have been performed, the results should be explained and interpreted as well as expressed. The report writer has the option of indicating possible responses to the results, or alternative courses of action that might be taken. It is important for the writer to separate his or her values from his or her interpretation of the findings in order to present unbiased information and data-based alternatives from which the report recipients may choose. Opportunities for bias may be minimized if the writing of the evaluation report is a team effort and if the various drafts of the report are reviewed by diverse others.

A NEEDS ASSESSMENT RATIONALE

There is no question that what we have described up to now requires a great deal of thought and work. Considering that this is only the first phase of the leisure programming cycle, you may be asking yourself why you should do all this.

There are several reasons why an organization should be responsive to its constituent groups. First, if indeed leisure programmers do identify themselves as human service professionals, then they must be committed to ongoing communication with their clientele so that they may provide the best possible service. Programmers use needs assessment to tap into their clientele's desires systematically.

Needs assessment allows programmers to be accountable to those whom they serve. When clientele members have participated in a needs assessment process, they know the questions they were asked and some of the responses that were given. It is up to the programmers to disclose those responses as a whole so that everyone involved may be fully informed. It is impossible to facilitate the kind of self-directed leisure that we have been writing about without full sharing of information. Government units and other agencies that deliver leisure services may be legally required to conduct and update large-scale needs assessments periodically. Even if you are not employed in public recreation and leisure services, it may be that your agency honors this mandate as part of the self-imposed obligations of this profession.

In commercial recreation enterprises in particular, it is important to "know your territory," as consumer-oriented decision making may mean the difference between prosperity and failure. Knowledge of one's clientele is also extremely important in therapeutic recreation service delivery systems. For that matter, can you imagine trying to program leisure experiences successfully for any population without knowing something about its members' interests, attitudes, and tastes?

If you work for an agency that does not make a distinction between leisure and education (or that considers leisure education and counseling to be part of its mission), then the results of a needs assessment can show you where you need to do some heightening of leisure awareness, leisure values clarification, or leisure skills training. Whole new avenues of service may open to you as they emerge from the expressed needs of your constituents. This implies your being able to respond to, if not anticipate, change. In part, that is why we devoted a chapter of this book to trends and issues. We are living at a time when the rate of change is very rapid. In order for programmers to make sure that they are in touch with the current needs of their constituents, they must look on needs assessment as a continuous process that reflects the dynamic natures of human beings and human institutions. Miniassessments may be just the thing to allow them to remain in contact with their clientele over time.

From the viewpoint of program management, needs assessment helps programmers to plan, to prioritize among competing interests, to allocate limited resources, to custom-design programs, and to provide basic information that may be useful in later evaluations.

SUMMARY

The primary focus of this chapter has been on the instruments and techniques used in needs assessment, a systematic information collection process that enhances programmers' responsiveness and capacity for innovation. In order to enable programmers to stay attuned to the current and future needs of their clientele, the needs assessment procedure must emphasize inquiry. What should result from a successful needs assessment are some priorities for action. These priorities form the basis for the next phase of the leisure programming cycle: program development.

FOOTNOTES

1. Peter A. Witt and Rhonda Groom, "Dangers and Problems Associated with Current Approaches to Developing Leisure Interest Finders," *Therapeutic Recreation Journal*, First Quarter 1979, pp. 20-21.
2. Seppo E. Iso-Ahola, "Intrinsic Motivation: An Overlooked Basis for Evaluation," *Parks & Recreation*, February 1982, pp. 32-33. Reprinted by special permission of the National Recreation and Park Association.
3. Christine Z. Howe, "Leisure Assessment and Counseling," in *Leisure Counseling: Concepts and Applications*, ed. E. Thomas Dowd (Springfield, Ill.: Charles C Thomas, Publisher, 1984), p. 235. Courtesy of Charles C Thomas, Publisher, Springfield, Illinois.
4. Peter A. Witt, Peg Connolly, and David M. Compton, "Assessment: A Plea for Sophistication," *Therapeutic Recreation Journal*, Fourth Quarter 1980, p. 6.
5. Larry C. Loesch and Paul T. Wheeler, *Principles of Leisure Counseling* (Minneapolis, Minn.: Educational Media Corporation, 1982). pp. 111-112.
6. Howe, "Leisure Assessment," p. 235.
7. Larry C. Loesch, *Leisure Counseling* (Ann Arbor, Mich.: ERIC/CAPS, 1980).
8. Witt, Connolly, and Compton, "Assessment," pp. 5-8.
9. Loesch and Wheeler, *Principles of Leisure Counseling*.
10. Paul Wehman and Stuart J. Schlein, "Relevant Assessment in Leisure Skill Training Programs," *Therapeutic Recreation Journal*, Fourth Quarter 1980, pp. 9-20.
11. Howe, "Leisure Assessment," p. 237.
12. Loesch, *Leisure Counseling*, p. 16.
13. Witt, Connolly, and Compton, "Assessment," p. 7.
14. Loesch and Wheeler, *Principles of Leisure Counseling*, p. 134.
15. John R. Kelly, "Leisure Styles: A Hidden Core," *Leisure Sciences*, 5 (1983), 321, Crane, Russak & Co., Inc., New York.
16. Wehman and Schlein, "Relevant Assessment," pp. 14-15.
17. Loesch and Wheeler, *Principles of Leisure Counseling*, pp. 112-131.
18. Julia K. Dunn, "Assessment," in *Therapeutic Recreation Program Design: Principles and Procedures*, 2nd ed., Carol A. Peterson and Scout L. Gunn (Englewood Cliffs, N.J.: Prentice-Hall, Inc., 1984), pp. 298-318.
19. Howe, "Leisure Assessment," pp. 240-241.
20. Christine Z. Howe, "Leisure Assessment Instrumentation in Therapeutic Recreation," *Therapeutic Recreation Journal*, Second Quarter 1984, p. 17.
21. Witt, Connolly, and Compton, "Assessment," p. 6.
22. Wehman and Schlein, "Relevant Assessment," p. 12.
23. Howe, "Leisure Assessment," p. 242.

24. Howe, "Leisure Assessment Instrumentation," p. 16.
25. Ibid., p. 18.
26. Rabel J. Burdge, "The Development of a Leisure Orientation Scale" (master's thesis, Ohio State University, 1961).
27. Karla E. Slivken, "Development of a Leisure Ethic Scale" (master's thesis, University of Illinois at Urbana-Champaign, 1978), p. 9.
28. Dean R. Yoesting and Rabel J. Burdge, "Utility of a Leisure Orientation Scale," *Iowa State Journal of Research,* 50 (1976), 345-66.
29. John Neulinger, *The Psychology of Leisure* (Springfield, Ill.: Charles C Thomas, Publisher, 1974), pp. 169-183. Courtesy of Charles C Thomas, Publisher, Springfield, Illinois.
30. Loesch and Wheeler, *Principles of Leisure Counseling,* p. 115.
31. Slivken, "Development of a Leisure Ethic Scale," pp. 64-88.
32. Loesch and Wheeler, *Principles of Leisure Counseling,* p. 117.
33. Howe, "Leisure Assessment," p. 244.
34. Mounir G. Ragheb, "Interrelationships among Leisure Participation, Leisure Satisfaction and Leisure Attitudes," *Journal of Leisure Research,* Second Quarter 1980, p. 142.
35. H. Triandis, "Explanatory Factor Analyses of the Behavioral Component of Social Attitudes," *Journal of Abnormal and Social Psychology,* 68 (1964), pp. 420-30.
36. Howe, "Leisure Assessment Instrumentation," p. 19.
37. Gary Ellis and Peter A. Witt, *Leisure Diagnostic Battery: Theoretical and Empirical Structure* (Denton, Tex.: North Texas State University, 1982).
38. Ibid., pp. 54-117.
39. Ibid., pp. 34-35.
40. Howe, "Leisure Assessment Instrumentation," p. 20.
41. Ibid., p. 20.
42. Willoughby A. Walshe, "Leisure Counseling Instrumentation," in *Perspectives of Leisure Counseling,* ed. David M. Compton and Judith E. Goldstein (Arlington, Va.: National Recreation and Park Association, 1977), pp. 113-114.
43. Ibid., p. 114.
44. Howe, "Leisure Assessment," p. 245.
45. C. Forrest McDowell, *The Leisure Well-Being Inventory* (Eugene, Ore.: Sun-Moon Press, 1983).
46. Howe, "Leisure Assessment Instrumentation," p. 20.
47. Ibid., p. 20.
48. Howe, "Leisure Assessment," p. 245.
49. Dunn, "Assessment," pp. 267-320.
50. Kenneth F. Joswiak, *Leisure Counseling Program Materials for the Developmentally Disabled* (Washington, D.C.: Hawkins and Associates, 1979).
51. Robert P. Overs, ed., *Avocational Counseling Manual* (Menomonee Falls, Wis.: Signpost Press, Inc.), pp. 106-36.
52. Howe, "Leisure Assessment," p. 246.
53. Susan M. Rimmer, "The Development of an Instrument to Assess Leisure Satisfaction Among Secondary School Students" (doctoral diss., University of Florida, 1979).

54. Seppo E. Iso-Ahola, *The Social Psychology of Leisure and Recreation* (Dubuque, Iowa: William C. Brown Company, Publishers, 1980).

55. Howe, "Leisure Assessment," p. 246.

56. Jacob G. Beard and Mounir G. Ragheb, "Measuring Leisure Satisfaction," *Journal of Leisure Research*, First Quarter 1980, pp. 20-32.

57. Ibid., p. 31.

58. Ibid., p. 31.

59. Howe, "Leisure Assessment Instrumentation," p. 22.

60. Edwina E. Hubert, "The Development of an Inventory of Leisure Interests" (doctoral diss., University of North Carolina at Chapel Hill, 1969).

61. Max Kaplan, *Leisure in America: A Social Inquiry* (New York: John Wiley and Sons, 1960).

62. C. Forrest McDowell, "Approaching Leisure Counseling with the Self Leisure Interest Profile" (master's thesis, California State University, 1973).

63. Howe, "Leisure Assessment," p. 247.

64. Wehman and Schlein, "Relevant Assessment," pp. 9-20.

65. Howe, "Leisure Assessment," p. 247.

66. George E. McKechnie, *Leisure Activities Blank Manual* (Palo Alto, Calif.: Consulting Psychologists Press, 1975).

67. Loesch and Wheeler, *Principles of Leisure Counseling*, p. 129.

68. Overs, *Avocational Counseling Manual*, pp. 106-36.

69. Howe, "Leisure Assessment Instrumentation," p. 23.

70. Patsy B. Edwards and P. A. Bloland, "Leisure Counseling and Consultation," *Personnel and Guidance Journal*, 58 (1980), 435-40.

71. Howe, "Leisure Assessment," p. 248.

72. Nancy Navar, "Leisure Skill Assessment Process in Leisure Counseling," in *Expanding Horizons in Therapeutic Recreation VI*, ed. David J. Szymanski and Gerald L. Hitzhusen (Columbia, Mo.: Technical Education Services, University of Missouri-Columbia, 1979), pp. 68-94.

73. Howe, "Leisure Assessment Instrumentation," p. 23.

74. Blaine R. Worthen and James R. Sanders, *Educational Evaluation: Theory and Practice* (Belmont, Calif.: Wadsworth Publishing Co., Inc., 1973).

75. Norman K. Denzin, *The Research Act: A Theoretical Introduction to Sociological Methods*, 2nd ed. (New York: McGraw-Hill Book Company, 1978) p. 28.

76. Ibid., pp. 28-33, 291-307.

chapter 7

Program Development
Phase Two of the Leisure
Programming Cycle

AGENCY PHILOSOPHY AND STRUCTURE

In this chapter we examine the second phase of the leisure programming cycle: program development. This phase necessarily follows the needs assessment phase because information must be gathered before development can be carried out.

Program development is the organization and administration of leisure experiences through systematic planning. When planning, you as a programmer must anticipate, coordinate, and implement. According to Harold Koontz and Cyril O'Donnell, "Planning is deciding in advance what to do, how to do it, when to do it, and who is to do it."[1] Planning functions are carried out within the confines of the organization in which you work. The unique philosophy and organizational structure of leisure service agencies determines the exact procedures under which they operate and offer programs to their constituents.

In Chapter 4 we discussed Knowles's "pool of needs" idea. You will recall that one area foremost in the pool of needs is organizational needs. Usually found among the written documents of leisure agencies are philosophical statements that set forth the agency's beliefs, values, and principles regarding the role of recreation and leisure in human experience. These statements form the foundation on which leisure program planning and development is built. One of the leisure programs offered by the Girl Scouts of Philadelphia, for example, is "Alive," which promotes adventure, fun, and learning for 12- to 17-year-olds. In order to integrate career education into "Alive" in accordance with the organization's philosophy, the program includes opportunities for Girl Scouts to meet professional women, examine career options, and develop leadership skills.

It is important for you to feel that there is a "fit" or congruence between your personal philosophy and the philosophy of your agency. Effectiveness in producing leisure experiences is increased when the leisure programmer concurs with agency beliefs, values, and principles. When this is the case, both you and your agency benefit, largely because your personal and professional energies are more clearly directed toward the accomplishment of organizational goals. A commercial recreation enterprise is in business to make a profit and the leisure programs that they promote are directed toward that goal. The leisure programmer employed by such an enterprise needs to have that organizational purpose in mind in order to plan successful leisure experiences.

Organizational structure can facilitate or inhibit leisure program development. Organizational structure refers to both the formal and the informal ways that leisure agencies are organized in order to accomplish goals. Aspects of an organization's structure include formalization (representation of operations on organizational charts), standardization (uniformity of organizational procedures), hierarchy (levels of management positions), span of control (number of people who report to a supervisor), and coordination (linkage between various work units).[2] Organizational structure may be viewed as existing on a continuum that runs from mechanistic (rigid) organization on one end to organic (flexible) organization on the other end.[3] Factors external to the organization that can affect organizational structure include government rules and regulations such as the Equal Employment Opportunity Act (EEO), which may affect personnel; rural or metropolitan location, which may determine the size of an agency; and sociopolitical pressures such as clientele discontent, loss of outside funding resources, or a mandate to be of service to a new interest group.

The organizational structures found in leisure and recreation agencies today vary as greatly as their program and service offerings. As with the philosophic fit discussed above, it is important that you feel comfortable with the organizational structure of your agency in order to be most effective on the job. If a leisure programmer prefers much structure and management direction but is working in an organization that provides minimal structure and has low-key managers, the incongruency will detract from overall productivity and program outcomes. Further, this discord can increase the programmer's stress and frustration levels and decrease personal and professional satisfactions.

Returning to Knowles's pool of needs (Figure 4-2), we can see how needs are screened through the filters of organizational philosophy and purposes and organizational structure on their way to becoming program objectives. Developing program objectives is one of the tasks that must be performed in the program development phase of the leisure programming cycle.

PROGRAM DEVELOPMENT TASKS

Leisure programmers often do their planning with the intention of improving program effectiveness. The old cliché "Practice makes perfect" is one reality they count on. The more often you systematically develop leisure experiences, the more likely you are to refine those skills that are important in successful programming.

We said earlier in this chapter that organizing and administering leisure experiences takes planning. Planning involves decision making. You do not make programming decisions in a vacuum. In terms of leisure program development, the decisions you make are based on three factors: (1) the information obtained during needs assessment; (2) the philosophical and organizational contexts; and (3) your professional training and experience. Programming decisions center on human and material resources, such as objectives, program formats, policies and procedures, scheduling of facilities, leadership, marketing and promotional efforts, and legal and financial considerations.

OBJECTIVES

The last screening filter in Knowles's pool of needs, constituent interests, has to do with the specific leisure preferences of the prospective participants whom you wish to attract. Although your knowledge of human development provides you with some general guidelines and expectations for leisure behavior throughout the life-span, individual leisure interests are fluid, fluctuating and changing quite often. The latest fads and trends will affect participants' leisure interests, as will their increased exposure to and experiences with leisure. The most precise information about the interests of clientele is obtained in the needs assessment process.

Once the interests are clear, you can initiate the process of translating them into objectives that address the needs of both the agency and the participants, individually and as a group. Objectives that address agency needs are usually called program objectives. Objectives that address participant needs are usually called performance or behavioral objectives. Programmers must ensure that the leisure experiences they facilitate serve the leisure organization as well as the leisure participant.

Ruth V. Russell provides some examples of specific program and performance objectives.[4] The differences between the two types of objectives are illustrated in Table 7-A. Program objectives are geared toward achieving agency purposes (organizational needs and institutional purposes); performance objectives are geared toward desired participant outcomes (fulfillment of individual needs and interests of clientele).

Program and performance objectives provide direction to leisure programmers. Once the objectives are established in written form, the other issues related to decision making throughout the entire phase of program development can be tackled. Referring to Table 7-A, if one of the program objectives is to provide adequate leadership for the program, directions must be given regarding leadership selection and staff scheduling. If the performance objective of a nature program is to enhance the quality of urban life, part of the program content must include communication of the names and uses of selected species to the participants.

Objectives are very important because they set standards for evaluating

Broad Direction of Program	**Specific Objectives**
Program Outcome	*Performance Objectives*
To make children safe while in or near the water	Each first-grade child will be able to pass the Red Cross beginner swimming course.
To enhance the quality of urban life	At the conclusion of the program, each participant will be able to identify flower species within a one-block radius of his/her home.
To encourage socialization among psychiatric patients	The psychiatric patients will demonstrate interaction with others by conversing with other patients twice during the rest break of the bicycle trip.
To develop psychomotor skills of kindergarten children	Each child in the kindergarten class will be able to perform the skills of running, walking, skipping, and galloping in different directions.
Program Operation	*Program Objectives*
To increase the number of scouts in the Boy Scout Council	There should be a 10 percent increase in the number of Cub Scouts, an 8 percent increase in the number of Boy Scouts, and a 5 percent increase in the number of Explorer Scouts in this district in the next two years.
To provide adequate leadership for the program	The program will maintain a minimum of two staff persons, each devoting at least three hours per week.

Table 7-A   Examples of Specific Objectives

From Ruth V. Russell, *Planning Programs in Recreation* (St. Louis: The C. V. Mosby Company, 1982), p. 119.

programs. You can find detailed guidelines for writing objectives in programming textbooks by Patricia Farrell and Herberta M. Lundegren; Christopher R. Edginton, David L. Compton, and Carole J. Hanson; and Ruth V. Russell.

FORMAT

Another task in program development is selecting the format for the leisure experience—that is, the kind or type of program that will be offered. The two main formats that have long served the leisure profession are activities and facilities. A third format that is gaining in popularity is leisure education.

If you decide to use the recreation activity format, a wide and varied range of options exists. Among the choices for programs are the arts (music, dance, drama, or crafts); sports (athletic leagues or events); games (vigorous activities such as New Games or sedentary activities such as table games); special events to highlight the agency or a holiday; social recreation (parties or street fairs); travel and tourism (outings or trips); outdoor recreation (camping or nature hikes); education experiences (lectures or workshops); spiritual activities (meditation groups); and hobbies (collecting or creating).

Another choice of activity often seen is volunteer service. Many people find leisure fulfillment in assuming leader or assistant roles in the provision of leisure experiences for others. For the volunteer, serving in this capacity becomes a recreational activity in itself.

The recreation activity format offers programmers four advantages. First, activity formats can be combined. You may plan a banquet (social recreation) in recognition of the work done by summer camp counselors (volunteer service). Or the agency may produce an open house (special event) that features program participants demonstrating their dance skills and displaying handicraft items (arts), a slide show of urban nature hikes (outdoor recreation), and a lecture on how to avoid job burnout (education).

A second advantage of the activity format is the opportunity for the sequential development of participant skills. The various activity modes can be planned so that the participant progresses through a series of leisure experiences that increase his or her skill in that activity. YMCAs, for example, provide a number of skill levels in their aquatic programs. These levels accommodate participants with different swimming abilities. Beginning swimmers are in the polliwog class. As the participants' skills improve, they progress through the minnow, fish, flying fish, and shark levels.

The third benefit of the recreation activity format comes about as a result of the wide variety of activities that exist. The challenge of producing a diverse range of leisure programs is one that many professionals feel. The activity format gives you a role in increasing the leisure repertoire of participants. Your constituents can choose to be exposed to and involved in many new activities or to develop increased competency in one or more.

And the fourth advantage of the recreation activity format is that the potential exists for activity analysis which is most frequently used in therapeutic recreation settings. According to Peterson and Gunn, activity analysis is a procedure for breaking down and examining a recreation activity to find inherent characteristics that contribute to program objectives. The programmer must consider the physical (psychomotor), cognitive (mental), affective (emotional), and social (interactive) requirements of participants which are inherent in different recreation activities. By developing a better understanding of activity components and participation requirements, programmers will find that activity analysis provides:

1. a better comprehension of the expected outcomes of participation;
2. a greater understanding of the complexity of activity components, which can then be compared to the functional level of an individual or group to determine the appropriateness of the activity;
3. information about whether the activity will contribute to the desired behavioral outcome when specific behavioral goals or objectives are being used;
4. direction for the modification or adaptation of an activity for individuals with limitations;
5. useful information for selecting an intervention, instructional, or leadership technique; and

6. a rationale or explanation for the therapeutic benefits of activity involvement.[5]

Face-to-face leadership plays an important part in the recreation activity format. Activities generally require a good deal of direction on the part of those staff members facilitating the program. In these leader-directed leisure experiences, the participant relies on a person trained in the activity to lead the program. The leader's knowledge and leadership skill will often determine the positivity of the outcome.

In contrast, the recreation facilities format usually provides for an almost totally self-directed leisure experience. Leadership is generally available, but often is not sought out by participants. Leisure spaces and environments are established and maintained for potential users to seek out. Parks, recreation centers, playgrounds, swimming pools, concert halls, and student unions are examples of facilities.

Commercial recreators maintain a variety of facilities programs. These include private health clubs and spas, racket-sports clubs, golf clubs, marinas, theme parks, ice and roller skating rinks, movie theaters, and nightclubs. Many restaurants have created elaborate leisure environments that feature dining, dancing, entertainment, and video games. Planned housing developments often feature leisure facilities as amenities and inducements to buy.

Renting or loaning recreation supplies and equipment can be considered part of this format. Although in some ways leasing can be viewed a separate format (the recreation supplies format), we view it as an extension of the facilities format because quite often it serves a leisure environment located nearby. For example, participants typically rent supplies and equipment for river rafting and snow skiing. There are also motor home and boat rentals. Outdoor adventure equipment programs (camping, back-packing, and climbing) exist on a number of college campuses.

Leisure education, the third major format, has to do with individual leisure development. Leisure education is concerned with the individual's life-style and the evolution of leisure values and functioning throughout the developmental stages of his or her life course. Participants in leisure programs, whether in the activities format or the facilities format, become more aware of the broad range of leisure experiences. But when programmers use the leisure education format, they do so with the primary intent of expanding the participants' exposure to and experience with leisure to promote optimal, independent leisure functioning. In leisure education, specific steps are taken to clarify individuals' leisure values, awareness, knowledge, skills, and experiences.

Once the decision has been made to use the leisure education format, a number of programming options are available. Leisure education can be conducted as a service that disseminates information about leisure opportunities in a given location (leisure knowledge); in a small group setting, as a series of exercises stressing clarification of leisure values and attitudes; in a school system, as a curriculum of study viewed as part of the students' entire educational experience (leisure awareness); as guided experiences with recently disabled persons who are redeveloping leisure competencies (leisure skill development); or as actual participation in leisure experiences designed with the individual's continued leisure development in mind.

Planning and implementing leisure education requires differing amounts of intervention, leadership, and skill. For example, leisure skill development among nondisabled persons is what the generally trained leisure professional routinely does when programming. However, the redevelopment of leisure skills among the recently disabled is the domain of therapeutic recreators who have specialized training. Individual and group counseling geared toward alleviating leisure dysfunction is also a function of leisure education. Leisure counselors are trained and certified leisure professionals who provide that service.

Figure 7-1 depicts the increasing amounts of leader intervention and skill required in various leisure education experiences, from the lowest level (conducting information dissemination services) through an intermediate level (conducting leisure experiences, leisure values clarification, leisure awareness modules, leisure activities, and leisure skill development) to the highest level (conducting individual and group leisure counseling programs).

Programmers interested in using any of the three formats discussed here

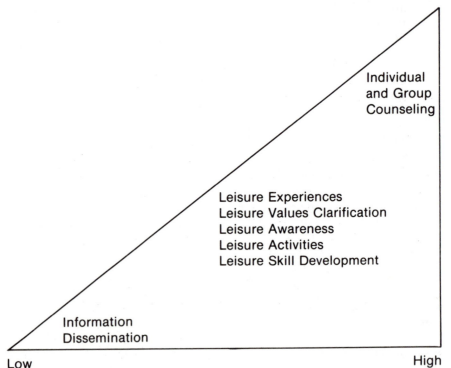

Figure 7-1 Amount of Leader Intervention and Skill Required in Leisure Education Experiences

will need to investigate further and can find a number of excellent textbooks that discuss each format in great detail. Our interest is in introducing you to accepted and productive modes that can be used in delivering leisure programs. Deciding upon the format or combination of formats to be used is of major importance at this point in the program development phase of the leisure programming cycle.

Application Section.   Take a few minutes to name ten different leisure service agencies with which you are familiar. List them in a column on the left side of a piece of paper. Next, decide which program format each agency uses, and write it next to the agency name, making a second column. Now do some careful thinking. Based on your perception of each organization's likely goals and purposes, decide whether or not its format is appropriate. If not, list in a third column your suggestions for an additional format or combination of formats. Finally, discuss your list and perceptions with at least one other person in order to clarify and confirm your own thinking.

POLICIES AND PROCEDURES

The next step in program development, after selecting the format, is to decide on program policies and procedures. Policies and procedures stem from the overall purpose of the recreation agency. Leisure programmers are often involved in defining program policies and procedures in order to establish program guidelines and practices. When policies and procedures are determined and published, agency supervisors and constituents can readily see indicators of program structure. If the organizational purposes are the soul of a program, and the selected program format is the heart, then the policies and procedures are the skeleton that supports the other aspects of program development.

Using the well-accepted programming steps advanced by Richard G. Kraus—philosophy, principle, policy, and procedure[6]—Figure 7-2 shows how policy and procedure statements could be written. When the agency philosophy (organizational purpose) stresses adventure, programmers enter the picture during program policy and procedure development. The guideline (policy), which suggests that the agency will promote a full range of adventure activities, guides the programmers in determining the kind of leisure experiences that will become specific program ideas. Then the programmers are responsible for ensuring that the practice (procedure)— offering bicycle motocross, for example—is realized.

Some leisure service agencies have well-formulated policies and procedures to which programmers must adhere. For instance, at Camp Tamarack, a privately owned and operated resident camp in central Oregon, policies and procedures that conform to American Camping Association (ACA) standards for accredited camps are in operation. ACA standards reflect professionally accepted guidelines and practices for camps, addressing such areas as facilities, leadership, transportation to and from the camp site, and camping activities. These standards serve to help define actual program practices.

The development of policy and procedure statements is far more

Concept	Examples of Statements
Philosophy Fundamental Beliefs of the Organization	• Individuals should be afforded opportunities for adventure in leisure experiences.
Principle Specific Statements About Those Beliefs	• Our agency/business will provide adventurous leisure experiences led by skilled individuals.
Policy Guidelines for Implementing Principles	• We will promote a full range of adventure activities for each segment of our clientele. • Programs offering skill development will be provided for clients having little or no previous experience. • Only leaders with demonstrated skill in the adventure activity will be hired to facilitate programs.
Procedure Program Practices That Can Assure Policy Realization	• Bicycle motocross will be offered the first Saturday of each month for children ages 7–12. • A beginning cross-country ski class will be offered this program year. • The over-65 camping program will include water-based activities this year. • Program participants must pay an additional fee to enroll in the group insurance policy. • Leaders of programs must have passed the skills test three months prior to leading the activity.

Figure 7-2   The Evolution of Policy and Procedure Statements

specific and concrete than the development of an agency's statements of philosophy and principle. While programmers usually have input into the latter, it is the former in which they have the most input and with which they are most involved on an ongoing basis.

SCHEDULING

Another task performed during the program development phase of the leisure programming cycle is the scheduling of sites and facilities. Questions about when programs should be offered, for how long, in what location, and so on fall at programmers' feet like nuts and bolts waiting to be assembled.

Decisions about scheduling must be made daily. These decisions have to do with the allocation and reallocation of existing and acquirable spaces and resources. Programmers, along with their co-workers, must determine which agency resources are available and which other resources can be made available for use in the agency's program. Quite often one decision will be affected by another, and both will be made with a view toward the expressed needs of others.

Scheduling interacts with a number of program aspects. It may be affected by space of facility availability, because certain leisure programs need to take place in particular leisure environments, and by participant availability. Another consideration is equipment and supplies. You need to secure or arrange for the procurement of resources necessary for the activity or event. For an aerobic dancing program, you would need to obtain a record or tape player, speakers, records or tapes, a clip-on microphone with a long cord, and some exercise mats. Sign-up materials, including attendance records, printed rules and regulations, health tips, and informational flyers that explain the program, must also be readied. Not only will you need to decide on what and how many to have of each of these, but you will also have to keep an inventory so that declining supplies and deteriorating equipment can be replaced as the program continues.

Personnnel decisions include the number of leaders, what time they should report, what functions they will fulfill, how many volunteer assistants they need, and how assistance will be arranged for and recognized.

Environmental considerations are important too. Staying with our aerobic dancing example, the facility would need to be a large room with plenty of open space, with restrooms and a drinking fountain accessible, with an electrical outlet near the front of the room, and with a stage or risers available for the program leader to use in order to be seen by all participants.

Sometimes resources must be sought outside the agency. Facilities may be overbooked or nonexistent. Clientele interests may require that programs be held in different environments. Or programmers may deliberately choose facilities away from the agency to provide programs in new places and under differing conditions. Trips and outings to waterfronts, historic sites, museums, water slides, theme parks, community gatherings, and mountains or other natural areas offer opportunities that cannot be duplicated in the agency setting. In these cases, it is important for the programmer to gather information about the site or facility in order to program well while he or she is there.

LEADERSHIP

It is often argued that leadership is the most critical element of successful programming and achievement of goals. The ability of leisure programmers to attract, train, supervise, and retain quality paid personnel and volunteer leaders does have a considerable relationship to program success. These tasks also consume large portions of a programmer's time. In this section, we examine some issues surrounding leadership that have relevance to programming leisure experiences. The reader who wants to know more about leadership theory, style, functions, and principles should seek in-depth information from the sources listed in the references at the end of this chapter.

Program leadership interacts with several of the other elements of program development that we have discussed. Agency policies and procedures often spell out specific leader-participant ratios or leader aptitude requirements that must be followed by the programmer. We will see in our upcoming discussion of legal considerations that leadership has a role to play there. Many programmers involve leaders throughout the entire program development phase in order to increase their input into decision making in a participatory management fashion.

Frequently, the leaders needed to facilitate a particular leisure experience are sought by the programmer because they already possess the necessary skill or ability to conduct the activity. A person who has been collecting coins for several years would be more helpful in leading other coin hobbyists than a person who is just getting started. The programmer who does attract a skilled person to lead a leisure experience is not done with leadership considerations, however. No matter how skilled and knowledgeable the leader may be, the programmer will still want to supervise the leader in order to further develop his or her skills. This personnel-oriented function is undertaken by programmers as part of managing the overall delivery of the program.

Kraus, Gaylene M. Carpenter, and Barbara J. Bates suggest that the qualities of an effective recreation leader include the leader's personality and manner of relating to group members, enthusiasm for the activity, organizational ability, preparedness to conduct the activity, ability to view the activity as part of the agency's overall leisure program, and ability to teach the activity effectively.[7] None of these characteristics is directly related to the leader's inherent skill or ability to perform the recreation activity itself. Each of them can be enhanced through training sessions conducted by programmers. For example, the leader's personality, enthusiasm for the activity, and manner of relating to participants can be observed by the programmer and communicated to the leader. Successful and unsuccessful interactions can be noted and shared. Plans for overcoming difficulties can then be arranged between leader and programmer.

Organizational ability, preparedness, and the ability to teach are areas of leadership that can be developed through in-service or preservice training. The leader's ability to view the specific leisure activity within the context of the agency is one that generally evolves as the programmer helps the leader to feel a part of the agency and to understand agency goals and purposes. The programmer can ensure that both of these will occur by holding a leader orientation as well as by providing ongoing training experiences or "refreshers." Successful programmers see it as a part of their job to develop leaders, recognizing that leaders are made, not born.

The "art" of leadership has been examined often. Koontz and O'Donnell discuss leadership from a management perspective. Because the leisure programmer's role is often indirect (supervising leaders) rather than direct (leading the activity), it is useful for programmers to know the following three major ingredients of leadership: "The ability to comprehend that human beings have differing motivating forces at varying times and in different situations, the ability to inspire, and the ability to act in a manner that will develop a climate for responding to and arousing motivations."[8]

Leisure programmers should be very familiar with motivation theory and the various motivational models. Understanding what motivates people in satisfying ways can provide you with the information necessary for ensuring that program goals are achieved at the same time that the leader's objectives and the participants' needs are met. The more awareness that you have regarding the incentives that encourage high-level performance on the part of the leader, the better equipped you are to facilitate individual and program growth.

The ability to inspire has much to do with charisma. Koontz and O'Donnell explain that it is a rare quality that includes the elements of charm and appeal, which influence other people to feel loyalty, devotion, and a strong desire to follow.[9] While this ability to inspire may seem a bit mystical and innate, we believe that it is a quality that can be nurtured. Clearly, the programmer as a model leader who exhibits direction and confidence and makes it a practice to aid recreation leaders in the accomplishment of their personal goals will garner a following.

Designing and maintaining a work environment that is conducive to eliciting peak performances from recreation leaders is something that the programmer does have some control over. While those in other management positions throughout the agency will have much to do with overall conditions, programmers very often function as heads over their own domain. So it may be possible for you to establish a working climate that fosters a high level of responsiveness and involvement. You can do this by encouraging leaders to become involved in program-related decisions, providing training experiences for leaders, attracting and retaining qualified leaders, and creating a personally motivating work environment.

MARKETING

Program marketing is another task that needs to be completed during the program development phase. Marketing is gradually becoming an accepted practice within the parks, recreation, and leisure field. In the past, leisure professionals, with their philosophy of human service, had the notion that marketing and selling were synonymous and that selling was pushy and inappropriate. So, especially in the public, nonprofit sector, they limited themselves to promotion and public relations. But recently, as the concept of marketing has been successfully implemented and disseminated, more and more professionals have information and resources available to use in gaining expertise in the area. As a result, there exists the potential for seeing the systematic application of marketing strategies in the collection of information about constituent wishes and the establishment of leisure programs and services designed to speak to those wishes. In the future, successful leisure service agencies will have a well-developed marketing strategy to which programmers hopefully will have input. The agency's product is its leisure programs, so programmers must necessarily play a major role in creating and implementing the marketing scheme.

In terms of supply and demand, agency programs are the supplier of leisure experiences demanded by the consumer. Marketing is a method of directing the activities that take place in an organization toward the satisfaction of consumer (or participant) needs and demands.[10] There are a number of factors that indicate the importance of leisure experiences to individuals in society today. Suppliers have much to do just to keep up with user demands. Some writers suggest that agencies that are in business to package leisure experiences can be considered part of a growth industry. But this idea is greeted with caution by Theodore Levitt, who states: "There is no such thing as a growth industry, I believe. There are only companies organized and operated to create and capitalize on growth opportunities."[11]

The point here is that agencies must be organized in ways that capitalize on growth opportunities rather than ride on the crest of some imaginary wave.

To understand the concept of marketing in terms of the leisure programming process, it is necessary to define *marketing* and *marketing strategy*. Markets consist of individuals who have certain needs and are willing to exchange something of value to satisfy those needs.[12] According to Dennis R. Howard and John L. Crompton, "Marketing is the analysis, planning, implementation, and control of carefully formulated programs designed to bring about voluntary exchanges with target markets for the purpose of achieving agency objectives. It relies heavily upon designing offerings consistent with clients' wants, and on using effective pricing, communication and distribution to inform, motivate, and service the markets."[13]

In this definition, specific marketing tasks to be performed by the leisure professional become apparent. When performing needs assessment in actualizing the cyclical approach to programming, the programmer is automatically engaged in the process of marketing research. Equipped with your knowledge of human growth and development, and needs assessment, you are performing functions during program development designed to meet leisure wants. The leisure programmer, in facilitating the delivery of leisure experiences, is developing a user-oriented product. The programmer's concern is not with how many participants but rather with providing those who do participate with a satisfying experience.[14]

Marketing strategy has to do with pricing, distribution in terms of location and scheduling, and promotion or communication of the service which is to be delivered.[15] Price represents what the user must give up in order to obtain the services offered and typically emphasizes finding out how much people are (1) able to pay, and (2) willing to pay. Distribution is concerned with the availability of the services offered and emphasizes the time and location, or the when and where aspects of the program. Promotion, or communication, facilitates exchanges by disseminating pertinent information about the product, price, and distribution to the selected clientele. Leisure programmers will need to manipulate these elements depending upon their setting. For example, a therapeutic recreation specialist working in a hospital will find it unnecessary to spend as much time with pricing than would a leisure programmer planning for people accustomed to paying fees for leisure experiences.

To achieve comprehensive results, marketing strategies should be undertaken by the entire agency. Philip Kotler reported on one such marketing response focused on colleges and universities.[16] This response can be used to demonstrate the issues that must be examined as part of an agency's overall marketing effort. As can be seen in Figure 7-3, a number of important questions must be answered regarding market analysis, resources analysis, and mission analysis. In this example, these efforts are directed toward improving student and faculty recruitment and institutional fund-raising. All divisions and departments within the academic, student services, and administrative sectors have input into and major involvement with those portions of the planning effort that address their particular sector. The leisure programmer working in a college or university would be part of the student services sector, where he or she could conceivably be involved in coordinating new student orientation activities or campus-wide open houses as part of an overall organizational effort directed toward student recruitment.

College union programmers and student activities coordinators can apply this same institutional planning structure to their own recreation departments. For example, trends affecting student activities in higher education, the major market segments, leisure satisfactions of current students, program strengths and weaknesses, and each portion of market-oriented institutional planning can be addressed specifically as they relate to the nonacademic life of the student for which the programmer is responsible.

Assuming that you have had input into the agency's marketing plan and that you can apply marketing concepts to the programming sector, what

---

Market Analysis

1. What important trends are affecting higher education? (Environmental analysis)
2. What is our primary market? (Market definition)
3. What are the major market segments in this market? (Market segmentation)
4. What are the needs of each market segment? (Needs assessment)
5. How much awareness, knowledge, interest, and desire is there in each market segment concerning our college? (Market awareness and attitudes)
6. How do key publics see us and our competitors? (Image analysis)
7. How do potential students learn about our college and make decisions to apply and enroll? (Consumer behavior)
8. How satisfied are current students? (Consumer satisfaction assessment)

Resource Analysis

1. What are our major strengths and weaknesses in faculty, programs, facilities, etc.? (Strengths/weaknesses analysis)
2. What opportunities are there to expand our financial resources? (Donor opportunity analysis)

Mission Analysis

1. What business are we in? (Business mission)
2. Who are our customers? (Customer definition)
3. Which needs are we trying to satisfy? (Needs targeting)
4. On which market segments do we want to focus? (Market targeting)
5. Who are our major competitors? (Competitor identification)
6. What competitive benefits do we want to offer to our target market? (Market positioning)

Figure 7-3 Issues in Market-Oriented Institutional Planning Facing Colleges and Universities

Adapted from Philip Kotler, "Strategies for Introducing Marketing into Nonprofit Organizations," *Journal of Marketing*, (January 1979), 39. Used by permission of the American Marketing Association.

kinds of marketing functions will follow? Efforts at public relations, personal contact, advertising, incentives, and publicity are important ongoing promotional functions that affect you as a programmer. Figure 7-4 depicts the leisure programmer's marketing functions, beginning with input when the agency engages in market-oriented institutional planning. As the leisure experience is created within the context of the leisure programming cycle, your task during program development has to do with promoting the leisure experience.

Public relations concerns the image of the organization and specifically with the image of the program itself. Leisure programs and services that are perceived by market segments as positive create a favorable attitude toward the agency by users and potential users. A well-organized program responsive to client wants that demonstrates sound management, quality

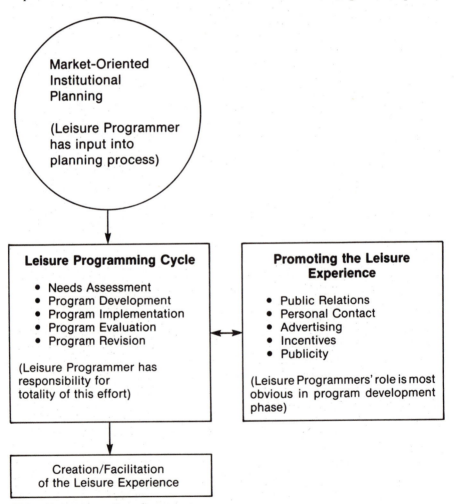

Figure 7-4   Leisure Programmer's Marketing Functions

facilities and equipment, and skilled leadership will also help to create a positive experience and image.

Promotional efforts are directed at the target market to let consumers know that services are available at a certain cost, location, and time. If you have developed something that your constituents want, promotion will communicate that fact to the potential participant who is willing to exchange money or time to satisfy that want. Promotion is communication that enables exchange between user and deliverer. It usually includes personal contact, advertising, incentives and publicity. Howard and Crompton distinguish among these functions in this way:

> Personal Contact: Direct oral presentation to one or more present or potential clients for the purpose of facilitating exchange.
>
> Advertising: Any paid form of nonpersonal presentation about an agency or its programs, which is paid for by an identified sponsor or developed by an identified sponsor and communicated through media as a public service.
>
> Incentives: Something of financial value offered to encourage participation in a program or use of a service.
>
> Publicity: Nonpersonal favorable communications in either print or broadcast media in which the sponsor is not identified and for which there is no payment.[17]

Marketing is a complex area, one in which leisure programmers often have underdeveloped skills. Much of its terminology is unfamiliar to programmers. Comprehensive marketing schemes have only recently been implemented by noncommercial leisure agencies. Those wishing to refine their techniques are encouraged to seek additional competency by attending some of the many marketing seminars offered by professional societies and by training and development specialists. Also, the authors cited in this section offer volumes of information and resources, much of it geared specifically to the park, recreation, and leisure professional.

Application Section.   In groups of four, identify one well-known leisure agency with which you are familiar. Attempt to isolate those factors that you believe are part of its marketing techniques and that you believe are effectively in operation. List these factors. Then identify another agency with which you are familiar but that is less well known. Now identify marketing techniques that you feel it is failing to use but could use to its benefit.

LEGAL CONSIDERATIONS

Next we turn to legal considerations to which you must pay attention during program development. As with marketing, legal issues have moved to the forefront of concerns that programmers need to make decisions about in order for successful programs to be realized. Articles about law and legal liability are appearing in professional magazines because new information is continually being compiled and applied to leisure settings.

Many claims of negligence involve the actual program design and content.[18] It is a responsibility of programmers to ensure that procedures are established to serve as specific guidelines for safety and accident prevention. These procedures must detail the responsibilities of both the programmer and of leaders involved in supervising leisure experiences and maintaining proper equipment. Agency policies and procedures may itemize prudent practices that must be followed in the planning and delivery of leisure programs.

Janna Rankin points out that programmers should develop a checklist of concerns that meet or exceed known safety standards for leisure experiences.[19] This checklist should be created during program development. Programmers need to be aware of potential problems and to determine methods for handling these problems prior to program implementation.

In identifying potential legal problems, it is helpful to review recent court cases. Arthur Frakt reports that the majority of cases concerning parks, recreation, sports, and games activities in which damages were awarded fall into the following categories:

1. Activities that, by their nature, involve high risk of serious injury (football, diving, trampolining, and to a lesser extent alpine skiing represent a disproportionately large number of cases).
2. Manmade or substantially man-altered activity sites (diving boards and swimming pools, prepared and groomed athletic fields with hidden holes or concealed sprinklers, prepared ski slopes, and modified "nature" areas).
3. Activities involving machinery or complex safety gear (snowmobiles, dune buggies, football helmets, and complicated games and gadgets).
4. Insufficient professional supervision, particularly of children.
5. Failure to use or understand approved emergency or first-aid techniques.
6. Failure to meet national or local standards or regulations for equipment and personnel.[20]

Risk management is the systematic prevention and reduction of accidents through the design and selection of safe equipment, elimination of unsafe conditions, and provision of information that effectively describes the nature of potential risks and ways to avoid injury.[21] The leisure programmer who has systematically considered the minimum legal and safety issues related to risk management has a process in operation that includes

- maintaining records of all accidents and steps taken to minimize their frequency and seriousness;
- conducting regular safety checks of any equipment or area involved in the program,
- running skill-building programs to qualify participants for more advanced activities;
- using staff members who are qualified to supervise the activity and who understand safety procedures; and
- involving the agency attorney in the activity planning process.[22]

It behooves programmers to stay alert to legal matters affecting programs. For example, programmers used to program under the assumption that signed liability waiver forms were protection against lawsuits. But it is a well-established fact today that waivers do not protect agencies or agency personnel if negligence can be proved. The knowledgeable programmer will accumulate safety information, integrate that information into policies and procedures, and see to it that these standards are adhered to. Being responsible in this way still allows for the planning and development of creative and innovative leisure experiences.

Beyond safety and liability, you are mandated by law as discussed in Chapter 3 (if not your conscience) to provide leisure programs that are equally accessible to all, without discrimination based on race, sex, or creed, particularly if you work for a public agency. Further, you are required to provide accessible and appropriate programs, services, and facilities to all individuals with disabilities. Those disabled persons who may be mainstreamed into programs for the general population must be allowed to participate freely and fully.

FINANCIAL CONSIDERATIONS

Leisure spending continues to increase even in times of inflation when personal budgets seem to grow tighter. Consumers whose purchasing power is diminished still pursue their leisure, and leisure professionals need to recognize that they work in a competitive environment in terms of obtaining a portion of those consumer dollars.

Programmers must also be aware of the responsibility they have to their leisure agencies for producing cost-effective programs. More and more programs today are being developed in ways that render individual experiences and/or programming units financially self-supporting. Assuming fiscal responsibility, establishing fees and charges, and implementing the budget are important parts of the leisure programmer's job during the program development phase.

A programmer's fiscal responsibility is usually structured by agency budgetary policies and procedures, which serve as guidelines for program budgeting. For example, the line-item budget (a budget classified by function or object) and the performance and program budget are two types of budgets frequently used by leisure service agencies. In functional budgets, the entire leisure program is viewed as one agency function and its costs are classified separately from those of other agency functions, such as administration. Object classification budgets organize the entire agency costs in categories such as personnel or supplies. Program costs are subsumed under those categories. Performance budgets provide more details about each subunit (each leisure experience offered) and are developed within function or object classification budgets. Program budgets emphasize programs deemed desirable by the agency and identify the costs of these programs in terms of the resources necessary to carry them out.[23] This type of budget includes program statements along with program and financial plans.

The form of budgeting your agency uses determines the type of budget that you will be responsible for producing during the development of your program. The budgeting process itself involves these three basic steps:

1. developing a budget plan expressed in dollars that anticipates revenues of a future period;
2. coordinating these dollar estimates into a well-balanced program; and
3. comparing actual performance with the estimated balance programs.[24]

Charging participant fees is an increasingly popular practice in leisure service agencies. In fact, some users think that the product must be inferior if it is free! The ability to assess the full costs associated with delivering a program is essential to making decisions about fees and charges.[25] In considering the full costs, the leisure programmer needs to itemize expenses related to factors like personnel, insurance premiums, upkeep or purchase of equipment and supplies, facility or space rental, and promotional efforts. Types of revenue producing activities that programmers use regularly are entrance fees, admission fees, rental fees, user fees, license and permit fees, special service fees, and sales. These are defined and examples are given in Figure 7-5.

Pricing methods can assist programmers in deciding the actual fee to be charged for a program or service. The two pricing methods we mention are examined in detail by Crompton.[26] In going-rate pricing, the programmer charges a fee that is consistent with the fee charged by other organizations for the same program and service. In demand-oriented pricing, the agency determines what price user groups are expected to pay for a program or service. The collection of fees and charges will in all probability be controlled by agency policies and procedures. So the programmer's responsibility is to implement agency methodology.

Besides fees and charges, programmers can look to other sources for revenue. In some instances, cooperative or synergetic forms of programming can compensate for budgetary restrictions.[27] For example, the Hershey Corporation cosponsors a track and field program in conjunction with public agencies. Corporate cosponsors provide program supplies, promotional resources, and training materials necessary for conducting local, regional, or national events; in exchange for its contribution, the corporation receives publicity. In other instances, program monies can be secured in the form of grants from government or philanthropic foundations. Donations from private industry or an individual can be secured to finance entire programs or some portion of user fees, such as "scholarships" for campers.

Once you understand the concept of fiscal responsibility, you will be expected to develop a budget that identifies incomes and expenditures consistent with agency operations. Then comes budget implementation. You will need to analyze your budget constantly as the program is being planned and offered. Changes may be required that can affect other tasks in program development. You may need to alter a program objective if enough funds are not forthcoming. Changes like this can occur during the actual delivery of the program or might come as the program concludes and before it is reoffered. What is certain is that budgeting consists of careful analysis and decision making. The better able you are to determine potential incomes and expenses, identify fixed and variable costs, and isolate direct and indirect costs that the program will incur, the better able you will be to make sound decisions throughout the budgetary process.

1. *Entrance fees* are levied to enter a large park, botanical garden, zoological garden, or other developed recreational or historical area. The areas are usually well defined, but are not necessarily enclosed. The entrance is usually the patron's first contact with the area and the area may contain additional facilities or activities for which fees are charged.

2. *Admission fees* are charges paid to enter a building, structure, or natural chamber. Facilities such as arenas, museums, conservatories, grandstands, and historic buildings usually offer an exhibit, show, ceremony, performance, demonstration, or use of special equipment. Entry and exit are normally controlled and attendance is regulated.

3. *Rental fees* are payments made for the privilege of exclusive use of tangible property of any kind. This fee gives the patron the right of enjoying all the advantages of using the property without consuming, destroying, or injuring it in any way. Examples include:

Cabins	Public address systems
Boats	Portable tables and chairs
Coin telescopes	Strollers
Portable platforms	Portable recreation equipment
Golf carts and clubs	Portable bleachers
Party rooms	Garden plots

4. *User fees* are charges made for the use of a facility or for participation in an activity. The patron usually shares the privilege with others. Examples include:

Fishing lake	League entrance fee
Bathing pool	Field use fee
Boat launch ramp	Skateboard area
Trapshooting range	Golf course
Archery range	Campsite

5. *Sales revenues* are obtained from the operation of stores, concessions, restaurants, or other types of retail operations and from the sale of merchandise or other property. Unconditional ownership of the item passes from the seller to the buyer with each sale. Examples include:

Packaged Items	*Merchandise*
Snacks & soft drinks	Picnic supplies
Cigarettes & tobacco	Souvenirs
	Educational materials
	Recreation/sport supplies

Figure 7–5 Types of Revenue-Producing Activities

From National Park Service, "Fees and Charges Handbook," Revised Edition (U.S. Department of Interior, 1982), pp. 31–32.

Food and Drink Service

Banquets
Catering
Snack bar/soda fountain

6. *License and permit fees* are similar. A license ordinarily involves written permission to perform an action such as fishing, fire building, or exhibiting wares but it seldom grants authority to occupy space or property. It is usually issued by a government agency.

7. *Special service fees* are made for supplying extraordinary articles, commodities, activities, or services as an accommodation to the public. These accommodations must be unusual in character and not normally considered a required governmental service. Examples include night lighting, pay telephones, class materials, and equipment storage.

Figure 7-5 *(Continued)*

Application Section. You have been asked to begin a new program in ceramics at your agency. Participants are willing to pay a price for the activity and your director has asked you to prepare a budget for the program.

You begin by checking prices in a handicrafts catalogue. You discover that modeling clay is $9.95 for 50 pounds and that Clay-Bake (a product that can be fired in a kitchen oven) is $4.75 for 5 pounds and $13.95 for 20 pounds. You figure that each participant will need at least 5 pounds of clay. Clay modeling tools are priced at $11.50 for a set of eight, and ceramic brushes are $10.95 for a set of six. Glazes run $1.50 per 2-ounce jar (one color) and $4.75 for an eight-color set of regular glazes. You know of a local agency that will rent you their kiln for 25 cents per piece to be fired, and you figure that each participant will create two or three pieces that need the kiln. Don't forget to consider leadership, publicity, and insurance costs.

Your task is to develop a program budget showing probable income and expense line items and totals. Indicate the cost per participant and the number of participants who need to pay and attend in order for your activity to break even financially.

INTERRELATED NATURE OF TASKS

Program development is a critical phase of the leisure programming cycle. The tasks involved are many and varied. Each requires special attention to detail by the programmer and often is carried out in conjunction with other tasks. The interrelated nature of the tasks is what makes planning and decision making most difficult. Securing the right leadership can contribute to marketing because some leisure programs can be promoted by the leaders involved. The program format can have an effect on leadership skills and abilities sought in recruitment. A new law that mandates special requirements for programming facilities can divert monies that the programmer may have intended to direct elsewhere, or it could require that additional policies be established. Agency policies and procedures can influence program objectives. The cost of replacing program materials and supplies can be prohibitive.

You need to be aware of and accept this interactive quality in programming leisure experiences. While you might prefer to take on one task in program development and complete it before moving on to the next, in reality this will not occur. The programmer must direct the entire process, much like the maestro of an orchestra, and must see to it that all tasks are fine-tuned and performed in consort with one another.

SUMMARY

The setting in which a leisure programmer works creates a philosophical base and organizational framework from which programs evolve and in which decisions are made. Decision making is an activity that underlies all the tasks associated with program development: formulating objectives; determining program format; following policies and procedures; scheduling facilities; optimizing leadership; using marketing strategies; and carrying out legal and financial responsibilities. All these program development tasks are interrelated, and decisions about each affect the others. From this point, the programmer moves to the next phase of the leisure programming cycle: program implementation.

FOOTNOTES

1. Harold Koontz and Cyril O'Donnell, *Essentials of Management,* 2nd ed. (New York: McGraw-Hill Book Company, 1978), p. 56.
2. William F. Glueck, *Management,* 2nd ed. (Hinsdale, Ill.: The Dryden Press, 1980), pp. 395–402.
3. Christopher R. Edginton and John G. Williams, *Productive Management of Leisure Service Organizations: A Behavioral Approach* (New York: John Wiley and Sons, Inc., 1978), p. 169. Copyright © 1978 by John Wiley & Sons, Inc. Reprinted by permission of John Wiley & Sons, Inc.
4. Ruth V. Russell, *Planning Programs in Recreation* (St. Louis: The C. V. Mosby Company, 1982), p. 119.
5. Carol A. Peterson and Scout L. Gunn, *Therapeutic Recreation Program Design: Principles and Procedures,* 2nd ed. (Englewood Cliffs, N.J.: Prentice-Hall, Inc., 1984), p. 182.
6. Richard G. Kraus, *Recreation Today: Program Planning and Leadership,* 2nd ed. (Glendale, Ill.: Scott, Foresman and Company, 1977), pp. 84–85.
7. Richard G. Kraus, Gaylene M. Carpenter, and Barbara J. Bates, *Recreation Leadership and Supervision: Guidelines for Professional Development* (Philadelphia: Saunders College Publishing Company, 1981), pp. 91–92.
8. Koontz and O'Donnell, *Essentials of Management,* p. 440.
9. Ibid., p. 440.
10. Edginton and Williams, *Productive Management,* p. 254.
11. Reprinted by permission of the *Harvard Business Review.* Theodore Levitt, "Marketing Myopia," *Harvard Business Review,* September/October 1975, p. 3.

12. Edginton and Williams, *Productive Management*, p. 255.

13. Dennis R. Howard and John L. Crompton, *Financing, Managing and Marketing Recreation and Park Resources* (Dubuque, Iowa: William C. Brown Company, Publishers, 1980), p. 320.

14. Ibid., p. 317.

15. Ibid., p. 331.

16. Philip Kotler, "Strategies for Introducing Marketing into Nonprofit Organizations," *Journal of Marketing*, 43 (January 1979), 37–44.

17. Howard and Crompton, *Financing, Managing and Marketing*, p. 332.

18. Ibid., p. 175.

19. Janna Rankin, "Legal Risks and Bold Programming," *Parks & Recreation*, July 1977, p. 68. Reprinted by special permission of the National Recreation and Park Association.

20. Arthur Frakt, "Putting Recreation Programming and Liability in Perspective," *Parks & Recreation*, December 1979, p. 44. Reprinted by special permission of the National Recreation and Park Association.

21. Seymour M. Gold, "Risk Management in Public Playgrounds," *Journal of Park and Recreation Administration*, 1, no. 3 (1983), 3.

22. Rankin, "Legal Risks," p. 68.

23. Edginton and Williams, *Productive Management*, pp. 299–306.

24. Ibid., pp. 281–82.

25. National Park Service, *Fees and Charges Handbook*, Revised Edition (U.S. Department of Interior, 1982), p. 27.

26. John L. Crompton, "How to Find the Right Price," *Parks & Recreation*, March 1981, pp. 32–33. Reprinted by special permission of the National Recreation and Park Association.

27. Kraus, Carpenter, and Bates, *Recreation Leadership*, p. 261.

REFERENCES

Edginton, Christopher R., David M. Compton, and Carole J. Hanson, *Recreation and Leisure Programming: A Guide to the Professional*, Philadelphia: Saunders College Publishing Company, 1980.

Farrell, Patricia, and Herberta M. Lundegren, *The Process of Recreation Programming: Theory and Technique* (2nd ed.). New York: John Wiley and Sons, Inc., 1983.

Mundy, Jean, and Linda Odum, *Leisure Education Theory and Practice*, New York: John Wiley and Sons, Inc., 1979.

Niepoth, E. William, *Leisure Leadership: Working with People in Recreation and Park Settings*. Englewood Cliffs, N.J.: Prentice-Hall, Inc., 1983.

Russell, Ruth V., *Planning Programs in Recreation*. St. Louis: The C. V. Mosby Company, 1982.

chapter 8

Program Implementation
Phase Three of the
Leisure Programming Cycle

INTRODUCTION

At this point in the leisure programming cycle, the programmer is well engaged in the process of creating or facilitating the leisure experience. Program implementation is the actual provision or delivery of the leisure experience to participants. Having moved through needs assessment and program development, the programmer now stands at the brink of creating what Clarence Brown refers to as the exciting blend of experiences needed to motivate and drive the individual into the search for happiness and self-development in order to attain self-satisfaction.[1]

There are many factors operating in contemporary society that affect the kinds of programs that are implemented. While some factors might be viewed as fads, others represent significant changes in the life-styles and wants of leisure consumers over the past twenty years. A genuine cultural revolution, according to Daniel Yankelovich, is one that makes a decisive break with the shared meanings of the past, particularly those that relate to the deepest questions of the purpose and nature of human life. He writes:

> In the 1960s the search for new meanings was largely confined to young Americans on the nation's campuses and was masked by the political protests against the war in Southeast Asia. When the war ended in the early 1970s, the campuses quieted and the challenge to traditional mores spread beyond college life to find a variety of expression in the larger society: in the women's movement; in a further expansion of the consumer, environmental, and quality-of-life movements (small is beautiful); in the emphasis on self-help, localism, and participation; in the hospice movement; in the flood of books on cultivating the self; in the questioning of the scientific/technological world view; in greater acceptance of sexuality (nudity, sex outside of marriage,

homosexuality, and open eroticism of varied sorts); in a new preoccupation with the body and physical fitness; in a revival of interest in nature and the natural; and, above all, in a search for the full, rich life, ripe with leisure, new experience, and enjoyment, as a replacement for the orderly, work-centered attitude of earlier decades.[2]

We can note reflections of these cultural changes in leisure programs that are being implemented. Three specific examples follow. The Eugene, Oregon, Parks and Recreation Department coordinates a noon-hour fitness program in department store lounges, bank conference rooms, hospitals, dance studios, and government facilities for downtown employees.[3] The YM/YWHA Branch of the Philadelphia Jewish Y and Centers operates the Institute of Awareness. This program allows participants to examine their relationships, their dreams, their assertiveness, their friendships, their sexuality, dying, and contemporary family life. At the University of California at Davis, the Student Affairs Office offers a packaged workshop on the "superwoman syndrome." This program is geared toward dispelling the myth that combining career and family is an easy task for the working woman. These and many other leisure programs in operation today address the human search for new meanings and provide environments conducive to obtaining happiness and satisfaction.

The numerous types of programs that are now being implemented cover a very wide spectrum of leisure possibilities. This is partly the result of the diverse nature of the leisure field. There are many different kinds of agencies and businesses in the leisure industry producing many different kinds of programs and services. This diversity is also partly due to the wide variety of the types of leisure experiences that these businesses and agencies have traditionally drawn on in leisure programming. Rather than classify and itemize each program type in great detail, a task that other recreation and leisure studies authors have done exceedingly well, we will discuss leisure program patterns more generally.

LEISURE PROGRAM PATTERNS

A leisure program pattern is an established way of providing leisure experiences. Program patterns may be physical, intellectual, cultural, social, environmental, or personally developmental. They usually conform to a specific design or scheme. While each program pattern has a distinct character all its own, it is also broad enough to incorporate elements of other patterns.

To clarify this, let's say that you wish to offer swimming. This activity is usually classified as "physical." However, swimming offers a much broader context for programming leisure experiences. Swimming can be part of the social pattern if it involves lounging around a pool with others; or it can be part of the environmental pattern if it involves taking a dip in a river during a hot backpacking excursion; or it can be decidedly part of the physical pattern if it involves swimming laps. To classify swimming only as physical limits the broader potential of the activity for the participant and for the programmer wishing to integrate program patterns. When you implement a particular program pattern, you need to be aware that elements from the other program patterns are being included. Let's look at each program pattern in order to examine them in terms of their programming potential and in light of our previous discussion of cultural changes.

Physical Program Pattern.   The physical program pattern is one that is used often and successfully in leisure programming. What many considered to be a fitness boom a few years ago seems closer to a fitness ethic today. While interest in a given sport—say, tennis—may fluctuate, there is evidence that the participant replaces one physical activity with another. An individual may lose interest in a particular physical activity, but not in physical activities or movement altogether; different physical pursuits may be substituted. Persons may switch from team sports to individual sports or dance depending on the season, time, location, availability, expense, and so on.

Fitness centers are found in most urban and suburban areas; the more populated the area, the more centers. An increasing number of employers are providing exercise rooms and equipment at the workplace for their employees. Both the YMCA and the YWCA have traditionally offered programs focusing on physical development. Public recreation departments, colleges, and universities have long sponsored recreational sport activities, tournaments, and leagues. Television, both commercial and cable, provides exercise shows so that viewers can work out at home. Even movie stars produce video cassettes, tapes, and records for fitness and body building. Students help finance recreation centers at colleges and universities in order to have a place to pursue a variety of physical recreation activities beyond traditional sports. New Games staff members continue to cross the country giving training programs in how to play their noncompetitive games. Picnics and gatherings feature contests and relays. Dance as a physical pursuit is becoming a recreation program area for private enterprise. Swimming is consistently at the top of the list of most frequently pursued physical recreation activities. Various groups sponsor triathalons.

Clearly, the appetite of North Americans for physical recreation is not waning. The desires for challenge, cooperation, and competition, to achieve one's personal best, and to experience the enjoyment, well-being, and satisfaction obtained through physical recreation are strong motivators. Informed programmers will want to implement many activities from this leisure program pattern.

Intellectual Program Pattern.   Programmers do considerably less programming in the intellectual program pattern than in the physical program pattern. One reason for this imbalance is the strong tradition in the profession of emphasizing programming in the physical area. Another reason is that individuals tend to seek intellectual leisure experiences independently, in a very self-directed manner, and often from sources outside the organized park, recreation, and leisure field. When individuals specifically seek learning experiences, they are apt to find what they are looking for in the strength and diversity of the educational community, which provides established and well-defined learning environments. The Georgia

Center for Continuing Education at the University of Georgia, for example, regularly offers inexpensive noncredit "courses" in leisure activities to members of the local community and residents of surrounding counties; areas of study range from microcomputers to foreign languages to short-story writing. The Adult Education Program in Columbia, Missouri, provides similar leisure opportunities, ranging from understanding automobiles to art and dance. Further, people may find their intellectual stimulation outside of any organized system. Reading is an excellent example of a very popular leisure pursuit that does not require an organized delivery system to enable the individual to participate. The increased purchase of electronic video equipment for home educational use is another example.

Lest programmers feel embarrased that their profession is not doing all that it could be doing in intellectual programming, let's remember that they are in business to encourage leisure, not educational experiences. While their primary focus is leisure, they also need to recognize that in leisure people learn. In this way, programmers do play a strong role in the intellectual development of their constituents. This pattern of leisure programming is perhaps found in all the others to some extent. For example, someone joins a softball team and learns about teamwork. Or a Seattle citizen attends a block party in a Vancouver neighborhood and learns about Canadian culture. If it is agreed that learning occurs throughout one's lifetime and that in leisure one learns, then programmers must also realize that the intellectual programming pattern is subtly in operation all the time.

When you implement leisure experiences that have intellectual development and learning as the primary focus, you may see the following kinds of programs in operation: a workshop on how to use a home computer, or a computer camp program for children; various special-interest classes, such as Gourmet Cooking, Conversational Spanish, Mastering Trivial Pursuit, Training Your Dog, Designing Your Backyard, Stamp Collecting for Fun; or any number of other activities that have a definite concentration on learning new leisure skills. Sedentary activities such as cards, word games, puzzles, and table and board games encourage people to use their intellectual capacities. Programs designed to train and develop volunteers for leisure service agencies fall into the intellectual program pattern. Finally, experiences in leisure education—those activities aimed at increasing participant leisure awareness and leisure functioning—may also be part of this programming pattern.

Cultural Program Pattern. Fourth of July news stories indicate the full strength and variety of the American people's interest in cultural leisure experiences. This nationwide celebration can include a harbor festival featuring Scandinavian music in New York City; thousands watching fireworks from Mount Rushmore in the Black Hills of South Dakota and in the Cotton Bowl in Dallas; country and western music at the May Fair Grounds in Dixon, California; basketball star Julius Erving reading excerpts from the Declaration of Independence and a Mummers' Parade in Phila-delphia; bathtub races and watermelon seed-spitting contests in Springfield, Illinois; and thousands of people running the Peachtree Roadrace in

Atlanta, Georgia. Barbara Palmer, citing U.S. Travel Data Center figures, reported that 38 million Americans celebrate the Fourth of July. "And only in America" she states, "could the celebrations of our common heritage reflect such diversity of interests and tastes. What they have in common— from the small towns to the big cities, from VFW halls to country club picnics—is a characteristically American mix of traditional values and pop culture."[4]

Far less clearly defined forces also give rise to cultural programming. Trips and excursions to theatrical and musical performances are often sponsored. Arts and crafts skill-building activities and fairs such as the Hiawassee Mountain Fair in Georgia are conducted. The city of Chicago puts on an annual tasting of Chicago foods at a waterfront fair. Community-based theater and dance groups attract performers and audiences. Music seekers find a variety of offerings, from massive concerts held in stadiums to entertainments on a smaller scale. Large numbers annually turn out for group singing of Handel's *Messiah;* smaller numbers participate in folk singing and perform in barbershop quartets. A wide range of dance programs exist that allow participants to experience many different forms of expression, again as either performers or viewers. Programs reflecting ethnic or national cultural heritages draw leisure consumers from all segments of the population; Hispanic celebrations in downtown Los Angeles are examples of this. Museums, art galleries, and historical monuments and districts (such as Savannah, Georgia, and Richmond, Virginia, which holds an Easter Parade in the Fan District) consistently attract visitors seeking to meet or develop their cultural interests.

Social Program Pattern.   Many agencies by tradition offer programs in the social pattern. One case is the YMCA, which was started in the mid-1800s by a young man who believed that the decadent social life of London threatened the morals of other young men and that there was a need for social alternatives. Organized social leisure experiences continue to be one focus of YMCA programs.

Leisure service organizations give the social program pattern wide exposure because it takes into account clientele wishes for social interaction. As Kraus states, social recreation tends to consist of the ordinary, the familiar, the informal and casual experiences and "The unique value of social recreation is its stress on informal and relaxed participation and group acceptance. It helps to draw people out, encourages them to take on meaningful social roles, and promotes a positive, accepting group climate that values human worth and dignity."[5]

The social program pattern is used in many different situations. Leisure environments that encourage and facilitate self-directed social interaction have been created and are being maintained. For example, a simple park bench placed in a comfortable location can encourage retirees to interact. Public restaurants that encourage leisure dining are another example. Examples needing some leadership include agency-organized clubs for youth; billiard games for young women in juvenile detention homes; company picnics; a senior center's Retired Senior Volunteer Program; a local street fair for residents of a psychiatric care facility; or a group of racquetball club members convening in the lounge to view the Superbowl on the club's wide-screen TV. The programming potential inherent in this pattern is limited only by the programmer's imagination. Some of the most innovative leisure experiences to date have evolved from the social program pattern base.

Environmental Program Pattern.   Leisure service professionals have established a fine record on sensitive use of the environment as a basis for leisure experiences. The increase in environmental awareness throughout North America has spawned many new programs that are being offered in a fashion respectful of the environment. Programmers need to remain mindful of the fragile balance at work in the ecosystem as they develop leisure experiences in the environmental program pattern.

The well-developed public park systems that crisscross North America provide outdoor settings for implementing leisure experiences. These areas and facilities are maintained for self-directed public use, such as picnicking, family and friendship camping, and backpacking. Park rangers or interpreters may provide leisure experiences that focus on the environmental or historical uniqueness of the site and may offer excursions through the park. Programmers can either implement programs themselves for their constituents or take advantage of established park programs coordinated by other park personnel.

Organized camping, resident and day, falls within this pattern. These leisure experiences are usually provided by private businesses or public agencies that use camping as an extension of their comprehensive leisure programs. Camps may offer a wide variety of outdoor leisure experiences or may focus their efforts on a particular theme, such as kayaking, outdoor crafts, rock climbing, and even music or soccer.

This program pattern probably includes the majority of the high-risk recreational experiences that are implemented today. The natural environment, along with the obvious sense of adventure and challenge that exists in the outdoors, has much to do with this. Other programs in this pattern are urban nature programs that extend to participants the opportunity to discover and interact with the ecosystem in densely populated areas; outdoor adventure operations, located on many college campuses and in the private sector, that make available equipment, supplies, and excursions; and river-rafting companies that provide direct leadership for beginning river rafters and rental resources for the more advanced. Outdoor spaces and locations are also set aside by utility companies for public use. Earth Day and other conservation-oriented activities that are designed to increase public awareness and responsibility toward the environment are sometimes implemented by local leisure personnel. Seemingly hundreds more examples could be given, but our intent is only to demonstrate the range of possible leisure experiences that can be provided with the environmental program pattern.

Personal Development Program Pattern.   This program pattern has emerged and taken on strength in recent years. Leisure programmers have responded to this aspect of the cultural revolution by implementing leisure experiences designed to add meaning and self-fulfillment to people's lives.

Yankelovich's studies show that nearly 80 percent of the population is engaged in the search for self-fulfillment. "On top of traditional demands for material well-being, seekers of self-fulfillment impose new demands for intangibles—creativity, leisure, autonomy, pleasure, participation, community, adventure, vitality, stimulation, tender loving care. To the efficiency of technological society they wish to add joy of living."[6]

Further evidence points to discrepancies between the importance people attach to certain aspects of their lives and their level of satisfaction with attaining or not attaining success in these areas. Researchers have noted wide satisfaction gaps in the areas of economic security, physical fitness, the use of one's mind and abilities, a positive view of self, and control of one's time.[7] Table 8-A shows the results of one recent nationwide poll conducted by Louis Harris and Associates.[8]

Leisure provides a vehicle for human development and self-fulfillment. Using the personal development program pattern, programmers can implement experiences that can add to both. To illustrate, let us reexamine the satisfaction gap described in Table 8-A in terms of leisure programming. Lectures and workshops dealing with financial planning and investments and career options and information are held. Physical fitness activities, facilities, equipment, and wellness programs have proliferated. There are individual and group experiences designed to assist participants to identify ways in which present and potential leisure experiences can further develop their minds or allow them to increase their skills and abilities. Self-help sessions focusing on dressing for success, substance abuse, or successful life strategies give participants the information, resources and even support groups that they need in order to feel more positive. Information services or seminars on burnout, stress, and personal time management provide participants with resources to better structure their time.

The personal development program pattern is one that we feel will become more common in the future. There are also linkages to the other program patterns. Stress management is an obvious example. When programmers implement programs in a way that provides the participants with leisure experiences designed to meet their desires for self-development

---

Many Americans say it's "very important" to have some of the following things. Fewer think they personally have them.

	Very Important	Very Satisfied	Gap
Economic security	80%	23%	−57
Physical fitness	89%	41%	−48
A life that makes full use of mind and abilities	93%	49%	−44
Positive view of self	91%	54%	−37
Full control of our time	75%	43%	−32

Table 8-A The Satisfaction "Gap"

From David Fink, "From Queens to California, We Want Help," *USA Today*, April 11, 1983. Section A, p. 2.

and self-fulfillment, they are first and foremost using the personal development program pattern.

INTEGRATING PROGRAM PATTERNS

As programmers develop program goals and objectives, rarely are desired outcomes limited to only one pattern. We mentioned earlier that elements from each pattern are incorporated into one another. This occurs because programs usually have more than one outcome and because programmers have traditionally fostered ways to integrate programming concepts in order to create better, more holistic programs. To conclude this section, we will look at three programs that have used more than one program pattern in the provision of leisure experiences.

The first example demonstrates the implementation of the social and intellectual program pattern. This pattern was implemented in a program designed to promote leisure education and leisure awareness. Called "Recreation Rendezvous," this day-long event was held in a shopping mall and offered the following activities: personality and leisure interest inventories; tests for physical fitness; a relaxation tent; a crafts fair where mall visitors could make things; risk activities such as "clothes try-ons"; a booth offering information on recreational eating for nutrition; sports areas for both indoor and outdoor activities; and an 8-foot-high enclosed nature booth with animal, rain, and howling wind sounds.[9]

The second example demonstrates combined use of the physical and the personal development program patterns. Michelle Celarier noted that hundreds of corporations offer wellness programs to employees in the hope of trimming health insurance costs, lowering absenteeism, and raising productivity. She reports that a typical wellness program consists of varying combinations of employee access to jogging paths, exercise machines, aerobic dance instruction, classes in stress-reduction techniques, smoking-cessation seminars, counseling for alcoholics, and nutrition advice such as tips on cooking without salt.[10]

The Lifestyle Information Network (LINK) is a special program of the Memorial Union at the University of California at Davis. This last example draws upon the physical, intellectual, social, and personal development leisure program patterns. LINK promotes healthful living, personal balance, and well-being by offering leisure experiences which integrate physical, intellectual, emotional, social, vocational, and value development. LINK's "Peak Week" ran for six days. It featured a multitude of programs relating to the various dimensions in LINK. Consistent with the theme, activities included Peak Performance (recreational sport clinics); the Courage to Peak (focusing on persons with disabilities); The Peak of Social Responsibility (volunteerism); and Peak Your Feet (foot massages).

The programmer who manages a comprehensive leisure program will find alternating between program patterns to be a common and desirable occurrence because it allows the establishment of a well-rounded, all-embracing program of leisure experiences for the clientele. On the other hand, programmers working for an organization with a single focus (for example, a sports group), or those who hold a departmental responsibility in a large agency (for example, arts and crafts director), may find that the majority of the programs they implement are from one pattern. Whatever the case, you will want to seek an appropriate balance, attempt to implement diversity and variety in programs, and remain flexible to meet the changing needs and wants of your participants.

Application Section. You are the leisure programmer for a newly opened residential care facility catering to mentally retarded adults in a city of 135,000. There are ten residents, ages 32 to 59, functioning at the fifth- and sixth-grade levels. There are six women and four men. The on-site facilities conducive to leisure programs include a large backyard and a good-sized family room. Off-site facilities include a neighborhood park eight blocks away and a small shopping mall four blocks away. Which of the program patterns we have just discussed might be most appropriate to use in programming leisure experiences for this population? For each program pattern selected, indicate how specific activities, facilities, and services can be programmed and implemented.

ADJUNCT FACTORS TO PROGRAM PATTERNS

We said earlier that program patterns are established ways to provide leisure experiences. There are some adjunct factors that programmers need to consider in implementing leisure experiences. While most programmers might prefer to select a pattern and then build program segments around that pattern, there are instances when certain realities take precedence. These adjunct factors include the ages of participants, the geographical area in which the program is located, the race or ethnicity of the clientele, and the homogeneity of the group. Each of these factors has the capability of altering the nature of the program pattern implemented.

Ages of Participants. Chronological age, or stage in the life-course, and its relationship to leisure within the context of human development are discussed in Chapter 2. In this section, our intent is to suggest good professional practice based upon the theories and research findings presented in Chapter 2. This is especially important because it has been customary for many years to implement leisure programs according to the participants' ages. Everybody knows that children like physical programs, youths like social programs, and adults like cultural programs best! Luckily, these assumptions are no longer the sole basis for program planning and implementation. Age myopia has been replaced by less stereotypical thinking, needs assessment, and the successful application of a variety of intergenerational programs. Innovative leisure programmers are using the work of developmental psychologists to guide their programming, along with the results of systematic needs assessments. Senior citizens like and are able to "rough it"; children enjoy interacting with sophisticated micro-computers; adults are playing "survival games"; and youths are interested in career exploration. Implementing programs based on age-related stereotypes does work, especially in terms of competitive team sports. But if you rely only on this kind of information, you will limit the leisure choices of your participants.

What conclusions can we draw about age? The age factor in leisure programming is one that programmers need to be aware of in terms of health and safety, but not in a manner that arbitrarily denies an otherwise deserving person access to a leisure experience. Programmers need to realize that while the North American population is getting older (the fastest-growing age group is between 35 and 44), less leisure programming for those in middle age is available from public and nonprofit organizations than from the private sector. The application of leisure education concepts, for example, is very important to this clientele group, as its members may be involved in reappraising their values.

Geographical Area.   Common sense indicates that the influence of geographical area on program pattern is related to the part of the country in which the program takes place and the geographical features of that region (mountainous or flat, rural or urban, seashore or desert, and so on). The local population is also a factor.

Various areas have unique features about them. The cultural amenities available in metropolitan New York City, for example, are far more numerous than those of Stillwater, Oklahoma. Location of the agency near a major metropolis can increase the programming options available in the intellectual or cultural patterns. Rock climbing or white-water rafting is more readily pursued in Washington State than in the Texas Panhandle. Outdoor waterslides are in use for more months of the year in warmer climates. Year-round downhill skiing can occur in only a few areas. We could go on, but the point is that activities to some extent are dependent on where the agency or business is located.

Local population, as an influence on program pattern, can mean the population of a neighborhood, an entire city, or a region, or the members of a particular organization. Social programs in Salt Lake City, Utah, the headquarters of the Mormon Church, are likely to have a different ethos than programs in the "anything goes" area around Venice Beach, California. Finally, because of membership interest, physical programs are more comprehensively developed in sports-fitness centers than in 4H Clubs, for example.

Frequently, the influences of the location and the population will interact. Two cities in southeast Pennsylvania, Norristown and Paoli, both have YMCA programs. Even though they are less than ten miles apart and belong to the same national organization, their programs have a very different look. The Norristown YMCA central branch is located in the deteriorating downtown. Its membership fluctuates and is typically made up of people with low and middle incomes. In contrast, the Upper Main Line YMCA is located in the hills above Paoli in a tree-shrouded area. Membership is steady, consisting of people in the middle- to upper-income levels. The facilities have a country club quality. The geographical factors of both location and population affect the application of program patterns for these two YMCAs.

Race or Ethnicity of Clientele.   Leisure is both a cultural product and a producer of culture.[11] Ethnicity is the ethnic similarity and affiliation of a group of people who are part of the larger society. The members of an ethnic group share a historical, cultural, linguistic, religious, and social background that is distinguishable from that of other groups. Because of these shared differences, the ethnicity in a given leisure service area or of an agency's membership will influence program patterns. Leisure programs that reflect the ethnic heritage of participants serve as a mechanism to further reinforce cultural identity. Multicultural, multiethnic leisure opportunities are thought to enhance the richness of diversity found in North America, allowing people to take pride in their heritage while having the joy of sharing it with others.

Most racial and ethnic groups in North America are concentrated in the larger metropolitan areas. Examples of these groups include Asians, blacks, Hispanics, Irish, Italians, Jews, and native Americans in the United States, and French Canadians and Eskimos and other native American groups in Canada. Some ethnic groups live in more rural areas, such as the Amish and Mennonite populations, some native American tribes, and migratory farm workers of Hispanic descent. Kraus points out that in those communities or regions where there are substantial numbers of residents of an identifiable ethnic or national background different from that of the majority population, it is essential that full efforts be made to recognize and meet their special cultural or ethnic needs and interests.[12]

Leisure programmers who implement leisure experiences that capitalize on ethnicity will find two notable outcomes. First, the leisure experiences will tend to strengthen national or minority group identification; and second, the programs will enrich the experiences of those participants not in the national or minority group by making them more aware of the country's diverse cultural and ethnic heritage.

Homogeneous Groups.   The last major adjunct factor that can alter the character of the program pattern implemented is homogeneous groups. These groups have similarities in structure or quality. We will explore two kinds of homogeneous groups: subcultural groups and situational groups. The population of a *subcultural group* is made up mostly of people who have chosen their affiliation. Individuals in *situational groups* in all probability did not choose affiliation. You need to be aware of subcultural and situational groups and to consider their leisure wants and preferences when implementing programs.

Subcultural groups reflect the variety of lifestyle choices and decisions that can be made in contemporary North America. They form a distinctive group within the larger social group. According to John R. Kelly, "While there are common symbols, language, and behavioral conventions in a leisure subculture, there are also signs of individuality and uniqueness."[13]

The potency of cultural changes has left many people with a feeling of separateness; as a result, identification with and acceptance in subgroups is taking on new meaning. The ongoing studies conducted by Yankelovich show this increased desire for acceptance and identification.

In 1973, the "Search for Community" social trend, whose status my firm measures each year, stood at 32 percent, meaning that roughly one-third of Americans felt an intense need to compensate for the impersonal and threatening aspects of modern life by seeking mutual identification with others based on close ethnic ties or ties of shared interests, needs, backgrounds, age, or values. By the beginning of the 1980s, the number of Americans deeply involved in the Search for Community had increased from 32 percent to 47 percent, a large and significant jump in a few short years.[14]

What are some of the subcultural groups that programmers need to consider? They are singles, members of the Moral Majority, Parents Without Partners, members of Mensa, members of sororities and fraternities, Vietnam veterans, self-help advocates, and surfers, to name just a few. To illustrate how subculture can alter program patterns, let's examine one group more closely: single adults.

It is reported that by 1990 the number of American households composed of unattached people (never married, divorced, separated, or widowed) will nearly equal the number of households of married people.[15] The number of single parents with children is also increasing. Tom Rogers cites the following statistics from the book *How We Live* written in 1983 by Victor Fuchs: "Nearly 25 percent of households in the USA have only one parent. And 2.8 percent of children in the USA live with a never-married mother—more than triple the percentage of 1970. Forty percent of children born since 1975 will live with only one parent at some stage of their lives before age 18."[16]

From this and other data we can infer that families are in a period of transition and diversity. In particular, households composed of a single person only, and households composed of a female single head-of-household (and dependents), are increasing. Households headed by single women, with or without dependents, are increasing, and when two adults are present (that is, a married couple), the likelihood that both people are employed is increasing. Obviously, periods of being single are occurring much more frequently for persons at all stages of life.

Single adults do have many of the same kinds of activities as their coupled peers. They read, travel, care for their homes, and watch TV. They also have many of the same social and psychological needs as others: love, affiliation, esteem, and so on. But because they are single, they may not have *long-term*, intimate, caring relationships with other adults not related to them by blood. So it is through leisure that some of their needs and interests may be expressed and met.[17]

In what kind of leisure programs are single adults participating? Commercial leisure enterprises have responded well to the singles market. The travel industry, noting that 40 percent of America's pleasure travelers are not married,[18] has responded with packaged tours, cruises, and weekend trips for singles.

Church-affiliated bodies are sponsoring programs for single adults. The Catholic Center in Athens, Georgia, once or twice every three months offers a weekend retreat for single adult members. Retreats are always held away from the home community and generally have a theme. Built around working people's schedules, they run from Friday evening until Sunday afternoon, for a total cost of fifty dollars, excluding transportation. Within the course of the weekend there are structured mixers that help people to meet one another, discussions on the theme of the retreat, and informal conversations about current events, social issues, and personal issues. Personal issues that may be addressed are feelings about divorce, choosing to be single, taking steps toward commitment, sexual mores, and the different meanings of love. There is also unstructured free time, group activities ranging from recreational team sports to hayrides and barbeques, and special events. The emphasis is on intermixing with others in a sincere, friendship-oriented way.

Lastly, employers are supplying recreation programs for both single and married employees. The bonds that are made during formal work-time interaction may be strengthened and deepened during informal free-time interaction.

According to *U.S. News & World Report*, a growing number of career women are delaying marriage until their late thirties and early forties.[19] "As their numbers grow, the live-alones—most of whom reside in or near big cities—are altering the nation's housing and leisure markets."[20] As evidence of this, several examples of such changes are cited, such as a condominium complex in Coconut Grove, Florida. This complex was designed, according to the marketing director, for single professionals who want to be able to go out the front door and jog, play tennis, run by the marina, and eat in the restaurants.

Advertising agencies on New York's Madison Avenue view singles as a burgeoning new consumer market with substantial discretionary income. They concluded from a study that singles, "especially those between 18 and 34, are above-average consumers of such commodities as liquor, stereo equipment, books, foreign cars, most sporting goods and casual apparel. They are also more likely to shop in gourmet and health-food stores and dine out."[21]

Turning our attention briefly toward single parents, we see successfully implemented leisure programs coming from public and private groups. The highly touted Parents Without Partners provides recreational and other programs geared to the single parent.[22] Other agencies implement leisure experiences directed to the parent and his or her children together. The YMCA's Indian Guide and Indian Maiden programs are examples of this. Programs that are developed around facilities such as parks and playgrounds afford opportunities for parent-led or shared leisure experiences. Numerous family camping programs no longer require that both parents attend.

Situational groups tend to be made up of people who did not choose membership. Among the subgroups included are the disabled, the unemployed, the economically disadvantaged, and displaced homemakers.

Almost twenty years ago, Thomas Goodale warned the leisure profession that it may be providing services for the wrong people. "We find among both young and old, that those best prepared to use leisure have the least leisure available, while those least prepared have the most leisure available."[23] Most people in situational groups do have vast amounts of free time (or, as it is sometimes called, enforced leisure). Being chronically unemployed, for example, has more to do with chronic depression and emotional instability than with prior training and ability.[24] You might do well to implement more experiences from the personal development program pattern for this situational group.

The displaced homemaker represents a situational group composed of about 5 million women, according to the latest figures.

> The displaced homemaker is a woman over 35, often in her 40s, 50s, or 60s, who needs paid work later in life after many years in the home. She has lost the support of a spouse through death, divorce, desertion, disability, or separation. Once children are grown, Aid to Families with Dependent Children and Social Security are no longer available and Social Security cannot be resumed until she is sixty-two.[25]

There are few examples of leisure programs geared to this growing group. A model one is in operation in San Jose, California. The San Jose YWCA's Career Outreach Program specifically focuses on the displaced homemaker. The program offers group counseling, social interaction, networking and support groups, and career identification and career development.

Application Section. Form small groups of no more than five people. Review the several subcultural groups that were identified in the homogeneous group section of this chapter. Based upon the explanation of subcultural groups, decide if there are others that could be added to our list. If so, add these to make up your total list of subcultural groups. Next, agree upon the selection of one of the groups you would like to explore further in your own discussion. Taking fifteen minutes, name and list leisure programs that would seem to be appropriate to your chosen group. Then identify the kind of leisure agency or business that can most effectively implement each leisure program that you have listed.

OTHER CHARACTERISTICS

So far, we have looked at six leisure program patterns and four major adjunct factors that relate to these program patterns. Over the years, as part of the profession's attempt to understand people's participation in recreational activities, other characteristics such as sex, education level, income, occupation, and marital and family status have been studied by leisure researchers to see if they account for differences in leisure pursuits. The results of these studies reveal that esssentially these characteristics do not account for much of the differences in style of leisure participation. As Kelly states:

> When a heterogeneous sample and activity list are employed, clear distinctions between activity types based on common participation and participant characteristics such as age, sex, education level, occupation, income, marital status, or race do not emerge. Only with the male-dominated youth team sports and the sex difference of drinking are even moderate correlations produced.[26]

Knowledge of these characteristics and major adjunct factors has proven helpful to program planning and leisure resource management. But these characteristics are by no means absolute determinants of peoples' leisure behavior. Once again, we caution that this information should not be used to prohibit persons from recreational participation. Nor should these data be used to limit leisure choices arbitrarily, in a manner reflecting stereotypical assumptions about people based on one or two observable characteristics. Kelly suggests:

> Styles and contexts of engagement, both in the core and differentiated choices, may change as the personal and social identities of the social self change through the life course. . . . A preferred model of leisure styles would then include both activities that are accessible and common to a large proportion of the adult population and those that are selected for a variety of reasons and are influenced by a person's complex socialization history. This model would still have a place for the individual who chooses a distinctive leisure style biased toward a single activity or set of similar activities.[27]

CONSTITUENT PARTICIPATION

The ideas expressed here and elsewhere serve to highlight the necessity of involving clientele throughout all phases of the leisure programming cycle. The leisure profession's constituency includes not only the participants who receive the direct benefit from leisure programs and services, but people who serve in management and support roles inside and outside the organization. We will conclude this chapter by examining constituent participation and defining constituent groups in greater detail.

The program population includes the casual, committed, prospective, and "dropped out" participant. The casual participant tends to come to the program on occasion. While such a person expresses the desire to participate by signing up or paying the program fee, his or her attendance is sporadic. In contrast, the committed participant rarely misses a session. This person consistently attends the program, whether ongoing or infrequently offered. The prospective participant is one who is either known to the programmer but not able to participate for some reason, or who is unaware that the program or service exists. The dropout is the participant who attends at some point during the program and then stops attending.

Management constituents include the programmer's supervisor, any programming board or committee to which the programmer has a responsibility, stockholders who have an investment in the provision of leisure programs, and the owners of the corporation or business.

Those in the support constituent group include program staff, program volunteers, related staff, and consultative staff. The program and volunteer staff are those persons who have accepted responsibilities for the operation of the program. They are basically distinguishable by salary: Those on the program staff receive a paycheck; program volunteers do not. Related staff are others within the agency or business who come into contact with the program, including the accountant, the clerical support unit, the maintenance personnel, and the building/facilities supervisor. The larger the agency or business, the more likely it will be that there will be more related staff for the programmer to involve. Consultative staff include such people as an attorney who is held on retainer by the organization to address legal matters, the local United Way budget officer for member agencies, and the program managers in other agencies or businesses with which synergetic programming is being done.

Gathering constituent input is pursued both formally and informally by the programmer. Obtaining input formally means collecting it in a systematic fashion; informal input is usually obtained in casual, face-to-face exchanges. Obtaining approval from higher management for a program idea at the beginning of program development should be done formally. Participant needs assessment and program evaluation should also be done formally. You should informally seek input from participants and staff while your programs are being implemented.

When, how, and how often constituent contact is made depend in part on the leisure program itself. For example, a program that carries with it an element of risk may require early input from the lawyer. One that demands a close leadership component will require more input from program and volunteer staff. One that has never been provided before may require more involvement with management, whereas one that is designed to increase participation will involve input from prospective and dropout clientele.

In order to clarify constituent input, Table 8-B shows the various constituent groups and at what phase of the programming cycle the programmer generally seeks their input.

Participant input is generally gathered formally during needs assessment and program evaluation from casual, committed, and dropout

Constituent Group		When the Programmer Generally Seeks Input	
		Formal	*Informal*
Participant	• casual • committed • dropout	Needs Assessment Program Evaluation	Program Implementation
	• prospective	Needs Assessment	
Management	• supervisor • program board or committee • stockholder • owner	Program Development Program Revision	Needs Assessment Program Evaluation
Support	• program staff • program volunteer	Program Development Program Implementation Program Evaluation	Program Implementation
	• related staff • consultative staff	Program Development Program Implementation	Program Implementation Program Evaluation

Table 8-B   Constituent Group Involvement

participants; management input is gathered during program development and program revision; and support input is gathered during program development, program implementation, and staff program evaluation. Informally gathered input is generally sought from participants during program implementation; from management during needs assessment and program evaluation; from support groups during program implementation; and from related and consultative staff during program evaluation. The key word is generally. Successful leisure programmers seek input from constituent groups at any time in the leisure programming cycle when program outcome is likely to be affected, with the ultimate goal of facilitating participant leisure awareness, choices, and functioning.

Application Section. Take a few minutes to think of a leisure program that you have helped implement. Using your knowledge of the program and Table 8-B, determine the extent to which constituent participation was carried out. Some questions that you may want to ask include the following:

Who were your participant constituents?

Were dropout constituents' needs assessed?

Was participant input informally gathered during program implementation?

Was your supervisor formally consulted during program revision?

Did a board or committee have to approve the program?

Did your staff have input during program development?

Were consultative staff utilized in any way?

Conclude your thinking by rating the program in terms of its involvement with constituent particiaption, using the following scale: A= excellent; B=very good; C=average; and D=below average.

SUMMARY

The life cycle of a program occurs within the context of cultural change. You can implement programs based on physical, intellectual, cultural, social, environmental, or personal development patterns. These program patterns often contain elements of one another and are frequently implemented in an interactive fashion. Major adjunct factors that affect the program during implementation include age of participants, geographical area, ethnicity of clientele, and homogeneous groups. Constituent involvement from participants, management, and support groups occurs throughout the leisure programming cycle; how often it is pursued, and whether it is obtained formally or informally, depends on the program.

FOOTNOTES

1. Clarence Brown, "The Business Experience," *AALR Reporter*, 8 (1983), 4.
2. Daniel Yankelovich, "New Rules in American Life: Searching for Self-Fulfillment in a World Turned Upside Down," *Psychology Today*, April 1981, p. 36.

3. Kim Sprague, "How to Avoid the Programming Rut," *Parks & Recreation,* July 1980, p. 25. Reprinted from permission of the National Recreation and Park Association.

4. Barbara Palmer, "We Fire the Whole Works on July 4," *USA Today,* July 1, 1983, p. 1A.

5. Richard G. Kraus, *Social Recreation: A Group Dynamics Approach* (St. Louis: The CV Mosby Company, 1979), p. 4.

6. Yankelovich, "New Rules," p. 39.

7. David Fink, "From Queens to California, We Want Help," *USA Today,* April 11, 1983. Section A, p. 2.

8. Ibid., Section A, p. 2.

9. Constance O'Connor, "Self-Awareness Programming: Should Recreation Get Into It?," *California Parks & Recreation,* October/November 1978, pp. 13, 15, 39.

10. Michelle Celarier, "Big Bucks in the Wellness Business," *Ms. Magazine,* May 1983, pp. 127–28.

11. John R. Kelly, *Leisure* (Englewood Cliffs, N.J.: Prentice-Hall, Inc., 1982), p. 242.

12. Richard G. Kraus, *Recreation Today: Program Planning and Leadership,* 2nd ed. (Santa Monica, Calif.: Goodyear Publishing Co., Inc., 1977), p. 137.

13. Kelly, *Leisure,* p. 248.

14. Yankelovich, "New Rules," p. 85.

15. Linda Wolfe, "Good News for Singles," *Sacramento Bee,* March 11, 1983, pp. C1, C4.

16. Tom Rogers, "Family Life Stymied by Lifestyles," *USA Today,* April 4, 1983. Section D, p. 1.

17. Richard G. Kraus, "Singles: A Large (And Largely Ignored) Target Population," *Parks & Recreation,* May 1982, pp. 50–51. Reprinted by special permission of the National Recreation and Park Association.

18. Martha Nudel, "ClubMed: At the Forefront of the Singles Tourism," *Parks & Recreation,* November 1982, p. 31. Reprinted by special permission of the National Recreation and Park Association.

19. *U.S. News & World Report,* February 21, 1983, pp. 53–56.

20. Ibid., p. 53.

21. Ibid., p. 55.

22. Kraus, "Singles," p. 50.

23. Thomas Goodale, "The Fallacy of Our Programs," *Parks & Recreation,* November 1967, p. 40. Reprinted by special permission of the National Recreation and Park Association.

24. Judith Hooper, "The Mental Health of the Unemployed," *Psychology Today,* December 1980, p. 31. Reprinted from *Psychology Today* Magazine. Copyright © 1980 (APA).

25. Ruth Harriet Jacobs, "Displaced Homemakers: An Adult Educator's Checklist," *Lifelong Learning: The Adult Years,* March 1982, p. 9.

26. John R. Kelly, "Leisure Lifestyles: A Hidden Core," *Leisure Sciences,* 5, no. 4 (1983), p. 334.

27. Ibid., p. 336.

chapter 9

Program Evaluation
Phase Four of the Leisure Programming Cycle

WHY EVALUATE?

The contents of our previous chapters imply that decision making is a responsibility that is ever-present in the professional lives of persons in the park, recreation, and leisure field. However, it is difficult to remember a time when making those decisions was harder than it is today. Not only are programmers faced with more leisure alternatives from which to choose, but they must meet ever-increasing leisure demands with (typically) decreasing resources. Thus it is critical that they make decisions as rationally and justly as possible.

But realistically, as human beings with emotions and biases, how truly rational and just can programmers be? A major means of helping them to get there, to make better decisions, is evaluation. Programmers should not hesitate to do evaluations. They should not hesitate to evaluate their programs themselves. For a number of reasons, they can no longer stand back and rely solely on persons external to their agencies or their field to evaluate for them. They must use evaluation as a legitimate means of systematically collecting data to serve as the basis for informed planning, analysis, and policy making. As public servants, entrepreneurs, and/or human service workers, leisure professionals do not exist in isolation. Rather, they are constantly engaged in dialogues with their clients, boards, interest groups, governing bodies, constituents, funding sources, and involved others. Thus, they make their decisions in concert with other people.

At present, representatives of other programs and services are competing with leisure programmers for access to the same "ears." Evaluation can be used to help programmers communicate better and perhaps be listened to just a bit more closely than the others. Michael Farley of the Portland, Oregon, Bureau of

Parks and Recreation suggests that this type of group interaction is an integral part of park, recreation, and leisure services. This interaction is the very heart of political activity—the use of power and influence to affect the allocation of limited resources in order to achieve desired ends. Evaluation helps programmers to monitor what they have, struggle to get what they need, and persuade others that what they propose is reasonable, efficient, effective, and worthy of investment. Evaluation can also be used to help programmers communicate within and among themselves.[1]

To help programmers be victors in the competitive struggle for dollars, a number of elements relevant to evaluation must be examined. First, just what is evaluation?

In its most basic sense, evaluation is the process of judging the merit, worth, or value of something. In their daily lives, people participate in a number of informal evaluations as they select one particular course of action from several alternatives. The formal evaluation of leisure programs requires programmers to be much more scientific and rational in their decision making. They strive to make choices based on objectively examined facts. They use systematic inquiry to determine the value of something. In a sense, they undertake a project in applied research. It is a situation-specific and often an immediate problem that they are trying to solve. As professionals in the leisure field, it is their responsibility to use this process to help themselves be of better service to their clientele. Thus it is no accident that the word "value" is heard when the word "evaluation" is spoken. Evaluation means making an appraisal of some phenomenon. In this case, the phenomenon is a leisure program.

What, then, is the purpose of evaluation? Why should programmers evaluate? A concern for evaluating park, recreation, and leisure programs has been evident in the writings of the leisure field for two decades. Historically, this concern was about setting and meeting standards of professional performance. This concern grew into a series of questions about what programmers were doing. Were they doing it correctly, enough, with equal opportunity for all, efficiently, and finally effectively? These concerns evolved into a full-fledged problem as the profession moved deeper into the "era of accountability."

Leisure service professionals are now in the position of having to compete with other human service agencies for shrinking resources. Ironically, this competition is occurring while the demand for leisure services in particular is on the rise. Thus leisure service professionals are compelled to be as efficient and effective as possible in providing or facilitating a full range of leisure experiences. It is through the process of evaluation that they can revise and improve their programs, decision making, and accountability while the demand for quality services increases. When programmers are accountable, they are responsible, and evaluation helps them to demonstrate responsible behavior. When they are efficient, they are able to show that they have used their resources in a prudent manner. When they are effective, they have facilitated some kind of leisure experience that is satisfying, fulfilling and meaningful to the individual or group participating.

By being responsible in this manner, programmers evaluate in order to improve, justify, and, if appropriate, expand their programs. They can meet the demands made on them by external authorities while at the same time documenting exactly what it is that they do. Then their decisions are indeed rational and factually based.

If evaluation is a process of systematic inquiry within which some judgment of merit or worth is made based on some criteria, then several very practical reasons for evaluation become obvious. Evaluation is useful in helping professionals to improve programs and in providing a defensible means of allocating or reallocating resources. Evaluation can lead to expanded support by grass-roots constituencies and can be used to help instill the ethic and value of a meaningful leisure life-style. Evaluation is a vehicle for two-way communication between an agency and its clientele and can help the professional to maintain sensitivity to the impact of the leisure experience on each and every participant. Evaluation can show how park, recreation, and leisure services contribute to the quality of life.[2]

Application Section.   Imagine that you have taken a summer job as a ride operator for an amusement park. It is a policy of this commercial recreation organization that early in the morning, before the park opens for business, operators must run maintenance and safety checks on their rides. Relate our previous discussion of evaluation to your responsibility for running a maintenance and safety check.

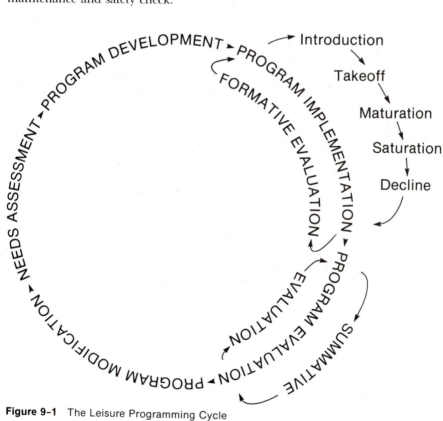

Figure 9-1   The Leisure Programming Cycle

WHERE EVALUATION FITS INTO
THE PROGRAMMING CYCLE

In Chapter 5, we gave an overview of the leisure programming cycle. We described the cycle—depicted again in Figure 9-1—as consisting of five phases. We stated that evaluation occurs in two of the phases of the cycle: program implementation and program evaluation.

The type of evaluation that happens during the program implementation phase as introduced in Chapter 5 and discussed in Chapter 8 is called *formative evaluation*. Formative evaluation is the judgment of program merit or worth in order to improve and revise the program while it is actually occurring. This enables the programmer to make adjustments and modifications while the program is being implemented. In this sense, evaluation is an immediate strategy for change.

The fourth phase of the cycle, program evaluation, should really be thought of (as we stated in Chapter 5) as *summative program evaluation*. Summative evaluation is the final judgment about program worth that occurs after a program has been completed. Generally, the decision to modify or terminate a program is based on the summative evaluation of the program. As stated earlier, the use of both formative and summative evaluation provides the programmer with greater depth of information about his or her programs than the use of one type of evaluation alone. The purpose of and the time frame for the evaluation are two important factors in determining whether formative or summative evaluation is the better choice.

CONCEPTUALIZING THE EVALUATION
OF A LEISURE PROGRAM

In order even to begin to conduct an evaluation, there are several things that a programmer must know about the particular leisure program or set of programs under study. An enlightened and professional leisure agency has some kind of written statement of *philosophy*, or mission, that guides the overall direction of the organization. Typically, the staff then writes general statements of the agency's purposes and *goals* that are in keeping with its mission. These goals are further refined into *objectives*, which are action statements to which the organization can be held accountable.

The philosophy, goals, and objectives of the organization may be used to determine what evaluation questions to ask, inasmuch as these written statements reflect what the agency is supposed to be providing in the way of programs and services. A well-functioning agency is expected to have a philosophical direction that gives rise to certain goals. The goals form the basis for the objectives of the actual programs. To identify and describe the programs and the degree to which they are congruent with the more general intent of the organization is an essential step in initiating program evaluation. This description lays the groundwork for the specific evaluation questions that the programmer will pose. Intelligent decisions about programs are more likely to be made when the nature of the programs being evaluated is fully described.

Application Section.   This series of questions is intended to help you to conceptualize the evaluation of a leisure program or set of leisure experiences and activities. The questions are appropriate both for the programmer who conducts his or her own internal evaluation and for an evaluator who is external to or independent of the program concerned, and apply to both formative and summative evaluation. Begin by assuming that the program you're going to evaluate reflects the philosophy and goals of the agency. Describe a hypothetical mission statement and a couple of goals of the organization. Then identify and select a specific leisure program to examine. Answer the following questions:

1. What is the *purpose* of this evaluation? Why evaluate? Provide a rationale.
2. For *whom* is the evaluation being done? Who are the most important or relevant audiences (commissioners) that are concerned with this program?
3. Do the audiences have any *special concerns* that they desire to see addressed? If so, what are they?
4. Can the program to be evaluated be precisely *described*, if possible including intents, transactions, and outcomes?
5. To what *extent* do the commissioners of the evaluation desire to be *involved* in the overall evaluation process?
6. How will the anonymity and confidentiality of the data and of data sources be *protected?*
7. Who will have *access* to the final evaluation report?
8. What *resources* (finances, administrative support, clerical help, equipment, supplies, participant cooperation, released time, and so on) are guaranteed to be available?
9. Are time lines, due dates, and other "contractual" necessities specified and understood?
10. Is the programmer or evaluator ultimately expected to *cease* his or her work after the evaluation results are reported and interpreted, or is he or she expected to *offer alternatives,* recommendations, and/or conclusions?

These kinds of questions are indicative of the types of activities that you will have to negotiate and clarify with others as you commence the evaluation process. The next series of questions relate to your decisions about the actual evaluation approach or model that you will employ.

1. Beyond any special concerns that the audiences have, what *issues* (evaluation questions) are you, as the evaluator, going to *pose?*
2. What *criteria* are you going to use to determine the value of the program?
3. What *evidence* (information) are you going to collect to shed light on how well the program meets your criteria?
4. From *whom* will the evidence be *collected?* Who are your sources of data?
5. *How* will the evidence be collected? What instrumentation or techniques will be used, under what conditions, and in what time frame?
6. *Who* will *collect* the data?
7. How will the information be *analyzed,* reduced, summarized, or synthesized?

8. *Who* will analyze the data?
9. How does this evaluation plan *allow* for the *unanticipated* or spontaneous events that occur during most leisure experiences? How is the ability to adjust for the unexpected built in?

Finally, as a programmer, you're probably concerned about your evaluation results getting put into practice. Thus you will have to address the following:

1. How will your results be reported? What mode or modes of delivery will be used?
2. Will the same report be given to all audiences? How will technical and nontechnical information be handled?
3. Is a plan of action expected to follow after the final evaluation report is made? If there are recommendations included, what assurance needs to be given that the recommendations will be implemented?
4. To what extent does the programmer or evaluator become involved as an advocate for change based upon his or her findings?

Providing the answers to these questions sets a general framework that is useful for conducting an evaluation without regard to what particular evaluation model or combination of models is selected to be used. This means of planning an evaluation necessitates the involvement of other people from the very beginning. When people are uncertain as to the meaning of an evaluation or are uninvolved, they are likely to be apprehensive about the process. Summative evaluation, particularly, signifies major changes on the horizon, and this may cause undue anxiety. But when people are truly a part of such an endeavor from its inception, and if they understand the intent, the process, and the results, it is more likely that they will feel less threatened and that they will act on the findings.

HIGHLIGHTS OF TECHNIQUES
FOR EVALUATING LEISURE PROGRAMS

Chapter 6 included an elaborate discussion of the various techniques of data collection, analysis, and reporting used in the needs assessment phase of the leisure programming cycle. Many of these same techniques may also be applied in the program evaluation phase. However, there are some things that are unique to evaluation. This section discusses these unique concerns and then reviews the previously mentioned techniques as they relate specifically to evaluation.

In evaluating a leisure program, judgments are made by systematically searching out the answers to the evaluative questions that the staff of an agency or some other audience holds to be important. Because the evaluation questions that are specific to the program under study are of the utmost importance, this topic merits further discussion. Evaluation questions are also called issues. They are the identifiable concerns that relate directly to the particular component or aspect of the leisure program that is being evaluated. Inherent in the evaluation questions are the beliefs and values that the developers of the questions hold. The criteria, or standards, that are based on these beliefs and values may be implicit or explicit and are the primary indicators of program worth.

It was stated earlier that evaluation is a value-laden undertaking. Judging worth is done within the context of some value system. It must be determined what or whose value system the evaluation questions will reflect. It must also be determined that the criteria selected and questions asked are truly indicative of a program's worth. J. Robert Rossman provides an excellent illustration of the need for valid evaluation questions and the criteria that underlie them:[3]

> No matter how well the evaluation is conducted, if the criteria selected are not appropriate indicators of a program's worth the evaluation will not be useful. An example of this is the use of attendance figures as the judgment criteria for determining the worth of a leisure program. Although attendance figures can tell you about the impact of a program, that is, how many people were served—they cannot indicate the quality of the leisure experience those who attended received.
>
> In selecting judgment criteria one should be aware of the following five points:
>
> 1. Criteria selection is a crucial step in evaluation and the usefulness of the evaluation is dependent upon how well the criteria you select as indicators of program success link with the substance of your program.
> 2. Making these decisions is a subjective undertaking.
> 3. Programs can be judged on a wide range of criteria, some of which are more important than others.
> 4. The more criteria that are examined, the more difficult it is to get good data and to be able to integrate the data into a summative judgment.
> 5. You will probably never be able to include enough criteria in an evaluation so someone cannot charge that something has been left out.[4]

A pluralistic social system such as ours makes the collective judging of worth even more difficult. For example, one group may deem a program a success, while another may consider the exact same program a failure. Unfortunately, the beliefs that groups hold may be implicit, *a priori* assumptions of which the group members are not consciously aware. Thus, judgment criteria often emerge from internally held viewpoints that may not even be discussed. These strongly held assumptions may concern the definition of what constitutes a "good" program, and as such may create a covert bias, according to Rossman[5] and Charles C. Bullock.[6] Rossman further cautions:

> Managers . . . must be aware of this value problem and be aware of competing value orientations and the judgment of worth that may have been rendered if a competing but just as legitimate value system had been applied. . . . Evaluations, if formally structured, can document program outcomes. But determining the value of these outcomes is more problematic and dependent upon a specific value orientation. It is disagreements over which value system should prevail that keep evaluations from providing the compelling conclusions about our social programs that we so often hope for.[7]

Evaluators must be sensitive to the divergent values and beliefs that may underlie the judgment criteria selected and the evaluation questions that are asked by the varying audiences or commissioners of the evaluation.

Beyond this, as suggested in the previous application section, a savvy evaluator should negotiate the "special" evaluation criteria (or concerns) prior to undertaking the actual project.

Furthermore, once the evaluation questions are decided on, the professional must also determine what information or evidence should be collected to provide answers to the questions. Such evidence may be descriptive or judgmental. Descriptive evidence may portray the nature of the participants in the program; describe the actual processes or interactions that occur in a recreational class; illustrate the context, setting, or environment of the leisure experience; or report the outcome or impact of the activity on the clientele.

Judgmental evidence includes statements of how well predetermined standards have been met. Judgmental evidence also includes professional judgments rendered by consultants or experts with regard to the merit or worth of the leisure program. Rossman suggests that day-to-day operations personnel are not especially interested in descriptive information as judgment data. As might be expected, day-to-day operations personnel are familiar with programs because of their contact with them. But governing boards, external funding sources, and so on do not typically have this level of familiarity. Judgments about programs that are presented to groups distant from the program need to be accompanied by enough descriptive information so that the groups may build a logical rationale for decisions and place decisions in a context.[8]

How is evidence best gathered? It is our belief that evaluation is very much like an applied research project, and that it is essential to use valid and reliable data collection instruments and procedures. Ken Mobily and Seppo E. Iso-Ahola believe that since survey techniques are the most widely employed means of gathering information in the leisure field, competence in survey research is critically important. Thus questionnaire construction and use must be carefully taught.[9]

A questionnaire is an information collection instrument that consists of questions or items to which a recipient responds. Questionnaires may be either mailed to respondents or handed to them in a face-to-face situation. However, the recipient is the one expected to complete the form. Thus questionnaires are generally self-administered. The questions or items consist of two types: (1) closed-ended, or fixed-alternative, and (2) open-ended. Sometimes the word "survey" is used to mean "questionnaire." Questionnaires are best used when the evaluator is interested in breadth of information—that is, collecting information relatively economically from a large number of people.

An interview schedule is an information-gathering device that generally elicits a greater depth of response from a fewer number of people. Interview schedules, like questionnaires, consist of questions or items to which a respondent answers. However, in an interview the *interviewer* completes the interview schedule by recording the respondent's responses on it. The interview questions may be of either the open- or the closed-ended type. Interviews may be conducted either over the telephone or in a face-to-face situation.

An observation schedule, or observation form, is a data collection instrument that allows the evaluator to record what he or she is actually seeing and hearing at a given time. The result is generally a written description of what actually occurs in an ongoing leisure program. The observations may be obtrusive or unobtrusive. The observation schedule may have closed-ended items to which the observer responds specifically, or more open-ended questions that allow the observer more freedom in selecting what he or she watches and records. Typically, a rather in-depth view of the leisure experience is gained through this data collection technique.

A final means of gathering evidence to be used in evaluation is the perusal of existing documents or artifacts. In this case, the evaluator reviews written information about, or the products of, a program to glean information about the program. Reviewing documents or artifacts allows the evaluator to determine what already exists "on the record" about a program. This adds to his or her body of knowledge about the leisure experience under study. For a further discussion of these and other data collection techniques, please refer back to Chapter 6.

Chapter 6 also includes detailed information on data analysis techniques. As with data collection, the procedures used in the analysis of needs assessment information may also be applied to *evaluation* information. Naturally, the nature of the information collected (whether it is numerical or verbal, for example) will be the primary factor in determining the way in which the information is analyzed. However, there are a couple of other things that need to be considered when you are analyzing information specifically for an evaluation report.

ANALYZING INFORMATION FOR EVALUATION

In Chapter 4 we talked about several kinds of "fits"—the fit between the agency's philosophy and the programmer's beliefs, for example. There is another fit that is extremely important in evaluation. That is the fit between the way in which the data collected in the evaluation are analyzed, summarized, and expressed, and the perceived level of understanding or "research sophistication" that the consumers of the evaluation results evince.

The evaluation of leisure programs occurs in the real world. In order to be meaningful, some action must come about as a result of the evaluation effort. Therefore, you want to make the undertaking—including the way in which data are treated—as straightforward as possible, so as to maximize the fit between the information and the recipients of the information.

Undoubtedly, once you come up with some results, conclusions, alternatives, or recommendations that stem from your evaluation effort, you want those recommendations to be implemented. This is more likely to occur if the audience of the evaluation fully comprehends both the results and the process of collecting and analyzing the information that led to the results. Since the evaluation audience probably will consist of lay people, the evaluator needs to convey what may be fairly technical procedures in a nontechnical, easily understood manner.

We are not discouraging the use of sophisticated, technical data analysis techniques. Rather, we encourage the use of the technique or techniques that are most appropriate to the data collected. But we also strongly urge the evaluator to be clear and simple when describing and reporting collection and analysis procedures. If this is the case, we believe that the evaluator will stand a better chance of getting his or her recommendations acted on, because the lay decision makers will feel that they understand what has occurred and that they are capable of rendering an informed decision.

Let us consider data analysis for a moment by taking a look at the relationship between descriptive and inferential statistics. A statistic is a summary value that is calculated from a sample of observations. Descriptive statistics involves the tabulation, depiction, and portrayal of collections of data. The function of descriptive statistics is to describe the characteristics of bodies of data. The data may be either qualitative or quantitative. This process is used to order or summarize masses of information in order to facilitate the interpretation of the information. A limitation of this process is that the findings cannot be generalized beyond the group sampled.

If one wishes to generalize, a rationale is needed. This is where inferential statistics enters. Inferential statistics addresses itself primarily to prediction within finite populations. It also has implications for more general predictability. Inferential statistics is the process of reasoning out the properties of a large collection of data by examining a sample of the data.

The difference between the two kinds of statistics is *not* one of statistical technique (inferential builds on descriptive); rather, it concerns the ways that the techniques are used and their purpose. Techniques that summarize data are said to be descriptive techniques. Techniques used to estimate parameters of populations of which the data are a sample are said to be inferential techniques.

An example of descriptive statistics is the use of the measure of central tendency called the mean ($\overline{X}$) to answer the question: "What was the average score on the mid-term examination in a selected recreation and leisure studies class?"

An example of inferential statistics occurs when a public recreation agency wants to determine what proportion of the residents of the local community has heard its public service announcement on the radio. It is unnecessary to question the total community population if the proportion could be estimated from a sample of, say, three hundred residents. How the proportion of residents in the sample relates to the analogous portion of the entire community population can be determined through inferential techniques.

So statistics are a primary means of analyzing the numerical or quantifiable information that has been gathered through the data collection process. Statistics are a set of techniques for reducing and summarizing data so that the characteristics or nature of the phenomenon under study may be more easily comprehended. But when you must make decisions based on data collected from a small portion—that is, a *sample*—of the group that you are evaluating, then you go beyond mere describing into making inferences. These "macro" decisions, involving inferences from a sample to the larger group or population, present one major problem. The sample must be an accurate representation of the population from which it is drawn. Randomization and random sampling, which is discussed in Chapter 6, helps to ensure that the sample is indeed representative.

If numerical data are gathered, then quantitative analyses, ranging from simple frequency counts and percentages to averages and correlations, may be done. However, in addition to considering the nature of the data, remember that the level of comfort and understanding of the audience of the evaluation must be taken into account. It is of no use to perform exotic statistical analyses if the persons for whom the evaluation is being done cannot base their decisions on the results because they do not know what the results mean.

If the information that is collected is of a verbal or qualitative nature, then data analysis techniques such as content analysis or critical review may be used. The volume of information must be reduced and summarized so that it is comprehensible to the audience to whom it is directed. This may mean that descriptive comparisons of program change over time should be made, or that an attempt to correlate program impact with participant satisfaction should be performed.

Finally, it would be meaningless to conduct an evaluation without making the results available to the audience in order for its members to have a set of facts on which to base their decisions. Thus it is necessary to select some organized means of reporting the evaluation findings. Again, the nature of the results affects the way in which the results are most effectively disseminated. However, the reporting techniques chosen must also be appropriate to the recipients of the evaluation information. Therefore, the nature of the audience must be considered at this stage of the evaluation process, too.

The evaluation results may be expressed in a variety of ways: written or oral, technical or nontechnical, descriptive or accompanied by recommendations. They may be in the form of a progress report or a final summation. Visual and audio aids, in the form of devices such as charts, graphs, overheads, slides, tapes, photographs, panel discussions, or testimony, may enhance the communication of the results. In sum, the use of the *most appropriate* dissemination technique will be likely to encourage the translation of the results into decisive action.

Application Section.   Most programmers have had to present information to a group. Typically, they rely on the old standbys: written and oral reports. Brainstorm some other ways in which programmers can get ideas across to people, and discuss the strengths and drawbacks of these ways. Think about how different communications media may be perceived by different subgroups within North American society. Further, think about the differences in the ways that you present evaluation results to your superiors, fellow staff members, advisory board, funding source, clientele, parent groups, and care providers.

OVERVIEW OF SELECTED LEISURE
PROGRAM EVALUATION MODELS

In 1981, Robert E. Stake advocated the use of the term "persuasion" instead of "model" when referring to certain evaluation approaches. He contended that the use of the word "model" implies a methodology, or a specific and precise way of going about the process of determining value.[10] On the whole, it is our opinion that the models that have been applied to the evaluation of leisure programs, as they are described in the literature, are not especially specific or precise. But they do nevertheless represent systematic approaches or strategies to judging merit or worth. So for the purpose of our discussion we will use the term "model" and will use it interchangeably with "procedure," "strategy," and "approach." We consider the models to be frameworks for thinking about the entire process of evaluation, not paradigms or methodologies for conducting them.

It was during the middle part of the twentieth century that educators became extremely active in the development and application of evaluation models. In the 1960s, American educators and social scientists received a great deal of financial support from the federal government to evaluate educational curricula and social programs. Ten years later, leisure service professionals began writing about the evaluation models that had been developed or adapted for use with leisure programs. There are now several textbooks solely devoted to the evaluation of leisure programs and services. What we will do is highlight some of the more widely used program evaluation models.

The following categories of evaluation models are presented roughly in the chronological order of their development. Each category has one or more models in it. The categories serve mainly to order this discussion. They are not truly mutually exclusive, as some models placed in one category may contain elements of models found in other categories.

We have placed two of the earliest leisure program evaluation models under the category of *evaluation by standards:* the Harry P. Hatry and Diana R. Dunn evaluation model and the Betty van der Smissen evaluation model. In 1971 the Hatry-Dunn model was developed as a joint project of the Urban Institute and the Department of Housing and Urban Development. The developers stated that the mission of community recreation departments is to provide a comprehensive and diverse set of leisure experiences to its public. Thus the major purpose of their model is to help management monitor program efficiency for planning, organizing, directing, and controlling functions. The primary audience addressed by the model is the manager or administrator. Other potential audiences include other governing officials and the general public. The process of the model includes collection of information from departmental records and periodic surveys of citizens on twelve measures of "effectiveness." The emphasis is on the evaluation of the entire leisure service delivery system, using the prescribed standards.[11] The twelve measures of effectiveness reflect the values of professionals in the field at the time that the model was developed. No *evidence* of the relationship between recreation and these criteria is given.

In 1972, with the support of the National Recreation and Park Association, van der Smissen disseminated her evaluation model. The purpose of the model is to allow for accountability and the review of the entire service system through a self-administered study. The principal audiences are the agency's administration, policy makers, and the general public. The model examines six major categories of agency operations. Criteria (standards of effectiveness) are listed for each of the categories. The standards and categories were developed by a panel of park, recreation, and leisure professionals. Again, the evaluation is based on the professional values inherent in the predetermined standards.[12] The problems with this whole approach are that the criteria are static and too broad to be truly applicable to diverse situations.

The Bannon evaluation model, published in Joseph J. Bannon's comprehensive planning text in 1976, also relies on predetermined standards in that goals and/or judgment criteria are established prior to commencing an evaluation. However, we have placed it into the *evaluation by goals and objectives* category. The model emphasizes the equal weight of professional staff and lay persons in determining the criteria to be used for judging the worth of programs. Staff and citizens are equally important evaluation audiences. Evaluation is described as a cyclical process; insight and program improvement may occur with each cycle. The model follows the tradition of the public recreation movement by heavily involving lay citizens in the governance of public recreation services.[13] Bannons' model allows more participant involvement in shaping the criteria for the evaluation than the Hatry-Dunn and van der Smissen models. The model itself does not specify any judgment criteria but elicits criteria from the audience. The usefulness of the model for evaluation purposes depends on the meaningfulness of the program goals and objectives, as well as the judgment criteria that are determined by the staff and the participating public.

The Gunn-Peterson model also falls under this category. Published first in Scout L. Gunn and Carol A. Peterson's therapeutic recreation text in 1978, its purpose is to document accountability for persons in authority. The model, rooted in Malcolm Provus's Discrepancy Evaluation Model, also seeks to provide information necessary for improving service delivery techniques. The intended audiences of the evaluation results include service providers, program administrators, and funding bodies.

Evaluation is one step in Gunn and Peterson's original comprehensive program planning model, and what is to be evaluated is determined within their comprehensive program planning methodology. The process of their model involves the identification of discrepancies between intended and actual program inputs, processes, and outputs. Expectations for client performance are expressed in written behavioral objectives. The Gunn-Peterson model does not suggest any evaluation criteria. It is a process to follow for the activity of evaluating.[14] The utility of the evaluation model depends upon the meaningfulness of the evaluation criteria, which are selected by the professional and tied to the behavioral objectives. The question remains whether all possible expectations can or should be translated into behavioral objectives.

The accreditation of park, recreation, and leisure studies curricula by the National Recreation and Park Association and the American Association for Leisure and Recreation became a reality in the 1970s. Although this particular formalized procedure is presently limited to undergraduate professional preparation programs, it is certain that through the years practitioners in the field have been relying on the professional judgment of their colleagues to "certify" their programs. Thus the third major category of evaluation models in leisure services is the *evaluation by professional judgment* approach. Turning from the accreditation of curricula per se to leisure programs in general, the purpose of an accreditation model is to tap the experience and training of recognized experts to judge the merit or worth of programs. Typically, the evaluation audience consists of the program administrators and staff, and the public as well (as the intended beneficiaries of the program). The process of the accreditation model consists of site visits in which a group of experts makes observations about the activities at hand. Typically, the agency's written policies, procedures, and other documents are reviewed, and constituents are interviewed. Then some kind of judgment is made, based on the observations and the intrinsic beliefs of each expert on the visitation team. A collective written or oral report with recommendations usually ensues. This is another evaluation approach in which the evaluative criteria are the intrinsically held beliefs of the professionals (experts) involved.

In 1981, Margaret L. (Peg) Connolly described her evaluation model in her doctoral dissertation. Although the Connolly model is predominantly one of evaluation by professional judgment, it too was influenced by Provus's Discrepancy Evaluation Model, and thus exhibits some characteristics of the goals and objectives category. The Connolly model does not require a team of experts who are knowledgeable about leisure yet external to the program. Rather, its purpose is to have someone internal to the program (the practitioner) describe the program and its transactions, operations, and client performance in connection with predetermined outcomes. As in the accreditation model, this is done in order to identify the strengths and weaknesses of a program as a step toward program revision and improvement.

The primary evaluation audience is the practitioner, followed by his or her coworkers and superiors. The process of the model is to facilitate positive change, with the practitioner as an evaluator, using a case-study technique. The process of the evaluation itself is an important component of Connolly's model. The judgment criteria that the practitioner-evaluator uses are culled from the literature and validated on the basis of the training and experience of the practitioner. Information is collected, analyzed, and interpreted in a systematic way. The model also examines the existing goals and objectives of the agency to determine their validity before examining client performance and making the overall evaluative judgment.[15] One problem with the model is that some practitioners may need the help of an external expert in making that initial judgment as well as in using case-study techniques.

The next category of evaluation is *evaluation by decision making.* Monica M. Nolan, in her master's thesis in 1978, developed the Program Evaluation Procedure (PEP) for the purpose of providing decision makers with a well-rounded view of a program. The model consists of a listing of data requirements for a description-based understanding of the program. Nolan's outline of important information is based on the management and programming literature in the leisure field. The obvious evaluation audience consists of those in the workforce who make decisions.

The process of Nolan's model involves collecting and analyzing information about program inputs and processes, actual and intended program goals, and so on, using questionnaires. The model mandates the evaluator to examine the program within the context of the organization in which it is housed. Nolan states that PEP is primarily an information-gathering tool. The model attempts to minimize the politics of the evaluation process by divorcing evaluation from the assignment of blame for absolute success or failure.[16] That may also be a problem with the model, because judging the merit or worth of a program on a continuum of "success" is the basis of evaluation (the assignment of blame is not). Although the model does identify a number of issues to examine, it gives no guidance about how to weight them or about what constitutes good programming. This model also serves to show how each successive model is a hybrid of its predecessors.

In her 1981 master's thesis, Margie Kenner tested her evaluation model, a hybrid in the decision-making category. Her model has the additional purpose of collecting information about the participant's satisfaction with the leisure experience gained through the recreational activity. This model emphasizes instruments for collecting data about the technical aspects of the program, the context or environment, the cost, and so on.

The evaluation audiences are program managers, leaders, and the participants themselves, as their satisfaction is an extremely important consideration. The collection of data from the participants constitutes the process of the model. Kenner's predetermined criteria and weightings are directly tied to the literature of both the leisure field and psychology. The criteria were subjected to validation by a panel of experts and received field implementation. The weighting of the evaluative criteria shows the influence of the goals and objectives category. But the added emphasis on participant satisfaction stems from Rossman's work in leisure theory-based evaluation.[17] The Kenner model is a more sophisticated data collection process than Nolan's model.

Ernest G. Olson and Christine Z. Howe developed their *evaluation by triangulation* models in 1978. Triangulation involves the combination of several research techniques for the purpose of studying a single phenomenon. Triangulation may be applied to data collection techniques, sources of information, and numbers of investigators or evaluators, as well as to methodologies. The advantage of triangulation, or use of multiple data collection and analysis strategies, is that the strengths of one strategy can offset the weaknesses of another. If something can be confirmed by two or more independent measures, the certainty of interpretation is greatly increased.

Olson's transaction-observation or qualitative evaluation model has the purpose of portraying, in a free-flowing and responsive style, "data bits" about the antecedents, transactions, and outcomes of a recreation program. Using several qualitative data collection techniques, such as audio- and videotapes, simple observation, participant observation, journals and photographs, the evaluator develops a case history of the program for in-house use. The evaluation consists of the compilation and interpretation of this evidence and the measurement of the degree to which it reflects participant satisfaction. Unintended or unanticipated outcomes typically emerge through this responsive type of design.[18]

While the Olson model is flexible, adaptable, and highly people-oriented, its lack of structure opens it to misinterpretation. For example, determining the relevant evaluation audience, the audience's specific informational needs, and the audience's values is part of the model's process. But no procedures for doing this in a systematic way are given, nor are any criteria for a "quality" recreation program given. The usefulness of such an open-ended evaluation model depends on the validity of the emergent criteria and the knowledge and integrity of the evaluator to minimize his or her bias. The only judgment that is inherent is that which is based on the way in which the data bits are organized and presented.

The Howe multimodal model of evaluation also falls under the evaluation by triangulation category. The purpose of the model is to describe a program so that judgments of merit or worth may be made in order to improve and revise the program and to provide accountability in decision situations. The primary evaluation audience is the program provider, followed by the rest of the staff and then by the participants. The process of the model is extremely triangulated, in that the design has both responsive and predetermined components.

Although the judgment criteria are left up to the practitioner-evaluator, there are some guidelines to follow. The data collection, analysis, and interpretation techniques are eclectic, typically using a synthesis of observation, interviews, questionnaires, and document analysis. The qualitative uses of these techniques are emphasized to get an in-depth portrayal of program transactions, context, and participant satisfaction, and to facilitate the production of journalistic evaluation reports. Emergent data are valued in this model, too.[19] Since judgment remains the territory of the primary evaluation audience, as in the Connolly model, the need for training is apparent. Although triangulation helps reduce the threat of subjectivity, it adds to the amount of data to be organized, reduced, and summarized. Thus this type of evaluation takes time.

The final category of evaluation is the *evaluation by leisure theory* approach. J. Robert Rossman was the first entry, in 1981. The purpose of the Rossman model is to measure outcomes of leisure engagement or participant satisfaction as a means of judging program worth. Rossman's model emphasizes his instrumentation; thus he does not feel that his procedure is actually a model.[20] But for the sake of consistency, and due to his clear reporting of the procedures he followed, we will refer to it as a model.

The process of the model involves using his closed-ended, leisure theory-based questionnaire to determine participant satisfaction with a program. The primary evaluation audience is the middle-level program manager. When the evaluator's paramount interest is knowing the degree of participant leisure satisfaction and using that as a specific criterion for judging program worth, this is a proven, valid, and reliable procedure to employ. Rossman's instrument has a predetermined series of questions to which the participant responds. Key factors based on the literature in the leisure field are probed to determine participant satisfaction. The results can be used by managers to form the basis for changing the program. In practice, some professionals are concerned that the prescribed questions are not relevant to their particular programs or their own specific context.

The following figure summarizes some of the key elements of the leisure program evaluation models that we have presented. Again, we caution you that the categories are not as discrete as they appear, and that the models, as frameworks for evaluation, may at times have characteristics associated with categories other than the one in which they are placed. This figure may be used as quick reference to the models that we have mentioned and as a guide to selecting models for use or further study.

Next we will consider some of the trends occurring in evaluation in parks, recreation, and leisure. There are some costs related to this process, both in economic and in human resources. The next section touches upon these.

THE EVALUATION MOVEMENT IN PARKS, RECREATION, AND LEISURE

In the not-too-distant past, professionals in the leisure field seemed content with explaining and justifying their existence on the basis of their presumed "good works," clichés, or lofty jargon about aspirations not yet fulfilled. The luxury of vagueness and ambiguity has gone, just like the ten-cent telephone call. Programmers have moved into an era in which the field must be assertive and competitive in order to survive along with other fields and must prove—that is, provide evidence of—its worth. The value of the field is measured by the models that are employed to evaluate leisure programs in terms of their contribution to the social, physical, psychological-emotional and economic health of North America. These processes are growing more sophisticated and more technical as time passes and will continue to do so.

Programmers have borrowed and adapted many of their leisure program evaluation models from other areas. That is fine; they operate in an applied area and have refined these strategies to suit the phenomenon with which they are concerned: leisure. In recent years, they have also developed instruments and approaches that use social science research techniques, but whose conceptual bases are grounded in leisure theory. Thus they are becoming more scientific in determining and demonstrating their worth.

Since the formal, systematic evaluation of leisure programs based on meaningful criteria is a relatively new practice, most large-scale evaluations have been conducted by persons external to leisure agencies. There is a debate in the literature of evaluation as to the relative merits of internal evaluation versus external evaluation. It seems that persons who are external to the leisure field do not entirely comprehend the full meaning of the leisure experience and environment and their impact on participants. The external evaluator may be prone to overlook the less obvious *intrinsic* aspects of the leisure experience.

The process of evaluation does more than just meet external mandates for accountability. It is an internal service responsibility for which appropriate models and approaches have been created. These approaches are relevant to the needs of and feasible for application by the internal evaluator. Currently, the internal evaluator is likely to be you, the same person who developed, implemented, and/or facilitated the leisure program. Since you are a programmer, and soon to be an evaluator, we assume that you have a professional's expert understanding of the leisure phenomenon. You should

Category	Models	Purpose	Primary Methodology	Outcomes
Evaluation by Standards	Hatry-Dunn	Program efficiency	Checklist	Comparison to standards
	van der Smissen	Program effectiveness and accountability	Checklist	Comparison to standards
Evaluation by Goals and Objectives	Bannon	Congruence between goals and outcomes	Part of Comprehensive Planning Process	Citizen input in goal and criteria determination
	Gunn-Peterson	Congruence between behavior and objectives	Part of Systems Approach to Programming	Indicators of degree of achievement of expected behavior
Evaluation by Professional Judgment	NRPA-AALR Accreditation	Professional colleagues judge and approve programs	Observations, interviews, and review of documents	Professional/peer acceptance and validation
	Connolly	Thorough description, achievement of outcomes, and judgment of program worth	Case-study technique	Detailed information on client outcomes as basis for program revision and improvement
Evaluation by Decision Making	Nolan	Data collection and program description	Multiple questionnaires	Data about program and its context
	Kenner	Efficiency and effectiveness of data collection	Questionnaire	Weighted data about program and satisfaction of participants
Evaluation by Triangulation	Olson	Multiple indicators of participant satisfaction through program description	Observation, interviews, and document reviews	Data bits about program that reflect emergent criteria for program success
	Howe	Same as above plus judgment of worth in decision situations	Observation, interviews, questionnaires, and document analysis	Comprehensive portrayal of program for judgment, revision, and improvement
Evaluation by Leisure Theory	Rossman	Evaluative judgment based on participant satisfaction	Questionnaire	Theory-based indicator of satisfaction as basis for judgment of worth

Figure 9-2 Taxonomy of Models for Leisure Program Evaluation

therefore be in the best position to have insight into the efficiency and effectiveness of the program. If you are trained to evaluate dispassionately, your credibility will not come into question.

Quality training, the use of evaluation for program revision and improvement, and the practice of documenting what has occurred should create an acceptable environment for undertaking this sensitive activity. When the effectiveness of a recreation program is evaluated, the persons closest to the leisure experience are best able, by virtue of their proximity and senses of context and history, to determine the participants' perceptions of leisure and their leisure behavior.

Further, as an internal evaluator, you can readily examine a participant's perceived freedom in selecting activities in which to become involved and the participant's feelings of personal competence in or preference for those activities that are commensurate with his or her abilities. Other intrinsic motivators for leisure behavior include relaxation; novelty; escape from stress or daily routine; optimal arousal; the interplay of achievement and avoidance; and social interaction. These complex psychological variables require subtle measurement, and subtlety regarding leisure may be more within the capabilities of an internal, rather than external, evaluator.[21]

Beyond being the person in the position to be most responsive to the evaluation of a leisure program in psychological terms, you as the internal evaluator can also use your firsthand knowledge of the agency, professional values, and standards of worth to be systematic and unbiased in judging the quality of the program according to those criteria. After this process is completed, you may still be the one left with choices and decisions to make. But the evaluation process provides a means for rational, factually based decision making.

The choices and decisions that the leisure programmer as an internal evaluator must make tend to be limited to items directly related to his or her own programs. Decisions at that level are typically about specific program goals and objectives; participant satisfaction with a particular experience; program leadership; costs; and specific strengths and weaknesses. What about collecting and using evaluative information beyond the operations levels and up to the policy level? This is where the results of a program evaluation can have an effect on the major decisions of the agency.

At the policy level, evaluation makes an agency accountable to its clientele. Evaluation information from the programmer helps the administrator to describe the capabilities of the leisure service delivery system and to explain and/or justify the activities, programs, and services provided or facilitated. Thus evaluation findings can influence policy when these findings are communicated throughout all levels of an agency.

Another change in the evaluation movement in the leisure field is the trend away from using design-focused evaluation in favor of utilization-focused evaluation.[22] *Design-focused evaluation* emphasizes a particular definition of evaluation; rigid adherence to predetermined goals and objectives; experimental or quasi-experimental design; and the use of a single method of data collection. It is useful in determining what a program *should* be or the degree to which the program is what it was officially intended to be.

In contrast, *utilization-focused evaluation* has as a primary consideration the fluid and emergent nature of the leisure experience. It is grounded in the real world constraints and events of a program's operations and structure. It considers actual program environments and interactions. It also responds to the information needs and processing capacity of the members of the evaluation audience as the ultimate decision makers and actors who implement or approve programmatic and policy change.[23]

When employing a utilization focus, in which it is important to be responsive to the dynamic and spontaneous aspects of leisure, it is appropriate to adopt an interactionist perspective that uses multiple methods of collecting data and nonexperimental evaluation designs. This helps the evaluator to determine what the program actually is, according to several persons or sources of information and in light of uncontrolled or unanticipated events that are known to occur quite often in leisure programs. The result is a broad-based description of what is happening in a program, instead of a determination of the degree to which the goals or objectives are being met. The descriptive information becomes explanatory, and from it are inferred the program "goals" as the program actually operates. Also, the leisure programmer has the necessary flexibility to change programs in midstream, free of any "penalty" for having unexpected things happen. Interactionism provides a penetrating examination of a leisure program that works well with the utilization-focused evaluation approach. It can also be used with the design-focused perspective when noncontrolled designs incorporating multiple methods are employed in the real-world environment.[24]

The final aspect of this movement that we need to consider is politics. We began this chapter by acknowledging that evaluation is a political process. Wherever there are two or more gathered together to compete for limited resources, there will be politics. Evaluation is a political activity and it occurs within a political context. As a result, the persons involved in evaluation need to be aware that decisions or outcomes may not be based solely upon "rational facts." Rather, the outcomes may reflect negotiation, compromise, ideologies, biases, and beliefs. In the final analysis, evaluations are conducted by people, and it is unrealistic to expect a single evaluator to make decisions in isolation. Rather, leisure decisions may very likely be based on something other than the systematically derived results of a valid and reliable evaluation process.

SUMMARY

Evaluation is a dynamic and systematic process of describing and judging the merit or worth of a program for the purpose of providing facts on which to base decisions. The process of evaluation occurs in the real world and uses the research techniques of the social sciences to collect, analyze, and interpret information to be used by the audience or consumers of the evaluation. Leisure and other human service agencies have endured some changes regarding varying levels of affluence and public acceptance and support. In terms of the leisure field, the process of evaluation has come to be thought of within the context of the program planning and development cycle and as an essential aspect of program management and human relations.

These types of realizations are leading the present-day change in emphasis from design-focused evaluation to utilization-focused evaluation in leisure programs. Many of the early evaluation approaches used in the field were designed on the basis of a particular definition of evaluation; they were intended to isolate program effects on behavior, as opposed to recognizing the contextual constraints of the evaluation setting, the information needs of the evaluation audience, and the vested interests of decision makers. As a result, the process of evaluation and the means by which results were obtained were often so incomprehensible, or seemed so arbitrary, to the evaluation audience that the evaluation findings went unused! Decisions were not based on the systematically collected and analyzed data. But as formal evaluations are increasingly being performed internally and viewed in relation to practical group decision making as well as methodological adequacy, the utility of evaluation is growing in importance.

The evaluation of leisure programs is a process that occurs within the ongoing management, decision-making, and planning cycle of the park, recreation, or leisure agency. Evaluation therefore has to be considered an integral part of the overall design and development of the agency. This enables the agency to be accountable to its clients, their families, and its funding sources. Evaluation needs to be addressed from the internal perspective in order for the agency to revise and improve its programs. Thus there is more emphasis today on a utilization-focused approach to evaluation that considers various aspects of a particular program from an internal perspective, in a holistic manner.

What implications exist for the practicing professional? It isn't all that new to say that programmers must conduct evaluations for all the reasons that are touched on herein and many more. What is new is that there are now a number of educators and practitioners who are developing, formalizing, using, and disseminating evaluation models and procedures for the systematic collection of information about the efficiency and effectiveness of leisure programs in order to enhance factually based decision making during this era of limited resources. What is essential is that we are leaders in this endeavor.

FOOTNOTES

1. Christine Z. Howe, ed., *Leisure Today: Evaluation of Leisure Programs* (Reston, Va.: American Alliance for Health, Physical Education, Recreation and Dance, 1980), p. 2. Reprinted with permission from The Journal of Physical Education, Recreation, and Dance. The Journal is a publication of the American Alliance for Health, Physical Education, Recreation and Dance, 1900 Association Drive, Reston, VA 22091.

2. Ibid., p. 2.

3. J. Robert Rossman, "Program Evaluation: Selecting an Appropriate Strategy" (1980). Cassette tape available from Management Learning Laboratories, 3337 Stoneybrook, Champaign, Ill. 61820.

4. Ibid.

5. Ibid.

6. Charles C. Bullock, "Interactionist Evaluators Look for 'What Is' Not 'What

Should Be,'" *Parks & Recreation*, February 1982, pp. 37–39. Reprinted by special permission of the National Recreation and Park Association.

7. Rossman, "Program Evaluation."

8. Ibid.

9. Ken Mobily and Seppo E. Iso-Ahola, "Mastery of Evaluation Techniques for the Undergraduate Major," in *Leisure Today: Evaluation of Leisure Programs*, ed. Christine Z. Howe. Reprinted with permission from The Journal of Physical Education, Recreation, and Dance. The Journal is a publication of the American Alliance for Health, Physical Education, Recreation and Dance, 1900 Association Drive, Reston, VA 22091.

10. Robert E. Stake, "Persuasions, Not Models," *Educational Evaluation and Policy Analysis*, 3 (1981), 83–84. Copyright © 1981, American Educational Research Association, Washington, D.C.

11. Harry P. Hatry and Diana R. Dunn, *Measuring the Effectiveness of Local Government Services: Recreation* (Washington, D.C.: The Urban Institute, 1971), pp. 13–37.

12. Betty van der Smissen, *Evaluation and Self-Study of Public Recreation and Park Agencies* (Arlington, Va.: National Recreation and Park Association, 1972), pp. 10–53.

13. Joseph J. Bannon, *Leisure Resources: Its Comprehensive Planning*, (Englewood Cliffs, N.J.: Prentice-Hall, Inc., 1976), pp. 280–292.

14. Scout L. Gunn and Carol A. Peterson, *Therapeutic Recreation Program Design: Principles and Procedures* (Englewood Cliffs, N.J.: Prentice-Hall, Inc., 1978), pp. 246–266. © 1978. Adapted by permission of Prentice-Hall, Inc, Englewood Cliffs, N.J.

15. Margaret L. Connolly, "Analysis of a Formative Program Evaluation Procedure for Therapeutic Recreation Services" (doctoral diss., University of Illinois at Urbana-Champaign, 1981, pp. 58–72.

16. Monica M. Nolan, "A Program Evaluation Procedure for Leisure Service Delivery" (master's thesis, University of Illinois at Urbana-Champaign, 1978), pp. 44–56.

17. Margie Kenner, "The Development of an Instrument for Evaluating the Effectiveness of Municipal Recreation Programs" (master's thesis, San Jose State University, 1981), pp. 62–77.

18. Ernest G. Olson, "A Conceptual Model for the Evaluation of Public Leisure Service Programs" (doctoral diss., University of Illinois at Urbana-Champaign, 1978), pp. 52–178.

19. Christine Z. Howe, "The Development and Evaluation of a Curriculum Evaluation Model for Master's Degree Curricula in Therapeutic Recreation" (doctoral diss., University of Illinois at Urbana-Champaign, 1978), pp. 48–69.

20. James Robert Rossman, "Development of a Leisure Program Evaluation Instrument (doctoral diss., University of Illinois at Urbana-Champaign, 1981), pp. 45–57.

21. Christine Z. Howe, "Evaluating Park and Recreation Programs in an Era of Declining Resources," paper presented at the annual meeting of the American Alliance for Health, Physical Education, Recreation and Dance, Houston, Texas, April 1982, pp. 16–19.

22. Michael Q. Patton, *Utilization-Focused Evaluation*, (Beverly Hills, Calif.: Stage Publications, Inc., 1978), pp. 275–291. Copyright © 1978 by Michael Q. Patton. Reprinted by permission of Sage Publications, Inc.

23. Ibid., pp. 119–147.

24. Ibid., pp. 199–238.

chapter 10

Program Revision
The Last Phase of the Leisure Programming Cycle

INTRODUCTION

Throughout this book, we have tried to emphasize our belief in the cyclical nature of systematic leisure programming. Program revision is the last phase of this cycle, if revision is considered to be the culmination of the programming effort. That is, revision is the activity that follows program evaluation. But revision is not the last phase of the cycle if, after some time has passed, you reconsider your program offerings—even those that have already been revised—by once gain initiating a needs assessment, either small-scale or large-scale. Under those circumstances, programming is really a never-ending cycle of discovery, delivery, modification, and rediscovery. That is why we have illustrated our concept of programming as a circle, even though we have discussed it in a phase-by-phase manner. So, how do programmers revise programs?

PROGRAM REVISION

In following this model, you can assume that a thorough and unbiased evaluation of your program has been conducted and that the results of this effort are available to you. This is what you base the revision of the program on—the results of the evaluation. What you do is carefully review the outcomes or findings of the evaluation. Some evaluations stop at the point of reporting the results. Others discuss the results and offer alternative courses of action. Others take the evaluation a step further and rank the alternative courses of action or make specific recommendations for further action. The key point is that program revision results in action—modification of the program based on the results of the evaluation. Thus revision occurs in response to evaluation.

There are several possibilities that may occur during program revision. A program whose evaluation results are highly positive may undergo little or no modification before it is offered again. A program that has mixed evaluation results should be modified in accordance with those results before it is offered again. Most leisure programs offered by an agency that hasn't conducted systematic evaluations in a while will fall in this category. Finally, a program that has highly negative evaluation results, indicating problems that cannot be remedied, should be terminated. Program revision can range, then, from the virtually intact repeat presentation of a viable program to the total withdrawal of a program that is no longer viable.

When we introduced the idea of the program life cycle under the section on program implementation in Chapter 5, we spoke of program death. Let us remind you that the demise of a program is a natural occurrence. It is a great mistake to perpetuate a program that is no longer satisfying to your clientele. It is better to terminate such programs until the need for them emerges again.

That idea also provides you with a key to the relationship between program revision and needs assessment. Without assessing needs from time to time, how can you know if the demand for a terminated program has been rekindled? Program revision allows you to be immediately responsive to your clientele as a result of your evaluation findings, while needs assessment keeps you informed of the changing demands for leisure programs and services, enabling you to remain responsive over the long run. In the end, program revision should lead to the improvement of your programs, whether that requires unchanged repetition, slight to major modification, or the termination of a particular offering.

Clearly, the interplay of these three phases is very important. But what if different audiences perceive the results of an evaluation in conflicting ways? How then can you arrive at some reasonable program modification?

REVISION WHEN DISAGREEMENT EXISTS

Almost all leisure service professionals work with other professionals in some kind of group. Whenever two or more disagree on something (in this case, on the results of an evaluation or how to act on them), then the politics of negotiation, compromise, and consensus enter in. What professionals strive for are open lines of communication between differing factions or special-interest groups so that issues may be clearly identified and fully discussed in order to enhance the probability of a rational decision. If you are working in a fairly democratic or participatory-management type of leisure service operation, then efforts will be made by coworkers and/or their supervisors or relevant clientele to explain, persuade, and negotiate various points of view. The ultimate intention is to arrive at a decision that is acceptable to a majority of the persons or groups involved. Most likely this will be a compromise decision that achieves support from or is the consensus of the people involved. Whether you are in the public sector, private enterprise, a therapeutic recreation setting, or the tourism/hospitality industry, there are some lessons to be learned in working with others to revise leisure programs. Conflict, when it is used in a healthy manner, can cause involved persons to be even more serious in their deliberations over program change. To pay close attention to programs and services is certainly desirable professional practice.

Application Section. Consider the following circumstance. You are in charge of community activities and relations for a large indoor mall on the edge of a major southwestern city. The results of some consumer surveys and observational studies made a couple of years ago indicated that young persons aged 14 to 20 were the largest single group of people coming to the mall and that they accounted for the highest dollar volume of purchases. Thus, teenagers were the major consumer group in both numbers and dollars at your mall. Based on this information, you decided to incorporate more programs and events that you thought would appeal to this age group into your community activities offerings. Programs that you added included a series of free short concerts highlighting popular local rock groups; autograph-signing parties by "name" professional and collegiate athletes; demonstrations of new (at that time) recreational activities such as aerobic dance, walley ball, disco roller skating, and disco rope jumping; and free tokens for new video games as they were introduced by the manufacturers.

However, this year, the evaluation you commissioned confirmed your worst suspicions. Not only were the young people not spending money at the mall anymore, they weren't even coming to it! Further, they reported dissatisfaction with the programs and events under your direction.

This caused you to ask yourself a number of questions. Should you be concerned with programs for such a fickle group as teenagers? For this age group in particular, how can you distinguish between a fad and a programming trend? If program revision is in order, how might you modify your current offerings? Should you consider new activities such as break dancing, "new wave" shows, or microcomputer exhibitions? Should you invest in the equipment to present video music? In sum, what are you going to keep, modify, delete, or add to meet the programming preferences of young persons, and how are you going to make these decisions? The way in which you answer these questions will to some extent be determined by the way in which you have by now come to look on recreation and leisure as a profession.

RECREATION AND LEISURE AS A PROFESSION

Professionals working in park, recreation, and leisure settings experience diversity at many points in their careers. Certainly, the variety in the lifestyles of their clientele creates part of that diversity. Diversity is also found in the various leadership modes required of professionals working with multiple populations during times of change. As a leisure programmer, you must have the capacity to "lead" leisure experiences in many ways, just as you must be able to employ the various program approaches or strategies we talked about in Chapter 4.

We're now ready to take a brief look at some different modes of leadership and programmer roles in light of participants' needs and capacities for self-directedness. Adults and persons with high skill development in certain activities generally require less intervention or direct leadership by the leisure programmer. Children and persons with low or no skill development in certain activities generally require more intervention.

SELECTED PROGRAMMER ROLES

In this section we are not discussing specific leadership tasks, functions, and styles. These are found in face-to-face situations that are comprehensively discussed in park, recreation, and leisure textbooks devoted solely to leadership. Instead, we are taking a broader look at the various roles you can assume in stimulating leisure engagement and in facilitating the activities that are the outcome of the leisure programming cycle. The roles examined are those of direct service provider, enabler, broker, advocate, consultant, and mentor. These roles should not be viewed separately from each other. Ideally, the effective programmer merges these roles together throughout the programming cycle. Our examples are concentrated in the program implementation portion of the leisure programming cycle and use leisure activity skill development to illustrate selected programmer roles.

Direct Service Provider.   In this role, the programmer exerts control throughout the programming cycle. The use of control here is not automatically to be viewed as negative. You may assume a very direct role in providing services when participants have little or no experience with an activity. For example, young children or recently disabled persons frequently require leisure activity skill development. Either these individuals have not had enough leisure life experience yet, or their leisure life has been interrupted by a traumatic event. In these instances, you may need to assume an active role in orchestrating the leisure experience in such a way that the participant is most likely to experience competency, enjoyment, and actual skill development. When individual participants or groups of participants are dependent (inexperienced), for any reason and within any portion of the leisure programming cycle, you are likely to have to guide or control the process directly.

Enabler.   The role of enabler can be adopted as the participants and participant groups begin to function more independently. Your approach is nondirective; yet you are available to intervene should the need arise. For example, a group of mildly retarded adults who interact socially on a regular basis do not necessarily need direct input from a programmer in order to plan a social activity. Their previous group experiences have given them the skills necessary to implement another social activity. Rather, you should facilitate the process of program implementation for them. In this case, the programmer encourages participative decision making and mutual planning while being there as a "backup" if needed.

Broker.   As broker, you are engaged in arranging, negotiating, and exchanging information. Your assumption of this role suggests that you have ready access to resources or information needed by potential or current participants. Let's say that a young adult wanders into your video arcade in search of "Dragon's Lair," the one electronic game that your arcade does not have. As a broker, you have several options. You could arrange to have one installed right away. Through negotiation, you could attempt to encourage the consumer to accept the play possibilities presented by the other electronic games in your arcade; or you might be convinced by him or her to install "Dragon's Lair" in your arcade at a later date. Further, you could inform the youth of where the game is available elsewhere in the area and refer him or her there.

Advocate.   The advocacy role is being assumed more and more by leisure programmers today. This is due in part to the limited availability of resources (or to what may be perceived as an unequal distribution of resources), which in recent years has come to require an advocacy stance by leisure professionals. It is also due to the increased encouragement of programmers to give constituents a greater participative role in programming. The advocacy role may have political elements to it because the programmer may have to work with program participants in an attempt to resolve conflict or to bring about change.

An example of a situation that requires a programmer's taking the role of advocate might be one in which there is competition over the use and cost of public space. As a leisure programmer employed by a public recreation agency, you become aware that the city school district is expanding its adult education program to include many of the same leisure programs geared toward activity skill development (or leisure education) that your agency already offers. Further, the school district is able to provide these programs for less cost to the participant because it does not have to pay the facility usage fee that your agency does. This is resulting in declining participation in your programs. The participants who remain fear that your programs will be canceled owing to low enrollment. In assuming an advocacy role, you and your remaining program participants actively seek to change the situation. You might collectively seek a fee adjustment to make your program fee competitive with the school district's fee. Or you might seek a clarification from the city council about which public agency's job it is to do leisure programming and leisure education in the community. Whatever means is adopted, the leisure programmer's role becomes that of an advocate for change.

Consultant.   In this role, you offer advice, give opinions, and make suggestions regarding programming matters. Like each of the other roles, the consultant's role can be applied within any portion of the leisure programming cycle. Suppose that you are approached by a group of individuals who want to develop the skill of wind surfing. They are seeking your professional advice, opinion, and suggestions. You interact with them and advise them after learning their needs and interests. Leisure programmers are often asked for assistance by clients and clientele groups, colleagues engaged in similar programming settings, and outside groups. Many leisure programmers have even decided to specialize in this role and have become independent leisure consultants, New Games consultants, therapeutic recreation consultants, adventure playground consultants, and so on.

Mentor. The role of mentor is based on concern for others and a personal desire to actualize that concern by forming a helping relationship. It is directed toward developmental, not therapeutic, ideals, and it is often the result of the interest programmers tend to take in individual participants. Another reason that programmers become mentors is the nature of the individuals who seek the field for their careers. Usually leisure programmers are sensitive to people, open with them, and desirous of improving the quality of their lives through the provision of fulfilling leisure experiences. A bit of mystery surrounds the role of mentor. It seems to evolve informally. It cannot be mandated and remain gratuitous. If it is part of a job description, then it may become a job responsibility, not engaged in by choice.

The functions of a mentor include teaching, sponsoring, hosting or guiding, exemplifying, and counseling. Say that in working on leisure skill development with a group you recognize leadership potential in one particular participant. The individual indicates interest in developing that potential, so you do all you can to enhance it. You use your influence and provide other outlets and experiences to enable the individual to develop and refine leadership abilities. You make certain that the individual has opportunities to meet influential people in your organization and that he or she has access to agency resources. You also provide the individual with a model—an example—to admire and emulate. Also, in times of stress or confusion, or in decision situations, you may counsel the individual.

As can be seen, the roles of a professional leisure programmer are multifaceted. Programmers seldom fill only one role at one time. Rather, leisure programmers must continuously demonstrate the ability to move in and among roles depending upon their skills, the given program realities, and the needs and interests of the participants. We hope that what you have learned up to this point, not just by reading this textbook, but from your other life experiences too, will make you better prepared to take your place in this profession. That is why we have highlighted the professional roles of the programmer after completing our discussion of the programming cycle—so that you may put together the information and experiences that you have collected to formulate your own way of practicing the profession based on a solid foundation of knowledge and experience.

Educators rarely can resist the opportunity to turn something into a learning experience. Now that you have come this far, we have one last exercise that will allow you to apply what you have learned about programming.

Application Section. Triathalons, which typically combine the events of swimming, biking, and running, are becoming a very popular leisure pursuit. Mini-triathalons, in which the distances of the events are shorter than full triathalons, are especially appealing to those who are in good shape, but not extremely rigorously trained. Mini-triathalons are being sponsored by a variety of groups including bicycling clubs, track clubs, military personnel associations, wellness councils, fraternal organizations, youth organizations, public recreation departments, and swim clubs. Frequently, these groups solicit co-sponsorship with business and industry with the proceeds from the event going to charity.

You are the Director of Campus Recreation at State University. Your division comes under the Office of the Vice President for Student Affairs. Based on the results of your biannual needs assessment, you have found a high interest in mini-triathalons among the students, faculty, and staff surveyed. In light of this information, and to commemorate the retirement of Dean McArdle, the beloved and respected Dean of Students, your boss has given you and your six graduate assistants total responsibility for the First Annual McArdle Mini-Triathalon.

The guidelines that your boss has given you are as follows: the ¼ mile swim will occur in State's Lake Kolesnik; the 12 mile bicycle course will be routed around the Keller Botanical Gardens and the Arnold Memorial Golf Course, using campus roadways as much as possible; and the 5 mile run will circle Lake Kolesnik and use campus pathways as much as possible. Entries will be limited to 150 people and be open to the community as well as people related to the university. You have a "seed money" budget of $150.00 and the free cooperation of State's Life Guard Service, the Hot Wheels Bicycle Club, the Front Runners Track Association, the Community Police Department, State's Campus Traffic Management and Security Patrol, and General Hospital's Emergency Services Squad. Financially, the event must at least break even.

According to the leisure programming cycle, your next step would be to develop this program. How would you begin? Be sure to consider the philosophy or rationale behind the McArdle Mini-Triathalon. Would you brainstorm program objectives with your assistants? How would you assign tasks among them and ensure their completion? At what point would you consider soliciting corporate co-sponsorship to subsidize T-shirt, awards, refreshments, publicity, and advertisements? What kinds of policies need to be made in order for procedures to be established? For example, under the area of health and safety of participants, should there be a policy regarding their level of fitness, age and sex related groupings, condition of bicycle, transition from event to event, safety in the water and first aid during biking and running? How would these policies be translated into procedures such as an orientation session for participants, bicycle inspection, the required use of brightly colored swim caps, partitioned transition areas, and "thirst aid" stations?

Are there ways in which the mini-triathalon might conflict with other previously scheduled events? What is the best time of year and day to schedule the program? What about organizing, training, and coordinating the volunteers needed for crowd and traffic control; safety in the water and on the roadways; first aid duty; registration and information responsibilities; and so on? Who will be the persons in charge (leaders) of these essential functions? What about communication between the various groups involved in the program, as well as publicizing the program to the potential participants? Will the co-sponsors work together with the media to publicize and cover the event? Will premiums, prizes, and awards be given? Since this first annual mini-triathalon is to honor the retirement of Dean McArdle, is a special ceremony in order? If so, what about the arrangements for that in terms of speakers, guests, time, place, content, and so on? How will sponsors or donors be acknowledged?

How much should an individual entry cost? Should there be a team competition? What will be done with any proceeds? What liability issues need to be addressed? How will the competition be timed? What rules for each event need to be established and how will the participants be informed of them? These are just a few of the questions that need to be addressed at the program development phase of the leisure programming cycle. Let us next turn to the program implementation phase.

Assume that it is the evening before the McArdle Mini-Triathalon is to take place. The sky is filled with clouds and rain threatens. Are you prepared to deal with the vagaries of Mother Nature? What are you going to do about any registrants who do not attend the pre-event orientation session that night? Are the swimming, biking, and running routes all well marked? On the day of the program are the trained volunteers at their stations? Are restrooms and concession facilities operational for the spectators? Are the participants being monitored for their safety as the mini-triathalon progresses? How are the transitions between events going? As the program draws to a close, is the time and record-keeping accurate? Are the results readily available? Is the contribution of all involved with the program appropriately acknowledged during the awards ceremony? Who has clean-up duty? Who is responsible for returning equipment and supplies?

These questions are appropriate for a single offering of a program. When a program is repeated, there are other implementation concerns to be addressed that are related to particular stages of the program life cycle. Formative evaluations are also helpful for on-going programs.

What about evaluating the effectiveness of this event? With only a $150.00 operating budget, what aspect of program evaluation are you going to emphasize and with what respondents? Again, the evaluation questions that may be focused on the single program itself will differ should the program occur continuously. Depending upon the nature of your program, purpose of the evaluation, and so on, you must decide what aspects of the program to focus on: participant satisfaction, achievement of objectives, degree of conformity to standards, responsiveness to participants, or some combination. Please refer to Chapter 9 for an extensive discussion of important evaluation considerations.

How will you use the evaluation results to revise the program for the future? How will you implement any possible changes? This exercise demonstrates that the process of leisure programming does not occur in a vacuum. If the cycle from needs assessment to program revision happens, it will not be as easy as a baker following a recipe. In park, recreation, and leisure services there are many cooks in the kitchen, as well as many flavors involved in the brew. While there may be consensus on the rules of food preparation, there may be conflict over seasonings and spices. That is, there may be agreement on the "rules of the leisure services game," but there may be conflict over the values that underlie certain policies. In decision situations like program revision, you can expect competition, compromise, discussion, bargaining, negotiation, reciprocity, and deference to authority to be standard fare.

Once it has been determined what should be done, you may have to become an advocate to ensure that it does get done. This means that the ability to work with all kinds of people is an essential skill to develop. It also means that you will have to be able to cope with losing when the position that you advocate is not a priority.

CONCLUDING COMMENTS

We have used a circle to try to impress upon you the cyclical nature of the leisure programming approach that this book is about. We have remarked that it is a rather simplistic illustration of a very complex process. The following figure captures more of the complexity inherent in leisure programming.

The act of programming, as it stands alone, is no easy task to perform. The reality of programming is that it very rarely occurs in isolation. Thus, there is an additional level of complexity that enters into the process when other people and the environment outside of your organization are considered. That is just one instance in which a good understanding of organizational administration and management is necessary for the leisure programmer.

Programming leisure experiences is a primary and unique function of persons involved in the park, recreation, and leisure profession. Whether you work in a family-owned camp, run a small sporting goods franchise, conduct white-water rafting trips, direct therapeutic recreation for a veterans' hospital, provide employee fitness programs, supervise cultural and performing arts for a city parks and recreation department, plan and design arenas, rinks, and other recreational facilities, or are in charge of youth services for a particular religious denomination, the programming of leisure experiences will be part of your job, or will directly relate to some part of your job. It is because aspects of programming are found throughout the profession and constitute such a critical element of the profession that we have tried to provide you with some fresh ways of considering the topic.

In introducing you to our concepts of leisure and leisure service delivery, we have tried to emphasize the importance of knowing about human growth and development and of using that information for making sound decisions about programs. We have discussed the various approaches that you may take as a programmer and introduced you to the steps followed in our leisure programming cycle. You have also read about numerous other program trends and issues relevant to programming.

From there, we looked at our approach to programming in depth, moving from needs assessment to program planning to program implementation to program evaluation to program revision. Finally, we shared with you some programmer roles and a few comments about the profession. Now we have reached the end of the process and of this book.

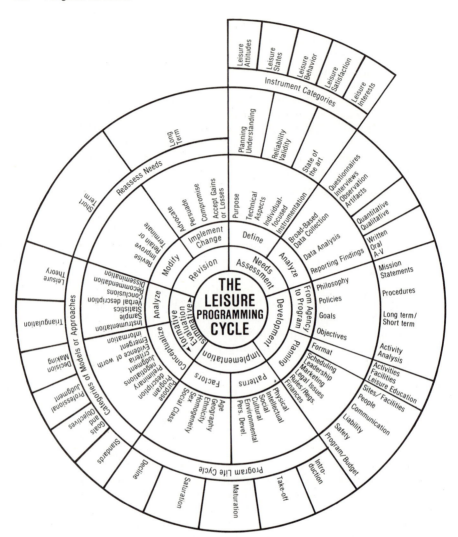

Figure 10-1   A Conceptual View of the Leisure Programming Cycle

Note: The authors gratefully acknowledge receiving the original idea for this figure from Mr. William Y. McKenzie, Jr.

No one source can say all that there is to be said about programming leisure experiences. The programming process by its very nature is fluid, dynamic, and ever-changing. Our contribution to you in this book is to offer one more way of helping you to move along the path to good professional practice. We have also tried to provide one more link in the evolution of programming theory and practice. We sincerely hope that this last page is not the end for you, but the beginning of yet another way for you to experience leisure and facilitate the leisure experiences of others. We welcome your commitment to a profession that plays a crucial role in the quality of peoples' lives and environment, now and in the future.

Index